A WHO'S WHO
OF
HULL CITY A.F.C.

A WHO'S WHO OF HULL CITY AFC
1904 – 1984

by
Douglas Lamming

HUTTON PRESS
1984

Phototypeset in ITC Garamond and Printed by
The Walkergate Press Ltd
Lewis House, Anlaby, Hull

Copyright © 1984
Hutton Press Ltd
130 Canada Drive, Cherry Burton, Beverley
North Humberside HU17 7SB

ISBN 0 907033 20 2

To
TIM JIBSON
of BBC Radio Humberside,
whose brain-child this book is
and who has been instrumental
in bringing the project to
fruition.

AUTHOR'S ACKNOWLEDGEMENTS

It has been said that books are written on the backs of writers who have gone before. This is in some senses true but the present book owes more to contemporaries. In particular my thanks go to J. A. Creasy and Christopher Elton. Jim, conveniently based near London, has made many forays to secure birth and death dates and, in the later stages, to the British Museum Newspaper Library at Colindale. Chris, a Hull City statistician, besides giving leads on a number of old time players, has made major contributions to the Tigers' Miscellany that appears at the end of the Who's Who. These are on the club's activities during both World Wars and the complete FA Cup and League Cup line-ups, features that will delight many enthusiasts.

Many correspondents and friends have provided valuable details and/or leads on individual players. In alphabetical order they are Michael Braham, G. J. Dykes, Michael Featherstone, Grenville Firth, Ray Goble, Malcolm Hartley, Bryan Horsnell, Barry Hugman, Paul Joannou, Trefor Jones, John Litster, Tony Matthews, Dr. Stephen Phillipps, Roy Shoesmith, R. J. Spiller, Keith Warsop, Michael Whelan, Alex Wilson and Sid Woodhead. Most of them are members of the Association of Football Statisticians, a body which in six short years has transformed the documentation of soccer data from a sketchy condition to an undreamed-of richness.

My good friend, Jimmy Ferguson, the Airdrieonians' chairman, has sent information on several Scots that would normally be unobtainable. Mrs. E. Cornett of Sherburn-in-Elmet must be thanked for the excellent 1910 team group photograph on which appears her grandfather and early City stalwart, J. B. McIntosh. So must Mrs. E. Thomas for ably coping with the preparation of a demanding typescript. The tiger on the cover is the work of Rosalind Baldwin and originally published by Accord cards.

Every care has been taken to ensure accuracy but in a work of this compass including so much new material it is perhaps inevitable errors have crept in. These, of course, should be ascribed to the author. Amplification of information on any pre-1940 player will be welcomed as will the sight of memorabilia of pre-1940 date.

The publisher wishes to thank the Chairman and management staff of Hull City AFC for their assistance in the production of this book; also *Hull Daily Mail* for providing the photograph of the 1984/85 season team.

FOREWORD BY HULL CITY CHAIRMAN

It is a great privilege to be asked to write this foreword. Hull City is a Club steeped in history. I have only been associated with the Club for the past 2½ years and so I am concentrating on the future rather than the past. However, I must make a special mention of Harold Needler and the Needler family who have done so much for Hull City over the years. I am pleased that we still have a member of the family involved with Christopher Needler currently on the Board.

Although the Tigers have never played in the First Division, it is my aim that we will soon be playing at that level of soccer. The Directors, Players, Staff and supporters are all a part of a great Hull City team. In the past two years we have played in Gibraltar and won the Three Nations Cup; we have played in America and won the Arrow Air Anglo-American Cup and Hull City have been great ambassadors both with publicity and public relations for Hull and Humberside. I feel very proud to be Chairman of a great Club and have such a good bunch of players, staff and supporters around me.

I hope you enjoy reading this book about the past history of Hull City. In five years' time I hope the publishers do a new edition showing that Hull City have become the First Division Champions and are playing in Europe. Some people will have a little chuckle at that but just watch out and don't say 'I didn't tell you so.' That's where we're going and what we're going to do.

Please keep supporting us.

DON ROBINSON
Chairman, Hull City AFC
November 1984

AUTHOR'S PREFACE

It is over half a century since I first saw a Hull City team in action. The date was January 31st 1931, the venue Sincil Bank, home of Lincoln City, my then nearest League club. The match is remembered with some clarity as it went into history. The reason – three players wore the Tigers' goalkeeper's jersey that afternoon. Geordie Maddison went off injured, Matt Bell filled the breech for a short while only to be knocked out, and finally Arthur Childs took over. Not surprisingly Lincoln won 3–0.

Two of those names, Maddison and Bell, are among the most illustrious of the 598 Tigers who have qualified to appear in these pages. Commentators keep reminding us that Hull is the largest centre of population never to have possessed a First Division club. Nevertheless during its 80-year span the local club has produced a continuous stream of distinguished players from 'Boy' Browell and Stan Fazackerley in the pre-1914 era to Peter Daniel and Brian Marwood in the present. The fact that such talent was usually sold must be a main reason why the top flight has never been attained.

Like most clubs, Hull City has an up-and-down history – never more so than in recent years. A quick descent from Second Division status to Fourth and then a steady revival under a dynamic leadership of a new Chairman, Mr. Don Robinson. This has been dramatic. In spite of the intense disappointment of 1983/84, failing to return to the Second Division by the narrowest of goal differences, one has a gut feeling Mr. Robinson will mastermind success in the future.

The six months spent in producing this book have naturally been somewhat taxing but also enjoyable. Threads have emerged in chasing individual details. For example, the amount of home-produced talent, the constant imports from Geordieland, an early rich seam of recruits from the Prescot/St. Helens locality. It is hoped readers will find enjoyment in these pages on a fascinating subject.

DOUGLAS LAMMING

North Ferriby,
7 September 1984

NOTES ON THE TEXT

SCOPE. The qualification for inclusion is an appearance for Hull City in a peace time League match but excluding the barely-commenced 1939/40 season. The seasons covered are therefore 1905/06-1914/15 inclusive, 1919/20-1938/39 inclusive and 1946/47-1983/84 inclusive. Actually, of course, the 1914/15 season took place largely in wartime but was run as a peacetime competition.

ABBREVIATIONS have been kept to a minimum and those occurring usually appear in works of this kind, viz:

Apps.	Appearances
cs	close season
Div.	Division
FA	The Football Association
FL	The Football League
Sub	substitute
WW1	The First World War
WW2	The Second World War

POSITIONS. Over recent times, since Ramsey's 'Wingless Wonders' triumph in the World Cup, players' positions have become blurred. Strikers and midfielders are terms that cover 8 of the former established system of 3 half-backs and 5 forwards. The precise labelling of Tigers who appeared up to the 'blurring' has been retained. An aside on the present-day labelling. It has thrown up some tortuous verbiage from radio commentators, who talk about 'left-sided midfield players' rather than 'left half' for example.

PHYSIQUES. Recording heights and weights can be a questionable exercise unless the date is given as well – a youngster may join a club as a skinny 17-year-old and a few years later be a six-footer with a weight in proportion. In the following pages where possible the measurements are those obtaining when the player was on City's books.

NOMENCLATURE. Clubs have been given the titles held at the time when the transfer or other event took place (e.g. Millwall was officially Millwall Athletic up to 1925 and Swansea Town did not become Swansea City until February 1970). Bradford refers to the now-defunct Bradford Park Avenue club and not Bradford City, which gets its full title throughout.

TRANSFER FEES are supposedly not for public consumption in spite of a widespread interest in amounts changing hands – an interest generously catered for in newspaper sports pages. Many of the fees quoted in the succeeding pages are know to be authentic. The remainder – and majority – have come from press reports and can be looked upon as being near the mark.

HONOURS chronicled are international caps, inter-league appearances and club honours (i.e. appearances in national cup finals and a qualification for a divisional championship medal). Regarding championships, the usual qualification is understood to be having played in a third or more of the matches. The fulfilling of this quota does not in fact mean a player necessarily receives a medal. I am told the England goalkeeper, Harold Pearson, didn't get one in 1938 (16 games for Millwall in a 42-match tourney). And, a more recent case, Bobby Seith of Burnley did not in 1960 after appearing 27 times out of a possible 42. The reason was reported to be because the player had asked for a transfer.

ACKERMAN, Alfred Arthur Eric (1950-51 and 1953-55)
Centre-forward/inside-left: 92 apps; 49 goals.
1950: 5ft. 9ins; 11st. 10lbs.
Born: Pretoria, South Africa, 5 January 1929.
Career: Pretoria Municipals; Clyde 1948; CITY July 1950 (£11,000); Norwich City July 1951 (£9,500); CITY again October 1953 (£5,000); Derby County March 1955 (£6,600 including Ken Harrison); Carlisle United November 1956 (around £3,000); Millwall January 1959 for a similar fee; Dartford as player/manager July 1961, later holding the appointment of manager to Gravesend & Northfleet FC.

Started as a centre-half and developed into a powerful grafting inside man, hard as they come. Alf had a keen eye for the scoring chance, building impressive goals totals with all his senior clubs.

ACQUROFF, John (1934-1936)
Centre-forward: 70 apps; 25 goals.
1935: 5ft. 10ins; 11st. 10lbs.
Born: Chelsea, 9 September 1911 of Scottish parents.
Career: Willesden Polytechnic; Tottenham Hotspur, who sent him to their then nursery club, Northfleet, from whence he joined Folkestone; CITY November 1934 (£250); Bury October 1936 (£1,500); Norwich City February 1939; played no senior football after WW2 and in 1949 emigrated to Tasmania.

Ideally built for leading the attack and showing plenty of verve, Jack was not, however, a particularly prolific scorer. With Bury he figured at inside-left also, laying on chances for their sharpshooting centre, George Davies. Had a cosmopolitan background — besides the above-mentioned Scottish parentage, was of Russian extraction too.

ADEY, Thomas William (1923-1925)
Centre-half: 16 apps.
1924: 5ft. 9ins; 11st. 12lbs.
Born: Hetton-le-Hole, Co. Durham, 22 February 1901.
Career: Bedlington United; CITY April 1923; Swindon Town August 1925; Northampton Town cs 1926; Durham City 1927.

All 16 appearances for the Tigers were in the 1923/24 season, when he was shown to be a useful player able to cope with Second Division demands. His name didn't arrive on a League score sheet until 1927/28, Durham City's last term in the big time.

AINSWORTH, Edgar Ward (1932/33 and 1935/36)
Goalkeeper: 2 apps.
1933: 6ft. 1ins; 14st.
Born: Hull, 1910. Died: 13 November 1952.
Career: Boulevard School, Hull, afterwards appearing in local junior soccer for Old Boulevardiers and Bridlington Town. Also assisted City Reserves on occasion, making a couple of appearances in the League side spaced by 3 seasons as above.
Honours: England amateur international vs Wales and Ireland 1933.

Big, burly 'keeper whose bulk was no bar to agility. A measure of his prowess was the winning of 2 international caps in competition with custodians from the crack London and Durham amateur clubs.

ALBERRY, W(illiam) Edward (1947-1948)
Centre-half: 1 app.
Born: Doncaster, 21 July 1922. Died 1978.
Career: Junior football to Doncaster Rovers during WW2; Leeds United May 1946; CITY April 1947; Gainsborough Trinity cs 1948.

Understudy to Harold Meens, his fellow Doncastrian and Tom Berry. Ted's Northern Section appearance in City's colours was the only one he made in League peace-time soccer.

ALEXANDER, Stanley (1926-1931)
Outside/inside-right and centre-forward: 98 apps; 41 goals.
1929: 5ft. 8½ins; 11st. 8lbs.
Born: Percy Main, Northumberland, 17 September 1905. Died: 5 June 1961.
Career: Percy Main Amateurs; CITY cs 1926; Bradford City November 1931 (City receiving Jack Hill in part exchange); Millwall October 1933; Tottenham Hotspur cs 1936; Accrington Stanley cs 1938, leaving that club in 1940 to join the Royal Navy and retiring from playing during WW2.

Honours: Toured Canada with FA team in 1931.

A noted sprinter who put his speed to good use on the football field as well as having the ability to fill 3 forward positions. His elder brother, Jack, was also on City's books between spells of sampling Northern Section soccer at Ashington. Stan settled in the Hull area after the war and coached City's juniors for a time.

ALLEN, Mervyn John (1931-1934)
Forward: 15 apps; 1 goal.
1934: 5ft. 9ins; 11st. 7lbs.
Born: Bargoed, Glam. 16 October 1909.
Died: 1976.
Career: Gilfach FC (Glamorgan); CITY during 1931/32 season; Carlisle United cs 1934-1935.

Made 10 appearances following his mid-season signing in 1931/32 but couldn't break into the 1932/33 promotion winning side which, naturally, was a pretty-settled one. Allen could also play in the half-back line.

ANNABLES, Walter (1936-1939)

Right or left-back: 62 apps; 1 goal.
1938: 5ft. 10½ins; 12st. 4lbs.
Born: Swinton, Yorks, 31 October 1911.
Died: 16 August 1979.
Career: Mexborough Athletic 1930; Grimsby Town April 1932; CITY June 1936; Carlisle United June 1939; retired during the war.

Unable to permanently break into a successful Mariners' side with the seasoned Jacobson, Hodgson and Ned Vincent around, Walter was an ever-present in his first term as a Tiger. A good back; efficient, dependable and well built.

ASKEW, William (1982-)
Midfield: 65 apps; plus 4 subs; 7 goals.
1983: 5ft. 6½ins; 10st. 2lbs.
Born: Great Lumley, Co. Durham, 2 October 1959.
Career: North-East junior football to Middlesbrough as an apprentice professional, turning full professional October 1977 (Blackburn Rovers on loan March 1982); Gateshead later in 1982; CITY October 1982 following a 6 weeks trial.

Has enjoyed an amount of senior football for City after infrequent outings during his Middlesbrough years. A purposeful little midfield man always trying to give full value.

ATKINSON, Charles (1949-1956)
Inside-forward: 37 apps; 2 goals.
1955: 5ft. 9ins; 10st. 6lbs.
Born: Hull, 17 December 1932.
Career: Played for 3 Hull junior clubs – Francis Askew YC, North Hull Juniors and Marist Old Boys – before joining CITY in 1949 as an amateur, turning professional May 1950; Bradford July 1956 (around £1,000); Bradford City July 1964 (£1,500) – 1965. After leaving the professional game assisted a Leeds Sunday League side, Real Santos FC, not retiring until 1975.

Played at outside-right too and, indeed, developed into a fine utility player. Gave 8 years excellent service to the now defunct Park Avenue Club (344 FL apps, 50 goals), spending much of the time at wing-half. Later a bookmaker in Bradford. Father of Paul Atkinson who appeared in the 1984 FA Cup Final for Watford.

ATKINSON, G(eorge) Arthur (1933-1934)
Outside-right: 5 apps.
1934: 5ft. 9ins; 11st.
Born: Goole, 30 September 1909.
Career: Goole junior football; Lincoln City 1930; CITY cs 1933; Mansfield Town June 1934; Southport cs 1937; Thorne Colliery cs 1938

Mostly played inside in his successful 3 years at Mansfield – missed but 6 League games out of a possible 126 and scored 31 goals – where he won a reputation as a constructive schemer with ball control and shooting ability. Earlier his wing play had chiefly been notable for speed.

ATKINSON, Peter (1947-1948)
Goalkeeper: 6 apps.
1947: 5ft. 9½ins; 11st. 4lbs.
Born: Middlesbrough, 13 September 1924.
Died: 1972.

Career: Billingham schoolboy football; Port Clarence Social Service Centre; Billingham Synthonia 1945/46; CITY June 1947—cs 1948.
Played centre-forward for his school, Billingham St. John's, but proved such a success when deputising for the Port Clarence goalkeeper he switched permanently to the position, graduating to Northern League soccer. Performed brilliantly for the Tigers on his debut in June 1947 – season 1946/47 was greatly extended because of the previous terrible winter.

ATKINSON, Trevor (1946-1948)
Outside-left: 2 apps.
1947: 5ft. 6ins; 10st. 6lbs.
Born: Dodsworth near Barnsley, 19 November 1928.
Career: Barnsley schoolboy football; Hull Amateurs; CITY May 1946; Barnsley August 1948-1949.
When at Barnsley Grammar School – that nursery of soccer talent – Trevor was in the team from the age of 13 and still at school when he signed for the Tigers. Did quite well on his League debut but didn't make the Barnsley first team.

BALDRY, George W. (1936-1937)
Outside-right: 5 apps; 2 goals.
Born: Cleethorpes, 1911.
Career: Grimsby junior football; Grimsby Town cs 1933; CITY May 1936. Assisted Chelmsford City in the late 1930's.
Made his League debut the season prior to joining City, his 20 Division One appearances bringing him 6 goals. A partner, with his brother, in a Grimsby fish business and at one time a saxophonist in Bob Walker's dance orchestra, for many years a leading Lincolnshire band.

BANKS, Francis S. (1966-1976)
Right-back: 284 apps. plus 4 subs; 7 goals.
1970: 5ft. 9½ins; 11st. 7lbs.
Born: Hull, 21 August 1945.
Career: Southend junior football to Southend United October 1962; CITY September 1966; Southend United again March 1976; retired 1978 subsequently joining the Southend Coaching Staff.
A case of the native returning, for Frank, though hailing from Hull, was educated at the Wentworth High School in Southend and learned his soccer in and around the Essex resort. Early looked upon as a half-back, he settled at right-back to give the Tigers a decade of sound defensive work. Wholehearted and a club man to cherish.

BANNISTER, Bruce I. (1977-1980)
Forward: 79 apps. plus 6 subs; 20 goals.
1978: 5ft. 7½ins; 11st. 5lbs.
Born: Bradford, 14 April 1947.
Career: Bradford Schools; Bradford City on amateur forms 1963, turning professional August 1965; Bristol Rovers November 1971 (£23,000); Plymouth Argyle December 1976 (£10,000 and another player); CITY June 1977 (£15,000); Union Sportive Dunkerque (France) July 1980 for one season.
Sturdy, assertive attacker. Chalked up over 500 League appearances and scored 168 goals in a 15 year period. Particularly noted when at Bristol for the prolific partnership with fellow Yorkshireman, Alan Warboys. They were re-united at Boothferry Park soon after Bruce's arrival. On leaving football entered the sportswear industry in a management capacity.

BARKER, Geoffrey A. (1964-1971)
Centre-half: 29 apps. plus 1 sub; 2 goals.
1972: 6ft; 12st.
Born: Hull, 7 February 1949.
Career: Hull schools football to CITY ground staff 1964, turning professional March 1967 (Southend United on loan December 1970 – May 1971); Darlington June 1971; Reading February 1975 (£5,000); Grimsby Town July 1977-1979; Bridlington Trinity later in 1979; Grantham Town player/manager appointed April 1980; Bridlington Trinity manager May 1981 – February 1982.
Strongly built – usefully so for his position -- and a strong all-round half-back. Gave excellent service on his travels, claiming first team status everywhere. In all Geoff made 322 League appearances plus 2 substitutions, scoring 11 goals in the process.

BARLEY, Henry Frank (1931-1932)
Outside-right: 13 apps; 2 goals.
1930: 5ft. 5ins; 9st. 10lbs.
Born: Grimsby 1905. Died: 1958.
Career: Grimsby junior football; Grimsby Town 1928/29; CITY cs 1931; New Brighton August 1932; Notts County January 1934; Scunthorpe United August 1934; Bristol Rovers May 1935; Barrow May 1936-1937.
Small and light, the smallness making him somewhat elusive for opponents. Skilful too, and he could cross a ball accurately.

BARRACLOUGH, William (1927-28)
Outside-left: 9 apps.
1929: 5ft. 4ins; 9st. 10lbs.
Born: Hull, 3 January 1909. Died: August 1969.
Career: Bridlington Town; CITY on amateur forms cs 1927; Wolverhampton Wanderers as a professional 1928; Chelsea October 1934; Colchester United August 1937; Doncaster

Rovers August 1938; retired during the war.
Honours: (Wolves) Div. 2 champions 1932.
Realised his full potential at Wolverhampton and Chelsea where he had a deal of top flight experience. Billy played inside-left with Bridlington but his slight physique made the wing a better proposition for the senior game. By the mid-'Thirties' he was a few inches taller and a stone heavier so his clever play could be more forcibly exploited.

BARRASS, James
The nome de plume used by J. W. Lodge (q.v.) in his early playing days at Anlaby Road.

BAXTER, William A. (1971-1972)

Centre-half: 20 apps. plus 1 sub.
1971: 5ft. 8ins; 10st. 6lbs.
Born: Edinburgh, 23 April 1939.
Career: Broxburn Athletic; Ipswich Town June 1960 (£500); CITY March 1971 (£12,500) (Watford on loan October 1971 – January 1972); Northampton Town May 1972 and their player/manager from the following October to May 1973.
Honours: (Ipswich) League champions 1962. Div. 2 champions 1961, 1968.
A distinguished Ipswich skipper signed after over a decade of success at Portman Road. Originally played right-half, eventually moving to pivot although physically small for the job. A tenacious player with an attacking flair that brought a number of headed goals in his 409 League outings for the Suffolk club.

BEARDSLEY, Donald T. (1962-1973)
Right/left-back: 128 apps. plus 2 subs.
1970: 5ft. 10ins; 12st.
Born: Alyth, Perthshire, 23 October 1946.
Career: Hull Schools; CITY on amateur forms August 1962, becoming an apprentice professional 2 months later and a full professional October 1964 (Doncaster Rovers on loan March-May 1972); Grimsby Town August 1973 (approaching £10,000); Louth United (Lincolnshire League) May 1975 for about 6 months thereafter playing in Grimsby Sunday League soccer.
Although Scottish-born, educated in Hull and a graduate from the fruitful local schoolboy ranks. A capable defender strong in both feet. Became an estate agent in 1975, subsequently obtaining a partnership in a firm.

BELL, Ernest (1935-38 and 1946-47)
Inside-forward: 27 apps; 5 goals.
1938: 5ft. 9ins; 10st. 7lbs.
Born: Hull, 22 July 1918. Died 8 December 1968.
Career: Hull Schools; CITY on amateur forms before signing as a professional in 1935; Mansfield Town May 1938 (Aldershot as a guest player during WW2); CITY for second spell cs 1946; Scarborough cs 1947, later assisting Hessle Old Boys.
A product of Blundell Street School, a lively forward who knew the way to his opponents' goal. Was a civil servant in the Inland Revenue Dept. and a brother-in-law of City's Dai Davies.

BELL, Matthew ('Ginger') (1919-1931)
Right/left-back: 392 apps; 1 goal.
1928: 5ft. 11ins; 13st. 3lbs.
Born: West Hartlepool 1897.
Died: 27 January 1962.
Career: Army football; West Hartlepool FC; Hull City August 1919, Nottingham Forest August 1931; retired in the mid-1930's and became manager/coach of Heracles FC, Holland. Later returned to live in Hull.
The 1920's in City's case might appropriately be dubbed 'the Matt Bell era' so closely was

his name and that of the club bracketed. The most prominent member of the celebrated Mercer, Gibson and Bell defence, his tackling was aptly said to be as fiery as his ginger hair. He had the other defensive requirements too and, in emergencies, proved himself an excellent goalkeeper. And, of course, Matt couldn't be surpassed as a loyal club man.

BELL, William Thomas (1932-1933)
Right-back: 4 apps.
1930: 5ft. 10ins; 12st 3lbs.
Born: North Seaton near Ashington 1903.
Career: Blyth Spartans; Sheffield United December 1925 (£200); Grimsby Town cs 1928; CITY cs 1932.
Went to Sheffield United as an inside-left; the Blades converted him to left-half and Grimsby to right-back. Unable to establish a regular place with any of his senior clubs – the aggregate number of League appearances came to only 20 – but obviously an adaptable player

BENNETT, Reuben M (1935/36)
Goalkeeper: 3 apps.
Born: Aberdeen.
Career: Aberdeen East End; CITY 1935/36; Queen of the South 1936/37 and with Dundee and Ayr United after WW2. Was Dundee's trainer 1950-53 and subsequently held appointments with Ayr United, Motherwell and Third Lanark before, in 1959, becoming Liverpool's trainer, a position he held for some years.
A reliable 'keeper but his name really became familiar through his Liverpool association when he was one of the architects of the Anfield Club's continuous success since the early 1960's.

BENNION, John Raymond (1957-1960)
Wing-half: 35 apps; 1 goal.
1958: 5ft. 10ins; 12st. 9lbs.
Born: Burnley, 2 April 1934.
Career: Junior football, becoming a professional with Burnley January 1952; CITY June 1957; Stockport County July 1960; Barrow July 1961; Netherfield as player/manager cs 1963, later having a spell as Goole Town's player/manager.
Fast moving wing-half owning a weight that let opponents know they had been in a game. Specialised in long throws. On leaving football became a bookmaker in Beverley. Son of Ray Bennion, the Manchester United and Wales half-back of the inter-war period.

BENNYWORTH, Ian R. (1979-1981)
Defender: 1 app.
1980: 6ft; 12st. 4lbs.
Born: Hull, 15 January 1962.
Career: Hull district schools football to CITY on schoolboy forms originally, apprentice professional July 1978, full professional January 1980. Given a free transfer cs 1981 and went to non-League football.
Tall defender, one of several players to leave during and after that troubled 1980/81 season. Produced by Cottingham High School.

BENTLEY, Keith J. (1957-1958)
Inside-forward: 4 apps.
Born: Hull, 27 July 1936.
Career: Junior football to CITY, signing as a professional November 1957; Scarborough July 1958.
Only briefly a League professional before transferring to non-League football. City were comparatively well off for inside men at the time with Bradbury in full spate and the likes of David Coates emerging.

BERRY, Thomas (1947-1957)
Left-back/centre-half: 276 apps; 1 goal.
1950: 6ft. 1in; 11st. 7lbs.
Born: Clayton-le-Moors, Lancs, 31 March 1922.
Career: Oxford City and RAF football during WW2; Great Harwood after demobilisation; CITY June 1947; Buxton October 1957.
Honours: (City) Div. 3 (North) champions 1949.
A City favourite for a decade. Cool and efficient, Tom's height gave command in the air and long legs enabled him to cover ground quickly enough although he didn't appear particularly mobile. With Oxford City had represented both Oxfordshire and the Isthmian League, and he appeared in RAF representative matches.

BEST, Charles (1911-1913)
Inside-forward: 35 apps; 4 goals.
1911: 5ft. 7ins; 10st. 8lbs.
Born: Margrove Park, Guisborough, North Yorks, 1888. Died: 1965.
Career: Eston United (Middlesbrough as an amateur 1910/11); CITY as a professional cs 1911-1913 (thought to have retired through injury). City's assistant trainer 1914/15.
Honours: (Eston United) FA Amateur Cup Finalists 1909.
Clever forward from a then crack amateur club, Eston United of Cleveland, who, incidentally, again reached the Amateur Cup final in 1912 with an almost different team. Best made 5 Div. 1 appearances for Middlesbrough in 1910/11 – a measure of his class as an amateur – and for signing him City were fined £25. They hadn't approached the Teessiders before doing so.

BEST, Jeremiah (1936-1937)
Centre-forward: 30 apps; 12 goals.
1935: 5ft. 9ins. 11st. 2lbs.
Born: Mickley, Northumberland, 23 January 1901. Died: 1975.
Career: Mickley FC; Newcastle United December 1919 (£100); Leeds United July 1920 (£100); retu rned to play in North-Eastern non-League football 1921 before going to America for a long spell, leaving Falls River (USA) to join Clapton Orient in August 1931; Darlington 1933; CITY October 1936 — cs 1937.
A versatile forward as effective on the wings and inside berths as in the centre. Very popular at Darlington where his speed and ability to manoeuvre in tight situations brought a haul of 68 goals in 109 League encounters.

BETTS, A(rthur) Charles (1914-1920)
Left-back/left-half: 52 apps.
1914: 5ft. 10½ins; 12st.
Born: Scunthorpe, 2 January 1886. Died: 1967.
Career: North Lindsey FC (Lincs.); Gainsborough Trinity cs 1905; Watford cs 1907; Gainsborough Trinity again May 1910; Newcastle United cs 1911; Derby County October 1911; CITY cs 1914; Scunthorpe United cs 1920; retired cs 1923 and became coach of a local club, Lysaghts Sports.
Honours: (Derby County) Div. 2 champions 1912.
Mostly figured at full-back although he was left-half during his Derby championship season. Charlie was a dashing and enthusiastic performer, quick to recover, calm and plucky. In 1906 represented Lincolnshire in the then popular county matches. A stone mason by trade.

BEW, Daniel Crombie (1922-1923)
Centre-half; 11 apps.
1925: 5ft. 10½ins; 11st. 8lbs.
Born: Sunderland, 1896. Died 1951.
Career: Lambton Star; Sunderland on amateur forms 1921; CITY May 1922; Swindon Town June 1923; retired cs 1930.
Made his League debut with the Tigers but in the 7 seasons at Swindon grossed a formidable 209 appearances, scoring 6 goals in the process. A stalwart pivot, powerful physically, energetic and a bustler. Settled in Swindon and worked in the coal trade there.

BLACKBURN, Edwin Huitson (1973-1980)
Goalkeeper: 68 apps.
1977: 5ft. 9½ins; 10st. 5½lbs.
Born: Houghton-le-Spring, Co. Durham, 18 April 1957.
Career: County Durham schools football; Easington Lane Under-19 team; CITY as an apprentice professional February 1973, turning full professional September 1974; York City April 1980 (£6000) (Hartlepool United on a month's loan December 1982 — subsequently signed permanently).
As a juvenile, in his junior school side when 11 and then in his grammar school side for 4 seasons, gaining representative recognition and playing in the English Schools' Shield tourney. Had quite a wait before getting many senior outings with City (only 2 League games up to 1977/78). On the small side as goalkeepers go, so accordingly more agile than many of his weightier brethren.

BLAMPEY, Stuart L. (1965-1976)
Wing-half: 61 apps. + 9 subs.; 1 goal.
1974: 5ft 8½ins; 11st. 4½lbs.
Born: North Ferriby nr. Hull, 13 June 1951.
Career: East Riding Schools; CITY on schoolboy forms October 1965, turning professional July 1968; retired through injury November 1976. Subsequently joined Scarborough and, in June 1979, Goole Town. Appointed the latter's player/manager November 1981, leaving this post January 1983. Manager of North Ferriby United (Yorkshire League) from August 1983.
Showed much promise as a schoolboy and first joined the Tigers at a tender age. Made 4 appearances for the Yorkshire Grammar Schools' representative side. Unlucky in the matter of injuries later, including a broken kneecap. A utility man, Stuart also played at full-back and forward in the League team.

BLEAKLEY, Thomas (1918-1930)

Left-half: 370 apps; 5 goals.
1925: 5ft. 6ins; 10st. 10lbs.
Born: Little Hulton nr. Bolton, 16 May 1893.
Died: 1 October 1951.

Career: Clegg's Lane FC (Farnworth League) for 5 seasons; Walkden Central (Bolton Wanderers on amateur forms); Army football; CITY 1918; Goole Town cs 1930 subsequently assisting Bridlington Town and Wombwell.

A magnificent club man and a model of consistency. Tommy's aggregate number of games for City totalled 418 (9 goals) from his debut in a wartime game against Huddersfield in October 1918 to his last, in April 1930 vs. Leeds United in the Hospital Cup. Played cricket professionally too, later coaching the East Riding and Hull University sides.

BLENKINSOP, Ernest (1921-1923)

Left-back: 11 apps.
1922: 5ft. 9ins; 11st. 7lbs.
Born: Cudworth nr. Barnsley, 20 April 1902.
Died: 24 April 1969.
Career: Cudworth United Methodists; CITY October 1921 (£100); Sheffield Wednesday January 1923; Liverpool March 1934 (about £5,000); Cardiff City November 1937; Buxton August 1939; Hurst during WW2 before retiring.
Honours: England international (26 apps). Football League (8 apps). (Wednesday) Div. 2 champions 1926. League champions 1929 and 1930.

One of the Tiger's finest developments, a great full-back for club and country – polished, cool, thoughtful and a supreme stylist. His zenith, of course, arrived some seasons after leaving the club. Latterly a licensee in Sheffield.

BLOOMER, James (1948-1949)

Outside-right/outside-left: 4 apps. 2 goals.
1949: 5ft. 9ins; 12st.
Born: Rutherglen, Lanarkshire, 10 April 1926.
Career: Strathclyde 1943-48 and he also played in Army football during WW2; CITY February 1948; Grimsby Town June 1949; King's Lynn during 1954/55 season.

Could perhaps have made a fair showing in any position – he played at centre-forward at Grimsby besides the extreme wings and was known to be an excellent deputy full-back. His son, James junior, had several seasons with the Mariners in the 1960s.

BLOXHAM, J(ames) Alexander (1947-1950)

Outside-right/outside-left: 33 apps. 2 goals.
1949: 5ft. 8ins; 11st. 4lbs.
Born: New Houghton, Derbyshire, 2 July 1923.
Career: Derbyshire Schools; served in the RAF in WW2 and had games for Mansfield Town, Leicester City and Nottingham Forest; Ollerton Colliery to CITY October 1947; Boston United cs 1950.

Compactly built forward, a performer on both flanks. A pretty regular choice in his first season, Alec made only 10 appearances thereafter and his delicate style was not to the liking of some City followers. In pre-professional days reckoned to be in the running for an amateur cap.

BLY, William (1937-1960)

Goalkeeper: 402 apps.
1951: 5ft. 9¾ins; 10st. 5lbs.
Born: Newcastle-on-Tyne, 15 May 1920.
Died: 24 March 1982.
Career: Newcastle Schools; Walker Boys' Club (Newcastle); Walker Temperance; Walker Celtic; CITY August 1937 (Guest player for Dumbarton and Hamilton Academicals 1942-3); retired May 1960 but joined Weymouth November 1961.
Honours: (City) Div. 3 (North) champions 1949.

One of the Tigers' all-time greats, Billy Bly's service to the club was both illustrious and lengthy. His build was slim but his courage became a legend, sustaining 14 fractures of various kinds among a multiplicity of injuries. Was selected for England 'B' but had to cry off through injury although he did represent the B.A.O.R. on a number of occasions during Army service. Billy settled in Hull, had a confectionery shop near Boothferry Park, worked for an estate agent, and then as a painter – his first occupation after leaving school.

BLYTH, James (1937-1939)
Centre-half: 72 apps.
1938: 5ft. 8ins; 11st. 4lbs.
Born: Edinburgh, 9 August 1911.
Career: Arniston Rangers; Tottenham Hotspur February 1936; CITY April 1937; Heart of Midlothian May 1939; St. Johnstone 1946; retired 1950.
Not tall as pivots go but his stocky build held him in good stead for the role. Quickly gained senior recognition after leaving the Scottish junior scene, having 11 League outings in his sole complete season with Spurs.

BOOTH, Dennis (1980-)
Defender: 121 apps. + 1 sub; 2 goals.
1983: 5ft. 7½ins; 10st. 5lbs.
Born: Stanley Common nr. Ilkeston, Derbyshire, 9 April 1949.
Career: Derbyshire Schools; Charlton Athletic as an apprentice professional August 1964, turning full professional April 1966; Blackpool July 1971 (£7000); Southend United March 1972 (£7000); Lincoln City August 1974 (£9000) after being on loan from the previous February; Watford October 1977 (£10,000); CITY May 1980 (£40,000), appointed club reserve team coach May 1984 but remaining as a signed player.
Honours: (Lincoln City) Div. 4 champions 1976. (Watford) Div. 4 champions 1978.
In a long career has played in several positions including full-back and inside-forward. Chiefly, though, a midfielder in berths which used to be called right- and left-half, and this was his role in the above promotion sides. A real professional and a skilled one.

BOWERING, Michael (1957-1960)
Outside-left: 45 apps; 7 goals.
1959: 5ft. 7ins; 10st. 6lbs.
Born: Hull, 15 November 1936.
Career: Junior football to CITY on amateur forms December 1957, turning professional September 1958; Chesterfield June 1960 (£350); Gainsborough Trinity May 1961.
The regular left-winger in the season of his senior debut, 1958/59, opponents finding him a speedy and elusive adversary. In the following (relegation) season Mike gave way to the emerging Cripsey and newly-signed Gubbins, and left during the ensuing close season.

BOWLER, Gerrard C. (1949-1950)
Centre-half: 38 apps.
1949: 6ft; 12st.
Born: Londonderry, 8 June 1919.
Career: Derry Municipal Training College; Derry City 1938; Belfast Distillery April 1943 (£1000, the first 4-figure fee between Irish clubs); Portsmouth August 1946 (£3500); CITY August 1949; Millwall June 1950 (£11,000) APV Co, Crawley (Sussex County League) as player/manager and as a reinstated amateur cs 1958, returning to APV Co as manager/coach for 1962/63, playing when required.
Honours: Northern Ireland international (3 apps.). (Distillery) Irish Cup finalist 1946.
Gerry possessed an easy action, brimmed with confidence and was extremely accurate in his passing, whether by head or foot. Had much experience at right-back and wing-half for other clubs, playing in the former position in wartime inter-league matches. Latterly worked as a storekeeper for the APV company.

BOWN, Herbert Arthur (1925)
Goalkeeper: 4 apps.
1921: 6ft; 12st. 10lbs.
Born: East Ham, London, 3 May 1893.
Died: 11 February 1959.
Career: Romford Town (during which spell he was associated with West Ham United); Leicester Fosse as a professional April 1913; Halifax Town May 1922; retired cs 1924 but signed for CITY in an emergency January 1925.
Soon became the first choice goalkeeper at Leicester where his reliability and sound judgment matured over the years. Did well for them in wartime football also. An ever-present in both Halifax seasons and, unusual for a 'keeper, Herbert's name appeared among their scorers in 1922/23. Ran a successful fish and poultry business in Leicester.

BOYTON, John (1913-1914)
Forward: 13 apps; 1 goal.
1913: 5ft. 9½ins; 11st. 3lbs.
Born: Glasgow, circa 1891.
Career: Kilsyth Emmett Rovers; CITY March 1913-1914.
Young Scot, stated to be 21 at the time of signing. Soon in the Tigers' League team – 10 of his 13 appearances were registered by the end of the 1912/13 season – he didn't command a place the following term.

BRADBURY, William (1955-1960)
Inside-right/centre-forward: 178 apps; 82 goals.
1957: 5ft. 10ins; 10st. 13lbs.
Born: Matlock, 3 April 1933.
Career: Modern Machines FC (Midland works side) to Coventry City ground staff, turning professional May 1950; Birmingham City November 1954 (in exchange for another

player); CITY October 1955 (about £4000); Bury February 1960 (£5000); Workington November 1960 (£3000); Southport July 1961 (£1500); Wigan Athletic as player/coach June 1962 for a season, then played 7 games for Kirby FC (Lancashire Combination) at the end of 1962/63 before retiring.

A real character possessing a great theatrical sense shown in mock exaggerated gesture to colleague, opponent and crowd alike. But there was a lot of footballing skill as well – for example, in the 1958/59 promotion season Bill's 30 goals were a post-war club record (surpassed 7 years later by Ken Wagstaff). Deservedly popular.

BRADFORD, Bernard (1927-1930)
Right-back: 1 app.
1929: 5ft. 11ins; 11st. 9lbs.
Born: Walker, Newcastle-on-Tyne, 13 February 1906.
Died: 1975.
Career: Walker Park (Newcastle); CITY cs 1927; Walsall 1930.

Tall defender whose 3 years at Anlaby Road coincided with City having both full-back berths more than adequately covered; accordingly Bradford's opportunities were minimal.

BRANDON, Thomas (1920-1922)

Right-back/inside-right: 56 apps; 3 goals.
1921: 5ft. 9½ins; 12st. 6lbs.
Born: Blackburn 1893. Died: 1 May 1956.
Career: Blackburn Rovers when 16; South Liverpool; West Ham United cs 1913; CITY June 1920; Bradford June 1922; Wigan Borough cs 1925-1926.

Gained inter-county honours at right-back, his essential position. A sturdy defender but it's in his other berth that Tom chiefly figures in City's chronicles. For he was an architect of the sensational 3-0 Cup victory over all-conquering Burnley in 1921, cracking in a goal from 25 yards. Son of the Scottish international, Tom Brandon senior.

BRAYSON, Joseph Hayes (1926-1927)
Outside-left: 3 apps.
1926: 5ft. 8½ins; 11st.
Born: Newcastle-on-Tyne, 12 December 1902.
Died: 13 May 1970.
Career: South Shields 1919/20; Newburn 1920/21; Ashington cs 1921; Scotswood; CITY April 1926.

Reserve winger receiving an opportunity when the two-footed and ever-present Billy Taylor tackled the troublesome opposite flank in the 1926/27 season. Joe got an early League debut with South Shields when a teenager, subsequently getting to know the North-East non-League scene.

BREMNER, William John (1976-1978)

Midfield: 61 apps. 6 goals.
1977: 5ft. 5½ins; 10st. 7lbs.
Born: Stirling, 9 December 1942.
Career: Stirling schools football; Gowanhill Juniors (Stirling); Leeds United as an amateur cs 1958, turning professional December 1959; CITY September 1976 (£25,000); retired May 1978; Doncaster Rovers manager November 1978; where in emergencies, he made 2 League appearances and 2 as substitute.
Honours: Scottish international (54 apps). Scottish Under-23 international (4 apps). Scottish schoolboy international. With Leeds United: European Cup finalist 1975. Inter-Cities Fairs Cup winner 1968. League champions 1969, 1974. Div. 2 champions 1964. FA Cup winner 1972; finalist 1965, 1970, 1973. FL Cup winner 1968.

The Tigers' gates were immediately boosted on this famous player's signing. Billy's long string of honours listed above is indicative of his quality. Skippered Leeds in the remarkable Revie era: a fiery little redhead sometimes at odds with authority but always resolute, brave and oozing skill. 'Player of the Year', 1970/71.

BRIDGES, Ben (1957-1960)
Inside-forward: 1 app.
1958: 5ft. 8ins; 11st.
Born: Hull, 3 February 1937.
Career: To CITY as a professional July 1957, graduating from the club's junior sides; Scarborough July 1960.

A single League appearance in his first season as a full professional was Ben's senior lot, this being the Bradbury, Coates & Co era. (Incidentally, the thought occurs that the band of ex-Tigers who later served Scarborough and Goole Town would make a sizeable Who's Who on their own!).

BRIGGS, Arthur Lionel (1921-1924)
Goalkeeper: 5 apps.
1922: 5ft. 10ins; 10st. 10lbs.
Born: Newcastle-on-Tyne, 1900.
Career: Jesmond Villa (Newcastle); Walker Celtic (Newcastle); CITY cs 1921; Tranmere Rovers August 1924 (after trials with Manchester City); Ashton National July 1932; Swindon Town 1933; Newport County June 1935-1936.

Found the job of understudying the consistent Billy Mercer somewhat unrewarding but proved his own reliability with 3 other senior clubs. Clocked up nearly 350 League matches for them, 233 in the 8-year Tranmere stint. Played for his county when an amateur.

BRIGGS, James (1912-1914)
Forward: 2 apps.
1912: 5ft. 8½ins; 11st.
Born: West Moor, Newcastle-on-Tyne, 1893.
Career: Craghead United; CITY August 1912-1914.

Recruited from the ever productive North-East when still a teenager. Both his League outings occurred in 1912/13 and Briggs found opportunities for young reserve attackers limited in his time at Anlaby Road.

BROWELL, Anthony ('Andy') (1907-1912)
Centre-half: 101 apps; 4 goals.
1912: 5ft. 9ins; 11st. 10lbs.
Born: Wallbottle, Northumberland, September 1888.
Died: 7 March 1964.

Career: Newburn Juniors; CITY 1907; Everton February 1912; West Stanley 1913, leaving this club in 1924.

Capable and solid pivot who followed brother Tom to Everton a couple of months after the latter's transfer. Andy eventually settled in Hull working first as a coal trimmer and then for a local bus company.

BROWELL, George (1905-1911)
Right-half: 194 apps; 3 goals.
1910: 5ft. 10ins; 12st. 7lbs.
Born: Wallbottle, Northumberland, 1884.
Died: 1951.
Career: West Stanley; CITY September 1905; Grimsby Town January 1911.

The eldest and heftiest of the Browell clan and also, incidentally, the one who wore City colours the longest. A solid and dependable wing-half, George's aggregate of League games was only bettered by John McQuillan and 'Stanley' Smith in the pre-WW1 period.

BROWELL, Thomas ('Boy') (1910-1911)
Centre-forward: 48 apps; 32 goals.
1912: 5ft. 8ins; 11st.
Born: Wallbottle, Northumberland, 19 October 1892.
Died: 8 October 1955.
Career: Newburn Grange (Tyneside League); CITY 1910 (£2); Everton December 1911 (£1,550); Manchester City October 1913 (£1,780); Blackpool September 1926 (£1,150); Lytham as player/coach cs 1930 – cs 1933; Morecambe December 1933 – 1934.
Honours: Football League vs. Irish League 1920. (Manchester City) FA Cup Finalist 1926.

One of the legendary names on the Tigers' roll-call, youngest of the Browells (hence the nickname, Boy, plus the fact he was a youthful prodigy). Did well everywhere, full of pluck and a consistent scorer: netted 206 goals in the League not counting any in wartime competitions. After leaving football worked as a tram-driver.

BROWN, Henry Stanford (1946-1947)
Centre-half: 2 apps.
Born: Workington, 23 May 1918.
Died: 27 April 1963.
Career: Workington FC as an amateur 1935; Wolverhampton Wanderers as a professional February 1937; CITY May 1946; retired through injury March 1947.

Had joined Wolves as an inside-forward and made his League debut for them at outside-right in 1938/39 following reserve team duty at full-back. So Harry came to Boothferry Park as a proven utility man, showing he was a capable pivot too. Later employed by the Hull firm, Priestman Bros., and acted as

Bridlington Town's trainer/coach for 4 seasons up to his death, which occurred as a result of a motor accident.

BROWN, Michael John (1954-1967)
Full-back: 8 apps.
1960: 5ft. 9½ins; 11st. 9lbs.
Born: Walsall, 11 July 1939.
Career: Gloucester schools football to CITY on amateur forms 1954, turning professional October 1958; Lincoln City, July 1967 (originally on 2 months' trial); Cambridge City 1968, holding appointment as the club's coach until joining Oxford United's coaching staff in 1969, becoming their manager September 1975 – July 1979; West Bromwich Albion assistant manager July 1979; Manchester United assistant manager June 1981. (In the last 2 appointments has worked as No. 2 to Ron Atkinson).
A City reserve for an unconscionably long time although his ground staff years were also occupied with an engineering apprenticeship, and he was a regular in his Lincoln season. Has become much better known as a managerial figure. Although hailing from Walsall, Mike's parents were both Hull-born.

BROWN, Ronald (1947)
Centre-forward: 7 apps; 3 goals.
1946: 5ft. 10ins; 12 st.
Born: Ballymoney, Co Wexford, 20 March 1923.
Career: Royal Navy football; Plymouth Argyle 1945; CITY March 1947.
An Irish leader of the attack, nicely built for the job and a bustler. Came with a good record for Argyle in the latter stages of wartime League football – in 24 matches Ron had slotted in 17 goals. Not retained at the end of the 1946/47 season.

BROWNSWORD, N(athan) John (1946-1947)
Left-back: 10 apps.
1957: 5ft. 8ins; 10st 6lbs.
Born: Campsall nr. Doncaster, 15 May 1923.
Career: Frickley Colliery; CITY September 1946; Frickley Colliery again 1947; Scunthorpe United cs 1947; retired cs 1965.
Honours: (Scunthorpe United) Div. 3 (North) champions 1958.
A one-time miner best known, of course, for a remarkable length of service with Scunthorpe – his 595 League appearances easily constitute a club record. Jack also established a national record there by converting 50 penalties, this being subsequently surpassed by David Peach of Southampton. Besides the obvious consistency, Jack was noted for speed and effective tackling.

BUCHAN, William Ralston Murray (1948-1949)

Inside-forward: 41 apps; 12 goals.
1949: 5ft. 10½ins; 11st.
Born: Grangemouth, Stirlingshire, 17 October 1914.
Career: Cowie Juveniles; Grange Rovers; Celtic January 1932; Blackpool November 1937 (£9,000) (guest player for Manchester United, Leicester City, Bath City, Aberaman and Hamilton Academicals during WW2); CITY January 1948 (£5,000); Gateshead November 1949; Coleraine as player/manager July 1953 – January 1954, later that year, when around 40, assisting East Stirlingshire in 16 matches.
Honours: Scotland wartime international vs. England 1943. Scottish League vs. Irish League 1936, 1938. (Celtic) Scottish League champions 1936, 1938. Scottish Cup winner 1937. (City) Div. 3 (North) champions 1949.
Distinguished Scottish footballer, lithe and graceful. Renowned as a penalty taker – with consummate skill he would trickle the ball in but nevertheless leave the goalkeeper stranded. On returning to his native Grangemouth in 1954, Willie worked as a process worker at ICI.

BULLESS, Brian (1949-1964)
Left-back/left-half/inside or outside-left: 327 apps; 29 goals.
1957: 5ft. 10ins; 11st.
Born: Hull 4 September 1933.
Career: Hull Schools; CITY as an amateur August 1949, turning professional October 1950; retired through injury cs 1964.
One of the best – and possibly the most versatile – of footballers ever produced in the Hull area. For Brian could fill any of the left

flank berths and, moreover, fill them with distinction. At full-back quick to tackle and clear, at half-back immaculate in distribution and as a forward he shone as a link man or when on a solo venture. And poised throughout – one felt he would have graced a First Division outfit.

BULLOCK, Arthur (1932-1934)
Outside-left: 18 apps; 3 goals.
Born: Hull, 1909.
Career: Southcoates Lane School (Hull); Hull Schools and then local junior football; CITY on amateur forms circa 1932/3; York City December 1934, subsequently assisting Bridlington Town.
Honours: England schoolboy international vs. Scotland and Wales 1924.
Never took the professional ticket, preferring a business career. This prevented advancement to top honours according to competent judges, Arthur's skills being comprehensive enough to reveal exceptional promise. The first schoolboy internationalist produced in the Hull area. England amateur international trialist January 1935.

BURBANKS, W(illiam) Edwin (1948-1953)
Outside-left: 143 apps; 20 goals.
1950: 5ft. 8ins; 10st. 8lbs.
Born: Bentley nr. Doncaster, 1 April 1913.
Died: 26 July 1983.
Career: Doncaster YMCA; Thorne Town; Denaby United; Sunderland February 1935 (£750); CITY June 1948; Leeds United July 1953; retired cs 1954.
Honours: (Sunderland) FA Cup winner 1937. (City) Div. 3 (North) champions 1949.
Actually a veteran of 35 on joining City but he gave several years splendid service – polished with an easy action and a hard shot in both feet. Played on the left flank all his career despite being naturally right-footed. Eddie settled in Hull, where he ran a sweet shop for 23 years prior to retiring in November 1979.

BURDETT, Thomas (1933-1935)
Centre-forward: 3 apps.
1937: 5ft. 10ins; 11st. 7lbs.
Born: Hetton-le-Hole, Co. Durham.
Career: Wheatley Hill FC (Co Durham); City cs 1933; Fulham cs 1935; Lincoln City July 1936; Bury May 1939.
Tom's best senior season was 1937/38 when he scored 8 times in 18 League outings for the Imps. But he didn't get many chances for the Tigers with the likes of McNaughton and Acquroff around. Could play on the wing too.

BURNETT, Denis H. (1973-1975)
Midfield: 46 apps; 2 goals.
1975: 5ft. 11ins; 11st. 12lbs.
Born: Southwark, London, 27 September 1944.
Career: North-West Kent Schools; West Ham United ground staff, turning professional October 1962; Millwall August 1967 (£15,000); CITY October 1973 (around £60,000) (Millwall again on loan March – April 1975); Brighton & Hove Albion August 1975 – February 1977, then having short spells with St. Louis (USA) and Shamrock Rovers before appointment as player/manager of FC Hagur, Norway.
Honours: (WHU) FL Cup finalist 1966.
A thoroughly tested and seasoned player by the time City acquired him, with over 300 League games to his name. Denis had played right-back in West Ham's fine mid-Sixties side and gave the Lions consistent service at wing-half. A true professional.

BURSELL, J(ohn) Clifford (1950-1956)
Inside-forward: 1 app; 2 goals.
Born: Hull, 16 January 1935.
Died: 27 July 1973.
Career: Hull schoolboy football (Newland Avenue School) and then a junior (Newland Youth Club) before joining CITY as an amateur during the 1950/51 season and he assisted Hull City Minors and then City Juniors, turning professional November 1952; Goole Town July 1956, later joining Bridlington Trinity.
Capable local. There cannot be many forwards who find the net twice on a League debut and this remains their sole senior outing. Such, however, was Cliff's experience.

BUTLER, Dennis M. (1963-1969)
Left-back: 215 apps; plus 2 subs.
1966: 5ft. 9ins; 11st. 10lbs.
Born: Fulham, 7 March 1943.
Career: Surrey junior football to Chelsea as an amateur cs 1958, turning professional May 1960; CITY June 1963 (£10,000); Reading December 1969 (£8,000); retired May 1974.
Honours: (City) Div. 3 champions 1966.
Strong, mobile defender. Was first choice left-back for most of his Boothferry Park span following an initiation into League football for Chelsea on the other flank. A first teamer at Reading too, clocking up a further 170 League outings before retiring.

BUTLER, Ian (1965-1973)
Outside-left: 300 apps; plus 5 subs; 66 goals.
1966: 5ft. 10ins; 11st.
Born: Darton nr. Barnsley, 1 February 1944.
Career: Barnsley Schools; Rotherham United

as an apprentice 1960, turning professional August 1961; CITY January 1965 (£40,000); York City July 1973 (£9,500) (Barnsley on loan October 1975 for a spell); Bridlington Town March 1976.
Honours: (City) Div. 3 champions 1966.
The youngest of the expensive trio of forward signings made by the Tigers in the space of 2 months (the other being Wagstaff and Ken Houghton). It's a matter of history that the expenditure paid off with 109 goals scored in the '65/66 championship campaign. Ian Butler was a fine winger – mobile, neat, thrustful and consistently good in his 8-year tenure at Boothferry Park.

BYRNE, Andrew (1913-1914)
Outside-left: 3 apps.
1913: 5ft. 6ins; 10st.
Born: Dublin.
Career: Shelbourne; CITY cs 1913-1914.

Irish forward, small and light. One of several players tried on the left-wing in 1913/14, Jack Lee easily claiming most appearances (23) despite, and unlike Byrne, having played only in minor football hitherto.

CAMERON, Kenneth (1935-1936)
Inside-forward: 30 apps; 12 goals.
1930: 5ft. 9ins; 11st. 2lbs.
Born: Glasgow, circa 1905.
Career: Parkhead FC (Glasgow); Preston North End cs 1926; Middlesbrough March 1929; Bolton Wanderers October 1933; CITY June 1935; Queen's Park Rangers August 1936.

Signed by Preston for his natural assets of speed, strength and control but, throughout his career, never seemed to quite fulfil obvious potential. As one commentator aptly said, 'a player of fitful brilliance'. Cameron's connection with the Tigers unfortunately coincided with a disastrous relegation season.

CAMERON, William Smith ('Kilty') (1914-1919)
Inside-right: 47 apps; 9 goals.
1908: 5ft. 8ins; 12st.
Born: Mossend, Lanarkshire, 1884.
Died: 15 October 1958.
Career: Burnbank Athletic 1902/03; Albion Rovers and Renton during the period 1903-04; Glossop 1904; Bolton Wanderers 1906; Blackburn Rovers 1907/08; Bury 1912/13 (£600); CITY January 1914 (guest player for Hamilton Academicals during WW1); Bury again May 1919 as manager (made 2 FL apps. 1919/20 until May 1923); Rochdale manager August 1930-December 1931.
Honours: (Blackburn Rovers) FL champions 1912.

A well known personality in English football circles for quarter of a century. Prominent as a junior, representing Lanarkshire in 1903, he made a successful transition to the first-class game. Had considerable experience at centre-forward and, in his Blackburn years, played in every position excepting goalkeeper and right-back. Outside football worked at different times as a licensee and as a firm's representative.

CAMPBELL, Austen Fenwick (1935-1936)

Left-half: 11 apps.
1935: 5ft. 9ins; 11st. 11lbs.
Born: Hamsterley, Co. Durham, 5 May 1901.
Died: 8 September 1981.
Career: Spen Black & White; Leadgate Park; Coventry City 1919/20; Leadgate Park again June 1921; Blackburn Rovers February 1923; Huddersfield Town September 1929; CITY November 1935.
Honours: England international (8 apps). Football League (5 apps). (Blackburn) FA Cup winner 1928. (Huddersfield) FA Cup finalist 1930.

An old warrior who completed his League career at Anlaby Road. Untiring, strong tackling, and a forceful forager who liked to dribble through at times and try a shot. Could hit a ball tremendously hard.

CAMPBELL, Joseph (1925-1927)
Left-half: 11 apps.
1927: 5ft. 11ins; 12st.
Born: Walker, Newcastle-on-Tyne, 31 October 1903.
Died: 14 September 1981.
Career: Walker Park FC (Newcastle); CITY cs 1925; Bradford City cs 1927.

Could take the other wing-half berth too. A well built reserve kept in the background at Anlaby Road by the consistency of Bleakley.

CAPEWELL, Ronald (1954-1955)
Goalkeeper: 1 app.
1950: 6ft. 3ins; 14st.
Born: Sheffield, 26 July 1929.
Career: Sheffield junior football to Sheffield Wednesday March 1950; CITY July 1954; King's Lynn July 1955.

Custodian possessing extra large dimensions both as to height and weight. Ron had 29 First Division outings under his belt from the two seasons prior to joining City, but at Boothferry Park was unable to supplant Bly and Teece.

CARTER, Horatio Stratton ('Raich') (1948-1952)

Inside-forward: 136 apps; 58 goals.
1949: 5ft. 8ins; 11st.
Born: Hendon, Sunderland, 21 December 1913.
Career: Sunderland Schools; Whitburn St. Mary's; Sunderland Forge; Esh Winning; Sunderland FC on amateur forms November 1930, turning professional November 1931; Derby County December 1945 (£8000) after being a guest player for that club during WW2; CITY as player/assistant manager March 1948 (£6000), appointed player/manager May 1948, resigned managership September 1951 and played until April 1952 when he retired; came out of retirement to assist Cork Athletic January-May 1953. Leeds United manager May 1953-June 1958; Mansfield Town manager February 1960 to appointment as Middlesbrough manager January 1963, an appointment held until February 1966, when he left the game.
Honours: England international (13 apps.). England wartime international (8 apps.). Football League (4 apps.). England schoolboy international (4 apps.). (Sunderland) League champions 1936. FA Cup winner 1937. (Derby County) FA Cup winner 1946. (City) Div. 3 (North) champions 1949. (Cork) FA of Ireland Cup winner 1953.

Arguably the greatest player ever to don a City shirt – he possessed marvellous ball control, and was a powerful marksman and a superb tactician. An excellent cricketer, Raich assisted Durham in the Minor Counties and, in 1946, Derbyshire.

CARTER, Joseph (1946-47)
Goalkeeper: 5 apps.
Born: Keighley, Yorks, 1920.
Career: Walsall pre-WW2; Notts County during WW2; CITY June 1946; Bournemouth & Boscombe Athletic March 1947; Bradford City August 1947.

The first full post-WW2 season must surely have created a record for the number of Northern Section players called upon. Half the clubs fielded 30 or more, City leading with an improbable 43. Joe Carter was one of the 4 'keepers used, and City was the only club for which he made appearances in peace-time League competition.

CARTWRIGHT, Philip (1929-1930)
Outside-right: 20 apps.
1929: 5ft. 8ins; 10st. 11lbs.
Born: Scarborough, 8 February 1908.
Died: 1974.
Career: Scarborough FC; Middlesbrough cs 1926; Bradford cs 1927; CITY cs 1929; Lincoln City May 1930; Bournemouth & Boscombe Athletic July 1933; Carlisle United 1934.
Honours: (Bradford) Div. 3 (North) champions 1928. (Lincoln) Div. 3 (North) champions 1932.

Played on the left-wing also in his Park Avenue days. Assertive and dangerous at his best, Phil liked to cut in and shoot – a successful ploy at Lincoln despite a blank scoresheet with City.

CASSIDY, Joseph (1935-1937)
Inside-left: 8 apps; 1 goal.
1935: 5ft. 6½ins; 11st.
Born: Glasgow.
Career: Glasgow Ashfield; CITY cs 1935, left 1937.

Signed from a crack Scottish junior side, a prime source for City recruitment since the days of John Boynton and Douglas Morgan. Joe made 7 of his 8 League appearances in the sad 1935/36 relegation season.

CHADWICK, Clifton (1946-1947)
Outside-right/outside-left: 23 apps; 7 goals.
1938: 5ft. 6ins; 10st. 6lbs.
Born: Bolton, 26 January 1914.
Career: Fleetwood; Oldham Athletic October 1933; Middlesbrough February 1934; CITY

September 1946; Darlington July 1947; Stockton August 1948.
An experienced campaigner by the time he joined City, having seen an amount of Div. 1 service at Middlesbrough. Assertive, two-footed and a consistent scorer. With Oldham had made their League side after only 2 games in the 'A' team.

CHAPMAN, Henry (1911-1913)
Outside/inside-right: 33 apps; 7 goals.
1911: 5ft. 8ins; 11st. 7lbs.
Born: Kiveton Park, Sheffield, 1879.
Died: 29 September 1916.
Career: Kiveton FC; Worksop Town; Sheffield Wednesday circa 1898; CITY April 1911; retired March 1913 on his appointment as City's secretary, a post he held until 1915 when his health broke down.
Honours: (Wednesday) League champions 1903 and 1904. FA Cup winner 1907.
At his peak Harry was considered by many to be the best inside-right in England, better even than the great Steve Bloomer. There seems little doubt he would have played for England but for being Bloomer's contemporary. A tremendous worker, extremely fast and imaginative. Brother of the celebrated manager, Herbert Chapman. Harry's early death was caused by tuberculosis.

CHARLESWORTH, Arthur Laurence (1919-1921)
Centre-forward: 15 apps; 7 goals.
Born: Hull 1898. Died: 4 January 1966.
Career: Junior football to CITY 1919; Worksop Town cs 1921; Doncaster Rovers cs 1922.
Bustling leader, understudy to Sammy Stevens and then Paddy Mills after joining the Tigers during season 1918/19. Son of A. P. Charlesworth, a noted cricketer of the Hull Town Club, Arthur lived in Cottingham.

CHARLTON, William (1934-1935)
Centre-forward: 3 apps; 1 goal.
Born: South Stoneham, Hants. 1912.
Career: Oxford University (Southampton on amateur forms December 1931); CITY 1934/35; Wimbledon August 1935 for 1 season; Queen's Park Rangers 1936-38. Also assisted Barnet and was on Fulham's books but made no League apps. for the latter.
Honours: England amateur international (4 apps. vs. Scotland 1936 and 1937, Wales and Northern Ireland 1936). Oxford Blue 1932-34.
Gifted amateur spreading his talents among a number of clubs, amateur and professional, during the Thirties. For the latter the greatest beneficiary was QPR (10 goals in 18 League outings). Employed by British Oil & Cake Mills after leaving university, which seems to account for his Tigers' connection.

CHEETHAM, Samuel (1920-1921)
Right-back: 28 apps; 1 goal.
1920: 5ft. 9½ins; 12st. 6lbs.
Born: St. Helens, 3 December 1896.
Died: 30 September 1967.
Career: Matt's Heath FC (St. Helens); CITY cs 1920; Bradford City November 1921; Yeovil & Petters United cs 1929.
Capable back of sturdy build, a member of the successful 1921 Cup side. The 8 years with Bradford City were spent mainly in the reserves, his League outings totalling only 57 (9 goals). Settled in Yeovil and spent the rest of his days there.

CHILDS, J(ohn) Arthur (1928-1931)

Centre-half: 74 apps; 8 goals.
1930: 5ft. 10ins; 11st. 10lbs.
Born: Acomb, York, 25 April 1899.
Died: 1964.
Career: Shildon; Darlington; CITY cs 1928; Exeter City cs 1931; Darlington again cs 1934; retired 1936.
A robust centre-half with attacking ideas and a good sense of constructive play. A contemporary critic wrote that Arthur was '... a relentless tackler, judicious purveyor, and exceptionally clever with his head'. Was for long a licensee in Darlington until about 1962 after which he had a year as steward at the Whitley Bay Golf Club.

CHILTON, Christopher R. (1959-1971)
Centre-forward: 415 apps; 193 goals.
1965: 6ft; 12st.
Born: Sproatley, East Yorks., 25 June 1943.
Career: East Riding schools football; Bilton FC (Hull Church League); CITY on amateur forms August 1959, turning professional July 1960; Coventry City August 1971 (£92,000); retired through injury December 1972. With Coventry's permission joined Bridlington Town December 1973; Highland Park (Johannesburg, South Africa) April 1974, later becoming player/assistant manager and then manager in the late 1970s. Eventually returned to City and joined the coaching staff; appointed assistant manager July 1982.
Honours: (City) Div. 3 champions 1966.
An imperishable name in City's history, a gifted centre-forward strong in both team work and individual goal scoring, whose partnership with the equally dangerous Waggy became legendary. In senior competition Chris actually played 475 games for the Tigers – the above 415 plus 39 FA Cup and 21 League Cup. Holds the club's aggregate goals' record (which includes 11 hat-tricks).

CLARK, W. (1919/20)
Outside-left: 1 app.
Career: Had been on Notts County's books as an amateur. Joined CITY from a Tyneside Alliance club during season 1919/20.
Young forward briefly at Anlaby Road. His only League outing was in the home game against Blackpool on March 20, 1920, which the Tigers lost 0-1.

CLARKE, Douglas (1955-1965)
Outside-right: 368 apps; 79 goals.
1960: 5ft. 8¾ins; 12st. 2lbs.
Born: Bolton, 19 January 1934.
Career: Bolton Wanderers as an amateur; Darwen; Bury February 1952; CITY November 1955 (about £2,000); Torquay United July 1965; Bath City July 1968; Bridgwater Town 1969; played for the Ex-Torquay United XI for charity from 1970. Returned to Torquay United as a permit player to coach reserves cs 1972. In September 1976 reported to be assisting Bodmin (South-Western League) when 42 years of age.
First choice right-winger at Boothferry Park for almost a decade after service with Bury as an inside-right. Doug always gave full value, a sprightly and thrustful performer who contributed a fair tally of goals. Made 521 League appearances plus 4 subs all told in which he scored 117 goals. While playing for Torquay, became partner in a carpet cleaning business.

CLELAND, J. H. (1914/15)
Inside-forward
Career: Had been on the books of Preston North End and played in the Southern League before joining CITY on amateur forms.
Stationed at Beverley Barracks as an Army private and played in the home game against Huddersfield Town on March 15, 1915 after a couple of outings with the reserves. He played for the Barracks against the City reserves in March 1916. A schoolmaster by profession.

COATES, David P. (1952-1960)
Inside-left: 61 apps; 13 goals.
1957: 5ft. 10ins; 10st. 8lbs.
Born: Newcastle-on-Tyne, 11 April 1935.
Career: Fatfield Juniors; Shiny Row FC (Durham); CITY November 1952; Mansfield Town March 1960 (around £1000); Notts County July 1964 (£2,250); retired cs 1967 and became the latter club's youth coach to the following December, when appointed Aston Villa's assistant coach for 9 years; Luton Town coach cs 1978.
At Boothferry Park 4 years before his League debut but a vital cog in the '58/59 promotion side with his prompting and foraging, missing only 5 games. Served Mansfield and Notts well, developing into a capable wing-half. A first-class coach.

COLLIER, John C. (1920-1926)
Right-half: 169 apps.
1923: 5ft. 9ins; 11st. 10lbs.
Born: Dysart, Fife, 1 February 1897.
Died: 28 December 1940.
Career: Victoria Hawthorn (juveniles); Denbeith Star; Inverkeithing United; CITY cs 1920; Queen's Park Rangers July 1926; York City as player/manager 1928-1930. Became York's manager 1933 and then their trainer/coach cs 1936 when a decision was made to dispense with a managerial appointment.
For 5 seasons a City regular, this canny Scot, along with Tommy Bleakley on the other flank, ensured there were no worries

concerning the wing-half spots. A summing-up by a contemporary critic reads '. . . could tackle with the best of them, and played with a vigour commanding respect of an opponent'. A licensee in York until appointed the local club's manager.

COLLINSON, Leslie (1953-1967)
Right-half: 296 apps; plus 1 sub; 14 goals.
1960: 5ft. 11¼ ins; 11st. 13 lbs.
Born: Hull, 2 December 1935.
Career: Local junior football to CITY on amateur forms August 1953, turning professional December 1956; York City February 1967 (£3,000); Goole Town July 1968; returned to Hull junior football in June 1970 when he signed for Hull Brunswick, and as late as 1975 joined Chilton Amateurs.
Long serving Tiger somewhat uneven in performance but, at his best, positively brilliant. His skills covered all the wing-half requirements — distribution, intervention, head work, speed and planning vision – and his lithe build abetted all these qualities.

CONWAY, Andrew (1947-1949)
Inside-forward: 6 apps; 5 goals.
1947: 5ft. 9ins; 11st.
Born: South Shields, 17 February 1923.
Career: County Durham Schools 1938; South Shields Ex-Schoolboys; Guildford City as an amateur during WW2; North Shields as a professional October 1946; CITY June 1947; Dartford cs 1949; Stockport County July 1950; Goole Town cs 1951.
Reserve with an excellent eye for the scoring chance – he had netted 28 goals for North Shields in 1946/47 before joining the Tigers, and 5 in 6 League outings speaks for itself. Did not make the Stockport first team during his one-season return to the first-class game.

COOK, Peter Henry (1946-1948)
Centre-forward/outside-left: 5 apps.
1947: 5ft. 7¾ ins; 11st. 2¾ lbs.
Born: Hull, 1 February 1927.
Died: 4 November 1960.
Career: Hull schoolboy football; Wath Wanderers; Kingston Wolves (Hull); CITY June 1946 (Scarborough on loan latter part of season 1947/48); Scarborough on transfer 1948; Bradford City May 1949; Crewe Alexandra August 1950.
Capable local forward who died tragically young. Bradford City signed him after a good stint at Scarborough – in his loan period there, for example, Peter scored 12 goals in 15 matches. Son of Jimmy Cook, one-time Hull Kingston Rovers' centre-threequarter.

COOKE, Albert (1930-1932)
Centre-half: 35 apps.
1930: 5ft. 10½ins; 12st.
Born: Royston nr. Barnsley, 1908.
Career: Scunthorpe United; CITY February 1930; Halifax Town July 1932-1936.
A sturdy and dependable half-back Aggregated 171 FL appearances in 5– seasons, 136 of them for Halifax. Played at left-half for the West Riding club to accommodate the ubiquitous Ted Craig who monopolised their pivotal berth right up to the outbreak of WW2. (For the record, Craig from joining in 1932 missed only 8 out of possible 297 League encounters).

CORBETT, Alexander M. (1948-1949)
Goalkeeper: 8 apps.
1949: 6ft; 12st. 4lbs.
Born: Saltcoats, Ayrshire, 20 April 1921.
Career: Annbank United; Ayr United 1945; New Brighton July 1946; CITY January 1948; Dartford cs 1949 and remained in non-League football until July 1953 when he joined Hartlepools United from Weymouth for a short spell.
Came to notice at New Brighton where he played some remarkable 'last ditch' performances with pluck and any amount of resource. The 4-year gap between Corbett's departure from and return to the League scene is a little unusual.

CORNER, J(ames) Norman (1962-1967)
Centre-half/centre-forward: 5 apps; 4 goals.
1964: 6ft. 2ins; 12st.
Born: Horden, Co. Durham, 16 February 1943.
Career: Horden Colliery Welfare; CITY August 1962; Lincoln City October 1967 (£4,000); Bradford City January 1969 (£4,000); Bradford cs 1972.
Norman's commanding height was an asset in both the pivotal and centre-forward positions. An enthusiastic player, after his years

as a City reserve, he was a recognised first teamer with his other two League clubs. (Bradford Park Avenue, whom he joined in 1972, was then a non-League outfit).

COVERDALE, Robert (1921-1924)
Wing-half/inside-right: 63 apps; 5 goals.
1922: 5ft. 8ins; 11st. 4lbs.
Born: West Hartlepool 1892.
Died: 7 January 1959.
Career: Rutherglen Glencairn; Sunderland 1912; CITY May 1921; Grimsby Town September 1924; Bridlington Town 1925.

Two footed so immaterial which flank he took. A gritty competent performer and a useful man to have on your side. Originally an outside-left. When with Glencairn, Bob represented Scotland in a junior international, the selectors not learning until afterwards he, being an Englishman, was ineligible. Played in Army football for the Durham Light Infantry.

COWAN, William (1925-1927)

Centre-forward: 11 apps; 8 goals.
1927: 6ft; 12 st. 7lbs.
Born: Gateshead, 28 November 1900
Died: 3 February 1979.
Career: High Fell FC (Gateshead); CITY 1925; Blackpool May 1927; Chesterfield cs 1928; York City circa 1929.

Could shoot with both feet and, in spite of his size, was very fast. Returned to live and work in Hull when his playing days were over.

CRAWFORD, John Forsyth (1919-1923)
Outside-right: 126 apps; 9 goals.
1921: 5ft. 5ins; 10st.
Born: Jarrow, 26 September 1896.
Died: 1975.

Career: Palmer's Works FC (Jarrow) before service in Navy during WW1; Jarrow Town; CITY December 1919; Chelsea May 1923 (£3,000); Queen's Park Rangers May 1934; retired cs 1937 and became a QPR coach until outbreak of war in 1939. Post-war coached Maldon Town (Essex) in his spare time.
Honours: England international vs. Scotland 1931.

Small in physique yet the complete winger — strong with both feet, a master at middling the ball and cutting in, and full of trickery. Played most of his senior soccer at outside-right, but capped on the opposite flank after moving there at Chelsea to accommodate the celebrated Alec Jackson. At this time Jackie was part of an all-international attack: himself plus 4 Scots — Jackson, Alex Cheyne, Hughie Gallacher and Andy Wilson.

CRAWSHAW, Cyril B. (1947/47)
Centre/inside-forward: 2 apps; 1 goal.
1939: 5ft. 8 ins; 11st. 5lbs.
Born: Barton-on-Irwell, Lancs. 2 March 1916.
Career: Fleetwood; Queen of the South cs 1938; Exeter City 1939 (after a trial with Rochdale); Stalybridge Celtic during WW2; CITY cs 1946.

A bit of an English rarity in that he made his senior debut in Scotland, playing a couple of Scottish League Div. 1 games for Queen of the South in 1938/39. The War, of course, robbed Cyril of much footballing life and he was already 30 on joining the Tigers.

CRICKMORE, Charles Alfred (1957-1962)
Outside-left: 53 apps; 13 goals.
1960: 5ft. 7½ins; 9st. 6lbs.
Born: Hull, 11 February 1942.

Career: Hull Schools; CITY as an amateur August 1957, turning professional February 1959; Bournemouth & Boscombe Athletic June 1962 (about £2,000); Gillingham June 1966; Rotherham United November 1967 (around £2,000); Norwich City January 1968 (£15,000); Notts County March 1970 (£7,500); retired June 1972.
Honours: (Notts County) Div. 4 champions 1971.
Always pretty fast, Charlie put on some needed weight after leaving City, developing into a sought-after wingman. He was a strong shot and the accredited penalty-taker for Notts County. A regular with all his clubs, he was an ever-present in his Notts championship season.

CRIPSEY, Brian (1951-1958)
Outside-left: 145 apps; 19 goals.
1958: 5ft. 6ins; 10st. 13lbs.
Born: Hull, 26 June 1941.
Career: Hull schools football then assisted three junior clubs in the area (Maybury Youth Club, Dansom Lane Police Boys Club and Bridlington Central United) before going on National Service. On returning he assisted Brunswick Institute (Hull) prior to joining CITY as a professional November 1951; Wrexham September 1958 (£4000); retired April 1960 but joined Bridlington Town the following July and subsequently played for Bridlington Trinity and Goole Town. Emigrated to New Zealand in 1963 and had a few games there.
A regular player after making his League debut in January 1953, Brian was a clever little winger skilled in ball control. Employed as a laboratory technician in New Zealand.

CROFT, Stuart D. (1972-1981)
Centre-half: 187 apps. + 3 subs; 4 goals.
1978: 5ft. 11ins; 11st. 5lbs.
Born: Ashington, 12 April 1954.
Career: Junior football to CITY as an apprentice professional, turning full professional April 1972; Portsmouth March 1981; York City cs 1981; Bridlington Trinity November 1981.
Developed into a very useful central defender, permanently supplanting Steve Deere in the mid-1970s. Mostly a regular thereafter until his departure to Pompey but left the League scene in a matter of months.

CROSBIE, Robert C. (1953-1955)
Centre-forward: 61 apps; 22 goals.
1951: 5ft. 9ins; 12st.
Born: Glasgow, 2 September 1925.
Career: Minor football to Bury May 1947; Bradford May 1949 (£11,000); CITY October 1953 (£4,000); Grimsby Town July 1955 (£1,425); Queen of the South August 1957-1958.
Honours: (Grimsby Town) Div. 3 (North) champions 1956.
Vigorous leader whose menace to opposing defences is well illustrated by his aggregate FL record: 144 goals from 273 games. Bury, it is said, had no great wish to part with Bob, but were enticed by Bradford's substantial offer. He played inside-forward also at Park Avenue.

CROZIER, James (1927-1928)
Outside-left: 3 apps.
1927: 5ft. 7ins; 11st.
Born: Glasgow.
Career: Glasgow Ashfield; CITY cs 1927-1928. Later assisted Derry City of the Irish League.
Sturdy reserve left-winger. Shared the deputy's duties in his Anlaby Road season with a promising amateur, Billy Barraclough, the latter getting the edge and finishing with 9 League outings.

CUBIE, Neil G. (1957-1958)
Right-half: 4 apps.
Born: South Africa, 3 November 1932.
Career: Clyde FC (Capetown); Bury October 1956; CITY July 1957; Scarborough July 1958.
One of several South Africans who followed in Alf Ackerman's footsteps to Boothferry Park in the 1950s. Neil could also take an inside-forward spot and, indeed, had joined Bury as an inside-man.

CUMMINS, George P. (1962-1965)
Inside-forward: 21 apps; 2 goals.
1964: 5ft. 8ins; 10st. 7lbs.
Born: Dublin, 12 March 1931.

Career: St. Patrick's Athletic (Dublin); Everton November 1950 (after 2 months' trial); Luton Town August 1953 (£8000); Cambridge City July 1961 (£3000); CITY November 1962; retired April 1965.
Honours: Eire international (19 apps). (Luton Town) FA Cup finalist 1959.
Much capped Irishman and a very clever one. A specialist in ball control and distribution – no great goal scorer himself but manufacturer of countless others for colleagues. George must be one of comparatively few players to go from a League to a non-League club for a sizeable fee.

CUMNER, R(eginald) Horace (1938)
Outside-left: 12 apps; 4 goals.
1938: 5ft. 8½ins; 10st. 10lbs.
Born: Cwmaman, Aberdare, 31 March 1918.
Career: Welsh Schools; Arsenal cs 1935, who sent him for development to their nursery club, Margate, from where he joined CITY on loan January 1938; Arsenal May 1938; Notts County July 1946; Watford July 1948; Scunthorpe United September 1950; Bradford City July 1953; Poole Town cs 1954.
Honours: Welsh international (3 apps.). Welsh Victory international vs. Scotland 1946. Welsh wartime international (5 apps.). Welsh schoolboy international.
Came to City as a bright young talent en route to a high destiny, but the War, of course, cancelled out much of his career. Clever, lively and a regular scorer, Horace could also play on the other flank and was at inside-left for his Victory international. Suffered serious burns while on service with the Royal Marines early in the War.

CUNLIFFE, Arthur (1938-1946)

Outside-left: 42 apps; 19 goals.
1935: 5ft. 7½ins; 11st. 7lbs.
Born: Blackrod, Lancs., 5 February 1909.
Career: Adlington when only 14; Chorley 1927; Blackburn Rovers 1928; Aston Villa May 1933; Middlesbrough December 1935; Burnley April 1937; CITY June 1938; Rochdale cs 1946, retiring from playing and becoming their trainer July 1947; Bournemouth & Boscombe Athletic trainer July 1950 and then that club's physiotherapist from 1971 until his retirement cs 1974.
Honours: England international vs. Northern Ireland and Wales 1933.
At the outset regarded as an outside-right but, after a rather halting start, made his considerable reputation on the opposite flank. Arthur was astonishingly fast, able to control the ball when going at full tilt and in a small space, and a frequent scorer. Cousin of J. N. Cunliffe (Everton and England).

DAGNALL, Walter (1906-1907)
Inside-left: 8 apps; 2 goals.
Born: Prescot, Lancs, 1883.
Career: St. Helens Recreational; CITY May 1906-1907.
Promising young forward whose year as a Tiger was dogged by bad health. So much so the club released him in May 1907 with a rider as to the possibility of re-engagement should his health improve. In the event, however, re-engagement did not materialise. Brother-in-law of City's W. S. Robinson, and a brother had an unsuccessful trial for City in 1914.

DALEY, Alan James (1947-1948)
Outside-left: 7 apps.
1947: 5ft. 7ins; 10st. 7lbs.
Born: Mansfield, 11 October 1927.
Career: Pleasley Boys Club; Mansfield Town September 1946; CITY July 1947; Bangor City cs 1948; Worksop Town; Doncaster Rovers March 1950; Peterborough United 1950; Boston United 1951; Scunthorpe United June 1952; Corby Town cs 1953; Mansfield Town again November 1953; Stockport County February 1956; Crewe Alexandra June 1958; Coventry City November 1958; Cambridge United January 1961; Burton Albion cs 1961.
A real rolling stone, flitting in and out of the League scene with an astonishing frequency (which keeps a soccer historian on his toes, if nothing else!). On his day could cause havoc to the opposing defence and he packed a blistering left-foot shot. Father of Steve Daley, whom Wolves transferred to Manchester City for £1.4m. in September 1979.

DANIEL, Peter William (1971-1978)
Right-back: 113 apps; 9 goals.
1975: 5ft. 8¼ins; 10st. 10lbs.
Born: Hull, 12 December 1955.
Career: Originally to CITY on schoolboy forms October 1969; City Juniors to CITY as an amateur 1971, turning professional September 1973; Wolverhampton Wanderers May 1978 (£182,000); Minnesota Kicks, USA, May 1984; Sunderland August 1984 (£15,000).
Honours: England under-21 international (7 apps.). (Wolves) League Cup winner 1980.
Also played at left-back for City and in midfield for Wolves. Among the most distinguished of the numerous Hull-born contingent; neat, intelligent and mobile in style. Peter's career had a setback in February 1981 when he broke his right leg in a match against Aston Villa. Worked as a painter and decorator before taking up the game professionally.

DARLING, Benjamin Stoves (1938-1939)
Goalkeeper: 2 apps.
1938: 6ft. 1ins; 11st. 11lbs.
Born: South Shields, 23 March 1916.
Died: 1974.
Career: South Shields FC; CITY June 1938-1939.
Tall performer who, along with the youthful Billy Bly, understudied John Ellis in season 1938/39. Was actually the No. 2 'keeper, Bly getting into the Midland League team when Ben sustained a head injury.

DAVIDSON, Andrew (1948-1968)

Right-back/right-half: 520 apps; 18 goals.
1958: 5ft. 10ins; 11st. 9lbs.
Born: Douglas Water, Lanarkshire, 13 July 1932.
Career: Douglas Water Thistle; CITY ground staff May 1948, turning professional September 1949; retired July 1968 and joined the club coaching staff, working in this capacity until appointment as Chief Scout December 1977-December 1979.
Honours: (City) Div. 3 champions 1966.
Such a remarkable length of service for one club inevitably produces records. Here are Andy's: a record number of League appearances for the club and of first team outings (598, which included an unbroken run of over 200); and he became the only Scot to put in 20 years playing service with a single Football League club. In May 1969 he was awarded a Football league statuette for this service. And, strange to relate, the number of games could have been even larger, for he sustained three broken legs and a bad knee injury in the course of his two decades. Younger brother of City's David.

DAVIDSON, David Craighogie (1946-1948)
Outside-right: 22 apps; 4 goals.
1947: 5ft. 7½ins; 10st. 7½lbs.
Born: Douglas Water, Lanarkshire, 19 March 1926.
Career: Cambuslang Rangers; Douglas Water Thistle; CITY November 1946 (month's trial with Crystal Palace during season 1947/48); Scarborough cs 1948.
Speedy winger with a degree of determination. Had 18 League outings in Major Buckley's first season when an astonishing 43 players were fielded and 20 other forwards didn't reach double figures. Elder brother of City's long-serving Andy and cousin of James Davidson, Partick Thistle and Scotland. Returned to Scotland not long after joining Scarborough and worked as a sub-postmaster.

DAVIDSON, Ian (1963-1969)
Wing-half: 5 apps; plus 1 sub; 1 goal.
1970: 5ft. 9ins; 11st. 6lbs.
Born: Goole, 31 January 1947.
Career: Goole junior football to CITY on amateur forms August 1963, turning professional February 1965 (Scunthorpe United on loan September 1968 — cs 1969); York City June 1969 (£2,000); Bournemouth & Boscombe Athletic July 1971 (in exchange for another player); Stockport County May 1972; Worcester City July 1974.
Showed he was League material with regular first team selection during his 'on loan' season at Scunthorpe. Did similarly well elsewhere apart from Bournemouth, where subsequent Norwich City notables, Benson and Powell, held sway.

DAVIES, David Daniel ('Dai') (1933-1948)
Inside-forward: 142 apps; 31 goals.
1938: 5ft. 7½ins; 10st. 7lbs.
Born: Aberdare, 5 December 1914.
Died: 13 October 1984.
Career: Aberaman Athletic; CITY 1933; Scunthorpe United September 1948; Barton Town (Lincs.) player/manager 1950 for a short spell.
The war robbed this thoughtful player of several matured years. Was consistent as well as crafty. Qualified as a telephone engineer, working for the Hull Telephone Dept. 23 years, and was also supervisor at the Wheeler Street Youth Club for 25 years. An excellent table tennis player good enough to represent both Hull and Yorkshire. Brother-in-law of City's Ernie Bell.

DAVIES, George Albert (1920-1922)
Left-half: 11 apps.
1921: 5ft. 8½ins; 10st. 6lbs.
Born: Prescot, Lancs, 1897.
Died: 1956.
Career: Prescot FC; CITY cs 1920; Merthyr Town cs 1922; Grimsby Town September 1923 - 1925.
Among the many recruits from the fruitful Prescot quarter, George found little profit in understudying an ever consistent Tommy Bleakley. Things were better in the Merthyr year and he proved his competence with 18 Southern Section outings.

DAVIES, Harry J. (1905-1907)
Full-back: 34 apps; 1 goal.
1905: 5ft. 11ins; 13st. 12lbs.
(Probably born in the Midlands).
Died: 23 September 1963.
Career: Wolverhampton Wanderers; Shrewsbury Town cs 1901; Gainsborough Trinity cs 1902; Doncaster Rovers cs 1904; CITY March 1905-1907.
Described as a 'back of the robust type', which must have disconcerted many an opponent considering the Davies dimensions quantified above. A tested performer by the time he reached Anlaby Road. Father of Harry Davies jnr., a famous Stoke and Huddersfield Town inside-forward of the Twenties and Thirties.

DAVIES, John G. (1980-)
Goalkeeper: 24 apps.
1983: 6ft. 3ins; 13st. 2lbs.
Born: Llandyssul nr. Swansea, 18 November 1959.
Career: Junior football to Cardiff City as an apprentice professional, turning full professional January 1978 (CITY on a fortnight's trial February 1980); CITY permanently June 1980 (£12,000).

Proved an excellent stand-in for Tony Norman. Has all the physical attributes needed for the 'keeper's job, especially in the way of reach. Troubled by injury in 1983/84.

DAVIN, Martin (1930-1931)
Inside-forward: 8 apps; 1 goal.
1930: 5ft. 8½ins; 9st. 10lbs.
Born: Dumbarton.
Career: Dumbarton FC; Bury August 1927; Bolton Wanderers cs 1930; CITY November 1930; Yeovil & Petters United 1931; Clapton Orient cs 1933.
Despite a slight physique had occupied the centre-forward position on occasion but generally regarded as an inside-right, playing a prompting and supportive role to his fellow forwards. In his longest League stint, the 3 Bury seasons, Martin scored 9 goals in 38 outings.

DAVIS, Ian (1981-)
Midfield: 25 apps plus 3 subs; 1 goal.
1983: 5ft. 11¼ins; 12st. 6½lbs.
Born: Hull.
Career: Hull Schools; CITY as an apprentice professional July 1981, turning full professional January 1983.
Highly promising young local player. Made the bulk of his League appearances while still an apprentice – a measure of his promise. Side-lined through injury in season 1983/84.

DEACEY, Charles (1914-1920)
Centre-half: 75 apps; 4 goals.
1919: 5ft. 8½ins; 12st.
Born: Wednesbury, Staffs, 6 October 1889.
Died: 1952.
Career: Wednesbury Town; Wednesbury Old Athletic; West Bromwich Albion May 1910; CITY June 1914; Grimsby Town December 1920 (£750); Pontypridd July 1923; retired circa 1925.
Also led the attack on occasion when at West Brom. Described by the club's historian as quiet and unobstrusive. Deacey was, of course, none the worse for that – an effective regular in 1914/15 and the first post-war campaign.

DEACY, Nicholas S. (1980-1982)
Forward: 80 apps. plus 7 subs; 7 goals.
1981: 6ft. 0½ins; 12st. 7lbs.
Born: Cardiff, 19 July 1953.
Career: Merthyr Tydfil; Hereford United September 1974 (£1,300) (Workington on loan December 1974-early 1975); PSV Eindhoven, Holland, June 1975 (£22,500); Beringen (Belgium) 1979; Vitesse Arnheim, Holland, 1979/80; CITY February 1980 (£93,600); Happy Valley FC, Hong Kong, March 1982; Bury (after month's trial) 1983.

31

Honours: Welsh international (12 apps. including 4 as a substitute). Welsh Under-23 international vs. Scotland 1976. Welsh Under-21 international vs. Scotland 1977.
Surely has had as cosmopolitan a career as any Tiger, past or present. Did especially well with Eindhoven, where he won almost all his caps, and brought to City by Mike Smith, who was acquainted with Deacy's abilities from his period as the Wales manager.

DEERE, Stephen H. (1973-1976)
Centre-half: 65 apps. plus 1 sub; 2 goals.
1974: 6ft. 2ins; 12st. 7lbs.
Born: Burnham Market, Norfolk, 31 March 1948.
Career: Norfolk junior football and Norwich City on amateur forms; Scunthorpe United November 1967; CITY May 1973 (£20,000 plus Ken Houghton and Stuart Pilling) (brief spells on loan to Barnsley October 1975 and Stockport County December 1975); Bridlington Town March 1976; Scarborough cs 1976; Scunthorpe United again February 1978 (£5,000) – 1980.
Left the League scene in March 1976 on taking up an appointment with a Hull finance company but returned after 2 years for another Scunthorpe run. Caught City's attention in the first, his sound and consistent displays warranting the investment. In all Steve appeared for Scunthorpe in 337 League encounters plus 6 as substitute.

DENBY, Stanley (1932-1937)
Left-half: 123 apps; 3 goals.
1935: 5ft. 7½ins; 10st. 1lb.
Born: Goole 1912.
Career: Goole Territorials; Goole Town; CITY April 1932; Guildford City cs 1937.
Honours: (City) Div. 3 (North) champions 1933.
Slight in build yet so effective and reliable in the aspects of wing-half play. Gave Guildford City fine service also, skippering the southern club's reserve side in the immediate post-war seasons when well into the veteran stage.

DENNISON, C(harles) Robert (1952-1958)
Full-back: 24 apps; 1 goal.
1955: 5ft. 9ins; 12 st.
Born: Hull, 12 September 1932.
Career: Hull junior football to CITY as an amateur 1952, turning professional July 1954; Scarborough July 1958, later with Bridlington Town, retiring from playing cs 1968. Was Bridlington Town's trainer in season 1968/69 and appointed their manager July 1969.
An efficient reserve back, Bob's best senior season was his first as a professional, 1954/55, when he had 16 League outings. Switched to centre-half during his Bridlington Town playing days.

De VRIES, Roger S. (1965-1980)
Left-back: 314 apps. plus 4 subs.
1975: 5ft. 8½ins; 11st. 5lbs.
Born: Willerby, Hull, 25th October 1950.
Career: Hull schools football to CITY as an amateur February 1965, turning professional September 1967; Blackburn Rovers June 1980; Scunthorpe United on trial October 1981.
Consistent and reliable defender, qualities which are revealed by the large tally of League appearances noted above. Came into the side in 1970/71 and for a decade his seasonal total was usually above the 30 mark. Among the best of City's local developments

DIAMOND, John James ('Legs') (1931-1932)
Centre-forward: 1 app.
1933: 5ft. 8½ins; 11st.
Born: Middlesbrough, 30 October 1910.
Died: July 1961.
Career: Junior football to CITY 1931; Shelbourne 1932; Southport cs 1933; Barnsley November 1934; Cardiff City May 1935; Bury June 1936; Oldham Athletic 1937; Hartlepools United 1938/39.
Made a reputation after leaving the Tigers by scoring 33 goals in the Irish Free State League for Shelbourne during 1932/33. Thereafter for the remainder of the 1930s half a dozen Football League clubs employed his speed, resolution and opportunism. Jack's nickname, derived from a notorious contemporary, the Chicago gangster, Legs Diamond.

DICKINSON, WILLIAM (1938-1939)
Centre/inside-forward: 18 apps; 5 goals.
1938: 5ft. 10ins; 11 st.
Born: Wigan, 18 February 1906.
Career: Wigan junior football; Wigan Borough 1925/26; Nottingham Forest June 1928; Rotherham United August 1934; Southend United May 1936; CITY May 1938.
A very experienced campaigner by the time of arrival at Anlaby Road. Was a regular with all his previous senior clubs, an aggregate of 370 League games bringing him a personal goal tally of 199. Thrustful, a good shot but, above all, consistent. Performed at outside-right in his last two Forest seasons.

DIMBLEBY, Stanley (1935-1937)
Half-back: 21 apps.
1935: 6ft; 12st. 7lbs.
Born: Killingholme, Lincs. 1917.
Career: Killingholme FC; CITY August 1935; Port Vale June 1937.

Not the first (nor the last) useful junior from North Lincolnshire to be acquired by the Tigers. Stan's stay, though, cannot match that of the recruit from neighbouring East Halton (Denis Durham) who crossed the Humber a decade later.

DIXON, E. 1907

Full-back: 3 apps.
1907: 5ft. 8¾ins; 11st. 8lbs.
Thought to have hailed from the North-East.
Career: Tynevale FC; Sunderland cs 1904; Lincoln City cs 1905; CITY March 1907.
Made his senior bow in Lincoln's colours. His League appearances for the Sincil Bank club totalled 36 – he was a regular in 1905/06 – before becoming a Tiger on March 23, 1907.

DIXON, E(dward) Stanley (1926-1930)

Centre-half: 98 apps; 3 goals.
1928: 5ft. 11ins; 12st. 8lbs.
Born: Choppington, Northumberland, 26 May 1984.
Died: August 1979.
Career: Barrington Albion; Newcastle United February 1914(£5); Blackburn Rovers March 1923 (£1,100); CITY May 1926 leaving 1930, and assisting East Riding Amateurs a short while as a permit player.
Originally an inside-forward, Stan played at right-and centre-half with Blackburn. He was a dour performer and quite fearless in the tackle. On leaving football he managed 4 Hull cinemas before retiring to Bedlington in his native Northumberland.

DOBSON, Ian (1974-1980)

Central defender: 86 apps plus 6 subs; 7 goals.
1977: 5ft. 10ins; 11st. 1lb.
Born: Hull, 3 October 1957.
Career: Hull Schools; Yorkshire Schools; CITY as an apprentice professional July 1974, turning professional October 1975; Hereford United June 1980 – February 1982.
In the old jargon would have been described as a centre – or wing-half. Nicely mobile, quick to the tackle and always in the action. Emigrated to Australia March 1982.

DODDS, Leslie Smith (1934-1935)

Outside-left: 20 apps; 4 goals.
1935: 5ft. 8ins; 10st. 10lbs.
Born: Patishead, Newcastle-on-Tyne, 20 September 1912; Died 29 November 1967.
Career: Newcastle Swifts; Grimsby Town 1929/30; CITY March 1934; Torquay United June 1935; Clapton Orient 1937; Hartlepools United cs 1939.
Had come under the eye of Newcastle United (the Swifts side was the United's nursery) but joined Grimsby when 17 years of age. Experienced a fair amount of Div. 3 soccer, both Northern and Southern Sections, playing the typical winger's game of his time. Son of a former Airdrieonians' player and nephew of Joe Dodds, Celtic and Scotland.

DON, Robert P. (1935/1937)

Right-back/right-half: 21 apps.
1935: 5ft. 10½ins; 11st. 7lbs.
Born: Glasgow.
Career: Glasgow Perthshire; CITY May 1935-1937
Principally a half-back, a supple and rangy build holding him in good stead for the wing-half role, but he could turn in a useful purely defensive game at the rear. Came from one of the best Scottish junior outfits which has supplied so much talent to the seniors over the decades.

DOWEN, John Stewart (1938-1939)

Left-back: 39 apps.
1938: 5ft. 8ins; 11st. 4lbs.
Born: Wolverhampton, 1914.
Career: Walsall Schools; Courtaulds FC (Wolverhampton); Wolverhampton Wanderers 1932/33; West Ham United briefly October 1935, then returning to Wolves; CITY cs 1938.
Honours: England schoolboy international vs. Scotland and Wales 1929. Birmingham FA vs. Scotland 1934 in the so-called junior international.
After a notable career as juvenile and junior Dowen was unable to break into an ultra-strong Wolves side, getting 6 League games in his several Molineux seasons. At Anlaby Road, however, he was a first choice back, an able partner to the redoubtable Cliff Woodhead.

DOWNES, Percy (1932)
Outside-left: 11 apps; 3 goals.
1931: 5ft. 8¾ins; 10st. 5lbs.
Born: Langhold, Notts, 19 September 1905.
Career: Gainsborough Trinity; Blackpool November 1924 (£500); CITY during the 1931/32 season; Stockport County August 1932; Barnley cs 1934; Oldham Athletic May 1936; Gainsborough Trinity cs 1938.
Honours: (Blackpool) Div. 2 champions 1930.
Won golden opinions at Blackpool with his speed, craft and powerful left-foot shooting after the club had paid what was then their record fee for a junior. Made 143 appearances in the Seasiders' League team including 37 in the Div. 2 championship term.

DOWNIE, John D. (1954-1955)
Wing-half/inside-forward: 28 apps; 5 goals.
1955: 5ft. 9ins; 11st. 11lbs.
Born: Lanark, 19 July 1925.
Career: Lanarkshire schoolboy football to Bradford ground staff 1942, turning professional 1945; Manchester United March 1949 (£18,000); Luton Town July 1953 (around £10,000); CITY July 1954 (£9,000); King's Lynn July 1955; Wisbech Town; Mansfield Town October 1958; Darlington June 1959; Hyde United July 1960.
Honours: (Manchester United) League champions 1952.
City used Johnny as a half-back as well as in the attack, where he had made a great reputation just after WW2. His fast, penetrative displays induced Matt Busby to sign him for the first great post-war Manchester United as replacement for the transferred Johnny Morris.

DOYLE, Dermot P. (1922-1923)
Outside-left: 6 apps.
1922: 5ft. 9ins; 11st. 7lbs.
Born: Dublin.
Career: Shelbourne; Pontypridd 1921; CITY April 1922; released at the close of season 1922/23.
Alec Thom's stand-in for just over a season, a usefully built Irish winger with a truly Irish name. The Humberside clubs had quite a connection with South Wales non-League outfits in the early 1920's – City's Charlie Deacy went to Pontypridd via Grimsby, whilst the latter secured several players from Mid-Rhondda including the great Jimmy Carmichael.

DREYER, Gordon (1935-1936)
Right-half: 5 apps.
1935: 5ft. 11ins; 11st. 7lbs.
Born: Sunderland 1914.
Career: Washington Colliery; Hartlepools United cs 1934; CITY June 1935; Hartlepools United cs 1936; Luton Town May 1937.
Attracted some attention in his initial senior campaign but didn't establish himself with the Tigers. However, another good season at Hartlepools was followed by a move to newly-promoted Luton and, by the outbreak of war, Gordon was their first-team centre-half.

DRYBURGH, Thomas James Douglas (1954-1955)
Outside-left: 23 apps; 3 goals.
1950: 5ft. 7ins; 11st. 7lbs.
Born: Kirkcaldy, 23 April 1923.
Career: Lochgelly Albert; Aldershot June 1947; Rochdale July 1948; Leicester City September 1950; CITY May 1954; King's Lynn July 1955; Oldham Athletic August 1957; Rochdale again November 1957-1958.
On returning to the League scene grossed only 6 outings from the Oldham and second Rochdale spells but had seen much senior action prior to 1955. Tom's neat, thrustful wing play in 95 appearances for Leicester had brought him 29 goals for example – perhaps his best feature was goal scoring potential.

DUNCAN, Andrew (1930-1935)
Inside-forward: 104 apps; 35 goals.
1935: 5ft. 5ins; 11st. 4lbs.
Born: Renton, Dunbartonshire, 25 January 1911.
Career: Renton Thistle; CITY May 1930; Tottenham Hotspur March 1935 (around £6,000); retired during the War but joined Chelmsford City for a spell in April 1946.
Honours: (City) Div. 3 (North) champions 1933.
Canny Scottish inside man mostly operating on the right flank. Brought the Tigers a tidy fee when transferred to the Spurs and gave them decent service too (93 League matches in which he netted 22 goals).

DUNCAN, Douglas ('Dally') (1928-1932)
Outside-left: 112 apps; 44 goals.
1930: 5ft. 7½ins; 11st. 2lbs.
Born: Aberdeen, 14 October 1909.
Career: Aberdeen Richmond; CITY August 1928; Derby County March 1932 (£2,000); Luton Town as player/coach October 1946; retired April 1948, then becoming Luton's manager for 10 years until appointment as Blackburn Rovers' manager October 1958 – June 1960. Later ran a guest house in Brighton, coached Brighton Schools for a year and did some scouting for Luton.
Honours: Scottish international (14 apps). (Derby County) FA Cup winner 1946. Scottish schoolboy international.

A brilliant stylist who carried his brilliance to the international arena, proving a worthy successor to the great Alan Morton. Dally's was a natural talent that appeared nonchalant but was deadly effective, doing the unexpected with masterly ball control.

DUNCAN, James R. (1953-1960)
Inside-forward: 26 apps; 3 goals.
1957: 5ft. 8ins; 10st. 10lbs.
Born: Hull, 2 April 1938.
Career: Hull Schools to CITY on amateur forms July 1953, turning professional April 1955; Bradford City June 1960; Bridlington Town July 1961.
Originally on City's books when only 15 on being spotted as a prospect from local schoolboy soccer. Compactly built with sound attacking ideas.

DUNNE, Leo (1935-1936)
Right-back: 8 apps.
1935: 5ft. 8ins; 11st. 7lbs.
Born: Dublin.
Career: Drumcondra; Manchester City September 1933; CITY June 1935.
Honours: Eire international vs. Switzerland and Germany 1935.
In spite of an international pedigree, Leo didn't win a regular place in English senior soccer, having only 3 League outings at Maine Road to add to the 8 with the Tigers. But plainly he was a good class defender with 55 games in Manchester City's Central League side before arriving at Anlaby Road.

DURHAM, R(aymond) Denis (1947-1960)
Left-back/left-half: 267 apps; 7 goals.
1955: 5ft. 11½ins; 11st. 7lbs.
Born: East Halton, Lincs, 26 September 1923.
Career: North Lincs schoolboy football; Army football; East Halton United; CITY April 1947 (had a trial in October 1946 but signing delayed because of appendicitis); Bridlington Trinity July 1960.
Honours: (City) Div. 3 (North) champions 1949.
Gave the Tigers 13 years excellent and loyal service. Denis was a stubborn defender with a yen to attack, when he was wont to employ a ponderous shot of surprising power. Had sampled many positions – inside-left at school, right- and centre-half in the Army and centre-forward for East Halton besides his Boothferry Park spots.

DUTHIE, James (1951-1953)
Centre-half/centre-forward: 17 apps. 3 goals.
1950: 5ft. 11ins; 13st.
Born: Trumperton, nr. Letham, Angus, 23 September 1923.

Career: RAF football; Grimsby Town as an amateur 1948, turning professional September 1949; CITY June 1951 (£500); Southend United May 1953; Bury Town (Suffolk) as player/coach June 1958.
Besides his utility value – the 5 campaigns at Southend usually found him at right half – Jim was a conscientious and reliable player. Had 160 League outings for the Essex Club.

ECCLES, Thomas Edward (1922-1923)
Centre-forward/inside-left: 9 apps; 2 goals.
1922: 5ft. 8ins; 11st. 12lbs.
Born: Hull, 1900.
Died: 21 October 1968.
Career: Army football: Hargreaves FC (Hull); CITY April 1922 – 1923. Subsequently with Bridlington Town.
Capable reserve forward, understudy to Paddy Mills and Joe Kitchen. With his junior side – which originated from the Gipsyville district of Hull – only briefly following 3 years Army service. Educated at the Williamson Street School in the city.

ECCLESTON, Stuart I. (1981-1982)
Defender: 22 apps. plus 1 sub.
1981: 5ft. 11ins; 11st. 5lbs.
Born: Stoke-on-Trent, 4 October 1961.
Career: Junior football to Stoke City as an apprentice professional, turning full professional October 1979; CITY January 1981; given a free transfer cs 1982.
Wore the No. 5 (centre-half's) shirt for all his City League outings and did reasonably well but lost his place before the half-way mark of season 1981/82 was reached. Made his senior debut with the Tigers.

EDELSTON, Joseph (1913-1920)
Wing-half: 89 apps.
1919: 5ft. 10ins; 11st. 5lbs.
Born: Appley Bridge, nr. Wigan 27 April 1891.
Died: 10 March 1970.
Career: St. Helens Recreational; CITY March 1913; Manchester City cs 1920; Fulham November 1920; retired cs 1926 and joined Fulham's office staff. After serving the Craven Cottage club for some years held appointments with Orient and Brentford and managed Reading during the War (appointed April 1939).
Honours: FA tour of South Africa 1920.
Nicely built half-back of proven ability. Skippered City during the Great War period. Father of the late Maurice Edelston, the England amateur and wartime international and BBC soccer commentator, who was born in Hull in 1918.

EDWARDS, Edmund C. (1936-1937)
Inside-right: 10 apps; 1 goal.
1938: 6ft; 12 st.

HULL CITY A.F.C. SEASON 1984-85

Back row: G. Swann, P. Olsson, A.J. Flounders, L. Pearson, R. M. McNeil, I. Davis, N. Williams.
Middle row: C. R. Chilton (assistant manager), M. Hollifield, J. Davies, W. Whiteburst, A.J. Norman, S. McEwan, P. D. Skipper, D. Booth (player/coach).
Front row: J. D. Roberts, S. Massey, G. W. Roberts, B. Horton (player/manager), D. Robinson (chairman), S. McClaren, W. Askew, J. Radcliffe (physiotherapist).

Born: Spennymoor, Co. Durham, circa 1912.
Career: Bury 1934/35; Clapton Orient August 1935; CITY May 1936; Mossley 1937; Carlisle United cs 1938.
Well proportioned inside man, his main contribution, however, being in the way of foraging rather than as a spear head. Had only 3 League outings elsewhere – 1 for the Orient and 2 at Carlisle.

EDWARDS, Keith (1978-1981)
Centre-forward: 130 apps. plus 2 subs; 57 goals.
1980: 5ft. 7 ins; 10st. 3lbs.
Born: Stockton-on-Tees, 16 July 1957.
Career: Joined Sheffield United from a Stockton youth club side in October 1975 following a 3-months' trial; CITY August 1978 (£55,000); Sheffield United again September 1981 (£75,000 plus a further £20,000 after 40 first team appearances).
Assuredly the finest signing made by Ken Houghton in his brief managerial reign – a razor-sharp opportunist, slightly built but skilled. City had no wish to lose the player even at a considerable profit, and rightly so for strike forwards of Keith's quality aren't exactly in abundance.

ELLIOTT, Harvey (1946-47)
Forward: 4 apps.
Born: Middleton, nr. Oldham, 21 January 1922.
Career: Manchester junior football to CITY 1946; given free transfer cs 1947.
One of the many 'first wave' recruits of Major Buckley and one of several from the Manchester area (of whom Jimmy Greenhalgh was the most noteworthy). Harvey arrived following good work in Mancunian junior circles but his stay at Boothferry Park was brief. Latterly worked as a window-cleaner.

ELLIS, John (1938-1939)
Goalkeeper: 32 apps.
1938: 5ft. 11½ins; 12st.
Born: Tyldesley, Lancs, 25 January 1908.
Career: Wolverhampton Wanderers 1930/31; Bristol Rovers cs 1934; CITY cs 1938; Clapton Orient July 1939.
An experienced 'keeper by the time he reached the Tigers, John had received a fair baptism of top flight football with Wolves prior to his 4 years in the West Country. Was Rovers' first choice until the arrival of Joe Nicholls from Spurs in 1936.

FAGAN, Fionan (Paddy) (1951-1953)
Outside-left: 25 apps; 2 goals.
1957: 5ft. 6ins; 9st. 11lbs.
Born: Dublin, 7 June 1930.
Career: Transport FC (Dublin); CITY March 1951; Manchester City December 1953 (£3,250); Derby County March 1960 (£7,500); Altrincham as player/manager cs 1961.
Honours: Eire international (8 apps). Eire 'B' international vs. Rumania 1958. (Manchester City) FA Cup finalist 1955.
Small, fast skilful Irishman and a real crowd pleaser. With Manchester City proved himself equally adept on the other wing. Son of J. Fagan of Shamrock Rovers, who was also an Eire international.

FARLEY, John D. (1978-1980)
Forward: 59 apps. plus 1 sub; 5 goals.
1979: 5ft. 7ins; 9st. 12lbs.
Born: Middlesbrough, 21 September 1951.
Career: Stockton; Watford July 1969 (Halifax Town on loan September-October 1971); Wolverhampton Wanderers May 1974 (£40,000) (Blackpool on loan October 1976); CITY May 1978; Bury August 1980; retired cs 1981.
Nimble left-winger, slight physically yet assertive and elusive. Attracted attention in his early senior years, occasioning Wolves' substantial outlay which was said in some versions to be £10,000 higher than the sum stated above.

FARQUHARSON, Hugh (1934-1936)
Goalkeeper: 7 apps.
1935: 5ft. 10½ins; 12st. 11lb.
Born: Glasgow, 1913.
Career: Renfrew Juniors; CITY September 1934; Dunfermline Athletic June 1936.
On returning to Scotland Hugh was involved in Dunfermline's unavailing fight against relegation from the top division of the Scottish League, but his brilliance in that struggle was favourably commented upon. Unorthodox in style (an unorthodoxy no doubt fuelled by 2 years of understudying Geordie Maddison!). Senior debut: vs. Fulham (away) 6 October 1934.

FAWCETT, Robert Elliot (1929-1931)
Centre-forward: 6 apps.
1929: 5ft. 7½ins; 10st. 9lbs.
Born: Usworth, Co. Durham, 31 July 1903.
Died: 1972.
Career: Usworth Colliery; CITY cs 1929 – 1931.
Appeared in 3 League line-ups in both seasons with City, the first being the historic Cup semi-final/relegation term. Another Fawcett had been on the Tigers' books in the Twenties – an amateur signed March 1922 from Harrogate FC along with pros Jock McGee and Harold Slater.

FAZACKERLEY, Stanley Nicholas (1912-1913)

Inside-right: 29 apps; 19 goals.
1915: 5ft. 11ins; 11st. 6lbs.
Born: Preston, Lancs, 3 October 1891.
Died: 20 June 1946.
Career: Accrington Stanley; CITY 1912 (£50); Sheffield United March 1913 (£1,000); Everton November 1920 (£4,000) establishing a new record; Wolverhampton Wanderers November 1922; Kidderminster Harriers 1924/25; Derby County August 1925; retired on medical advice April 1926.
Honours: FA tour of South Africa 1920 during which he twice played against their national team. (Sheffield Utd) FA Cup winner 1915. (Wolves) Div. 3 (North) champions 1924.
A big name in soccer immediately before and after the first World War, and one that commanded hefty transfer fees in both eras. Tall and graceful, Stan was an adroit dribbler and his shooting possessed power and direction.

FEASEY, Paul Cedric (1949-1966)
Full-back/centre and wing-half; 271 apps.
1958: 5ft. 8ins; 10st. 8lbs.
Born: Hull, 4 May, 1933.
Career: York Schools; York Railway Institute; CITY on amateur forms 1949, turning professional May 1950; Goole Town July 1966, appointed their player/manager May 1967 and remained with the club until cs 1970.
A long time City loyalist. Best remembered as a centre-half where, although short in stature by pivotal standards, he could match most opponents in the air, and his battling displays saved many a seeming lost situation. Although born in Hull, Paul spent much of his early life in York.

FENWICK, Alfred Randolph (1910-1914)
Left-half and centre-forward: 16 apps; 7 goals.
1914: 5ft. 10½ins; 12st. 4lbs.
Born: Hamsterley, Co Durham, 26 March 1891.
Died: 1975.
Career: Cragheart United (Co Durham); CITY 1910; West Ham United cs 1914 (Hartlepools United as a guest player 1918/19); Coventry City December 1919; Blyth Spartans 1921.
Continued to show his versatility at West Ham and looked upon there as a utility player. But the club recognised as did City, Alf was essentially a half-back where his vigorous tactics proved more valuable. He took the centre-forward role at Anlaby Road following the transference of Tom Browell.

FERGUSON, J(ames) Brian (1980-1982)
Midfield: 24 apps. plus 4 subs; 2 goals.
1981: 5ft. 10ins; 10st. 6lbs.
Born: Irvine, Ayrshire, 14 December 1960.
Career: Mansfield Town as an apprentice professional; Newcastle United January 1979; CITY December 1980; Goole Town cs 1982; Southend United August 1983.
Slim midfielder. Received his League baptism when at St James' Park in a then Div. 2 Newcastle United Side, in all having 4 outings and one substitution for the Geordies. Added to his senior experience with City before temporarily leaving the League scene.

FISHER, J(ames) Bernard (1955-1963)
Goalkeeper: 126 apps.
1959: 5ft. 11ins; 13st. 2lbs.
Born: York, 23 February 1934.
Career: York junior football; CITY, originally on amateur forms, turning professional November 1955; Bradford City July 1963 - 1965.
Weighty 'keeper, consistent and reliable. Understudied Billy Bly for 5 seasons, then first choice in 1960/61 and '61/62, totting up 87 League outings, before losing his place to Mike Williams. An ever-present for Bradford City in his first term at Valley Parade.

FLANNIGAN, Thomas (1929-1930)
Inside-right: 2 apps.
1929: 5ft. 9½ins; 10st. 1lb.
Born: Edinburgh, 27 April 1908.
Career: Edinburgh juvenile football to Dundee 1925; Stoke City cs 1927; CITY cs 1929 (£500); Loughborough Corinthians 1930/31; Rochdale and Buxton during 1931/32; St. Etienne (France) 1933 for 3 months; Shrewsbury Town 1933/34; left football 1934.
An article by him appeared in 'Topical Times' during October 1934 saying he had left the game disillusioned. According to the article, City placed a fee of £750 on his head at the

close of season 1929/30, a sum so high as to scare off any prospective buyer. The fee was lifted by the FL some 18 months later but Flannigan's unsettled career continued. A one-time hairdresser's apprentice.

FLETCHER, Peter (1974-1976)
Centre/inside-forward: 26 apps plus 10 subs; 5 goals.
1975: 6ft; 11st. 6lbs.
Born: Manchester, 2 December 1953.
Career: Manchester junior football to Manchester United as an apprentice professional, signing full professional December 1970; CITY May 1973 as part of the Stuart Pearson transfer deal, Fletcher being valued at £30,000; Stockport County May 1976 (£1,500); Huddersfield Town July 1978 - 1982.
Honours: (Huddersfield) Div. 4 champions 1980.
Led Huddersfield's attack in the 1980 championship side, finding the net 18 times in 30 matches and 8 substitutions, but wore the number 10 shirt as well at Boothferry Park. A tall player of rangy build, his height a handy factor in aerial work.

FLOOD, Charles William (1920-1922)

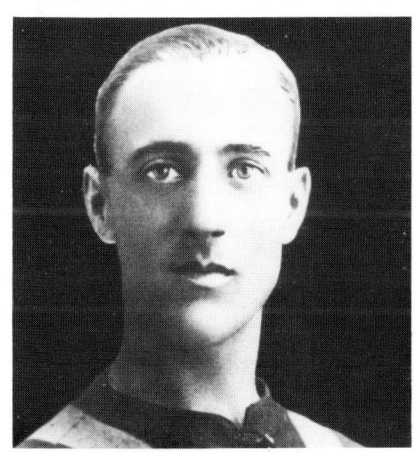

Inside-left: 54 apps; 24 goals.
1921: 6ft; 12st. 2lbs.
Born: Newport, Isle of Wight, 18 July 1896.
Died: 14 November 1978.
Career: Army football (Royal Garrison Artillery team); Plymouth Argyle (where he played as an amateur) 1919; CITY cs 1920; Bolton Wanderers May 1922; Nottingham Forest January 1923; York City cs 1926; Swindon Town February 1927; retired 1928.
Tall inside man possessed of an indomitable attitude that drove him at full stretch to the final whistle, helping out in defence besides giving his full weight to the attack. Settled in the Hull area and prominent in local cricket for many years after an earlier association with Notts CCC, Devonshire CCC and Sir Julian Kahn's XI. A fine wicket-keeper and attacking batsman, Charlie starred with Hull CC until the immediate post-war years, and was in 1963 appointed club coach.

FLOUNDERS, Andrew J. (1981-)
Forward: 54 apps. plus 16 subs; 27 goals.
1983: 5ft. 7½ins; 10st.
Born: Hull, 13 December 1963.
Career: Hull schools football to CITY as an apprentice professional, turning full professional December 1981.
Young and very promising striker establishing a reputation for consistent goal scoring. And he was said to have established a club record as the youngest Tiger to appear in the League team, coming on as a substitute in a match against Oxford United in October 1980 (age: 17 years, 296 days).

FORGAN, Thomas Carr (1949-1954)
Goalkeeper: 11 apps.
1955: 6ft; 12st.
Born: Middlesbrough, 12 October 1929.
Career: Middlesbrough junior football to CITY May 1949; York City June 1954 (£500); Gainsborough Trinity cs 1966.
A sound and sometimes brilliant custodian, ideally proportioned for the position. Must rank as one of the best and most consistent to represent York City – his League appearances there totalled a creditable 388. Emigrated with his family to Australia in March 1974.

FORWARD, Frederick John (1932-1933)

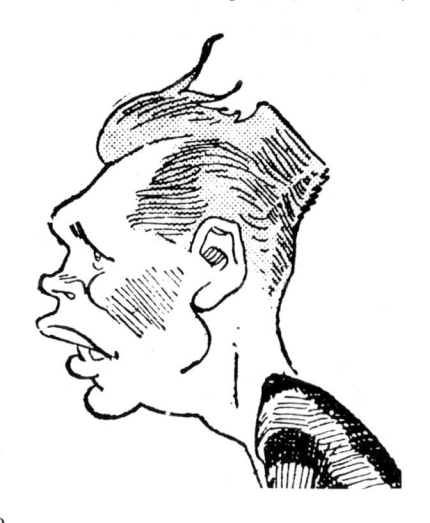

Outside-right: 38 apps; 6 goals.
1931: 5ft. 8ins; 11 st.
Born: Croydon, 8 September 1899.
Died: 1977.
Career: Crystal Palace 1920/21; Newport County cs 1924; Portsmouth February 1927; CITY July 1932; Margate October 1933 (following a trial with Bath City).
Honours: (Portsmouth) FA Cup finalist 1929. (City) Div. 3 (North) champions 1933.
Most appropriately named (a fact much latched upon by inter-war football writers), for Fred was a speedy, assertive forward with long service spanning all 4 divisions. Finished his League career in style, winning a Northern Section championship medal in his Anlaby Road season.

FOSTER, Thomas (1931-1938)
Centre-half/Wing-half: 25 apps; 1 goal.
1935: 5ft. 9½ins; 12st.
Born: Hull, 1913.
Career: Hull junior football to CITY cs 1931 on amateur forms, eventually signing as a professional.
Had been on City's books 3 seasons before making his League debut after useful service in the reserves. A good example of the talent produced in local amateur circles.

FOWLER, H(enry) Norman (1946-1949)
Right/left-back: 52 apps.
1947: 5ft. 8¼ins; 11st.
Born: Stockton-on-Tees, 3 September 1919.
Career: Stockton Schools; South Bank FC (Middlesbrough); Middlesbrough as a professional September 1936; CITY September 1946; Gateshead November 1949; Scarborough August 1952.
Honours: England schoolboy international vs. Scotland, Wales and Northern Ireland 1934, skippering the side for the Ireland match.
A notable career as a juvenile, his senior years lost a sizeable chunk because of the War. Being two-footed, Norman operated equally well on either flank. Cool and efficient.

FRANKLIN, Cornelius ('Neil') (1951-1956)
Centre-half: 95 apps.
1950: 5ft. 10½ins; 11st. 4lbs.
Born: Stoke-on-Trent, 24 January 1922.
Career: Potteries schoolboy football; Stoke Old Boys; Stoke City ground staff 1936, turning professional January 1939 (Guest player for Gainsborough Trinity during WW2); Santa Fe, Bogota, May 1950; CITY February 1951 (£22,500); Crewe Alexandra February 1956 (£1,250); Stockport County October 1957 (£1,250); Wellington Town as player/coach July 1959; Sankey's FC (Wellington) July 1960, having a year, 1961-2, as player/manager before retiring from playing December 1962. Coach to Appoel FC, Nicosia, Cyprus, February-November 1963; Colchester United manager November 1963 - May 1968.
Honours: England international (27 apps). England wartime international (3 apps). England 'B' international vs. Switzerland 1948. Football League (5 apps).
One of the great stars of the immediate post-war period; a pivot brilliant in heading, positioning and marshalling his defence, and stubborn withal. Became a licensee after leaving the game.

FRASER, David M. (1953-1958)
Outside-left: 11 apps; 7 goals.
1957: 5ft. 7ins; 10st. 5lbs.
Born: Newtongrange, Midlothian, 6 June 1937.
Career: Arniston Rangers; CITY On amateur forms 1953, turning professional July 1954; Mansfield Town July 1958; Third Lanark November 1959 (after month's trial); Cowdenbeath 1960.
Thrustful reserve winger. David, a Scot, certainly knew the way to goal, as the tally in his limited League opportunities while with City shows. Settled in Hull in 1963 after leaving the senior game and managed Brunswick and North Ferriby United.

FROST, W. Ben (1904-1906)
Right/centre-half: 1 app.
(Very possibly born at Hessle, nr. Hull).
Career: Hessle FC; CITY 1904-1906.
Local amateur half-back prominent in district soccer during the early 1900's. Played regularly for the Reserves in 1905/06, the

season when he played once in the League side. Represented the East Riding XI on several occasions and assisted both City and the Hessle club in the former's initial campaign.

FRYER, John L. (1937-1938)
Inside-right: 40 apps; 22 goals.
1938: 5ft. 10ins; 12st. 2lbs.
Born: Widnes, Lancs, 23 September 1911.
Career: Runcorn junior football; Everton 1930, originally on amateur forms; Wrexham cs 1933; CITY cs 1937; Nottingham Forest June 1938.
Well built attacker with progressive ideas which included plenty of hard shooting. Jack's best seasonal tally came in his Anlaby Road term although he scored frequently elsewhere too.

GALLACHER, Constantine (1947-1948)
Inside-forward: 18 apps; 3 goals.
1947: 5ft. 9ins; 11st. 4lbs.
Born: Londonderry, 25 April 1922.
Career: Lochee Harp (Dundee); Middlesbrough January 1947; CITY May 1947; Rochdale March 1948; Boston United cs 1948.
More the thoughtful linking-up man than a finisher of moves, as will be guessed from the above goal tally. Willie Buchan's arrival at Boothferry Park possibly shortened Con's stay.

GALVIN, Christopher (1973-1979)
Midfield: 132 apps. plus 11 subs; 11 goals.
1976: 5ft. 10ins; 12st. 3lbs.
Born: Huddersfield, 24 November 1951.
Career: Junior football to Leeds United as an apprentice professional, turning full professional November 1968; CITY July 1973 (around £25,000) (York City on loan December 1976 – April 1977); Stockport County April 1979 – May 1981. Later in 1981 went to Hong Kong and managed the Taun Wan FC.
Honours: England Youth international 1970.
An apprentice at Leeds when that club was continually among the honours, receiving an excellent grounding in the basics of his craft and eventually turning in sound performances for City. Elder brother of Tony Galvin, the well known Spurs and Eire forward.

GARDNER, Thomas (1932-1934)
Right-half 67 apps; 2 goals.
1935: 5ft. 9½ins; 11st. 4lbs.
Born: Huyton, Liverpool, 28 May 1910.
Died: 1970.
Career: Orrell FC (Liverpool); Liverpool FC as an amateur 1928, turning professional a year or so later; Grimsby Town cs 1931; CITY cs 1932; Aston Villa February 1934 (£4,500); Burnley April 1938; Wrexham December 1945; Wellington Town August 1947; Oswestry Town player/manager reverting to player/coach January 1952; Chester assistant trainer cs 1954-May 1967.
Honours: England international vs. Czechoslovakia 1934 and Holland 1935.
(City) Div. 3 (North) champions 1933.
(Blackpool) FL North Cup winner as a wartime guest.
A lively performer famed for massive throws which vied with those of the celebrated Sam Weaver. Played outside-right when at Wrexham. Latterly employed as steward at a club in Chester.

GARRETT, Sydney (1920-1927)
Wing-half: 8 apps.
1923: 5ft. 10ins. 12st. 2lbs.
Born: Hull, 1899.
Career: Hull junior football to CITY cs 1920; Goole Town cs 1927.
Seven seasons on City's books, for practically the whole of the time in the reserves. Useful to have around, though because Syd could play pivot as well as wing-half, and he was perfectly built for the intermediate line. His brother, Harold Garrett, was a Hull RLFC forward.

GARVEY, Brian (1953-1965)
Left-back/centre and left-half: 232 apps; 3 goals.
1961: 5ft. 8ins; 11st. 10lbs.
Born: Hull 3 July 1937.
Career: Hull junior football to CITY on amateur forms August 1953, turning professional January 1958; Watford June 1965; Colchester United June 1970; Bedford Town as player/manager August 1972; Wolverhampton Wanderers youth team coach cs

1974, remaining with this club until appointed Arsenal's reserve team coach July 1981.
Generally regarded as a half-back – usually wing-half – then made a successful switch to full-back. Another of City's excellent locals, a first teamer soon after turning pro for 6 seasons. The son of Bob Garvey, Hull RLFC wing-three-quarter 1925-29 and a professional sprinter.

GAYNOR, Leonard Alfred (1948-1951)
Inside-forward: 2 apps.
1949: 5ft. 7ins; 10st. 2lbs.
Born: Ollerton, Notts, 22 September 1925.
Career: Notts Schools; Giltbrook Villa 1944/45; Ilkeston Town 1945/46; Brinsley 1946/47; Eastwood Colliery 1947/48; CITY April 1948; Bournemouth & Boscombe Athletic June 1951; Southampton March 1954; Aldershot February 1955; Oldham Athletic July 1957.
Had also sampled the wing-half spots by the time he reached Boothferry Park, so a good man to have in reserve. Later moved round the Div. 3 circuit, having his best spells at Bournemouth and Aldershot.

GERRIE, Sydney (1950-1957)
Centre/inside-forward: 146 apps; 60 goals.
1950: 5ft. 9ins; 11st. 7lbs.
Born: Aberdeen, 14 June 1927.
Career: Inverurie Loco; Dundee June 1948; CITY November 1950 (£11,000); retired through injury 1957. Brechin City manager January 1968 – March 1969.
City paid what was then a large fee for this bustling, goal scoring Scot. He had received a first-rate apprenticeship in a Dundee side that was building up to notable cup success in the early 'Fifties. Syd found English football to his liking also, fitting in well with the Tigers' attack. Worked in the coal trade for 16 years to 1980, later that year becoming head storeman with an Aberdeen civil engineering firm.

GIBSON, Alexander (1950-1951)
Right-back: 21 apps.
1950: 5ft. 6ins; 12st.
Born: Glasgow, 25 January 1925.
Career: Arthurlie 1942; Clyde 1943; CITY March 1950 (£6,000); Stirling Albion July 1951 to circa 1960.
Honours: Scottish schoolboy international. (Clyde) Scottish Cup finalists 1949. (Stirling Albion) Scottish League 'B' Div. champions 1953 and Div. 2 champions 1958.
Short though stoutly built, employed a telling tackle and very fast (he had been an outstanding sprinter as a schoolboy). Father of John Gibson, Partick Thistle 1968-74.

GIBSON, David (1974-1978)
Midfield: 19 apps. plus 5 subs.
1977: 5ft. 7ins; 9st.
Born: Seaham, Co. Durham, 14 February 1958.
Career: North-East junior football to CITY as an apprentice professional July 1974, turning full professional December 1975; Scunthorpe United July 1978 – 1980.
Right-sided midfielder. Very lightly built so had to rely on skill rather than bustle. Like so many Tigers since WW2, moved across the river to pastures new at Scunthorpe.

GIBSON, Frederick William (1926-1932)
Goalkeeper: 102 apps.
1929: 6ft. 2ins; 13st. 4lbs.
Born circa 1907 (probably in the West Riding).
Career: Frickley Colliery; Denaby United; Dinnington Colliery; CITY 1926; Middlesbrough November 1932; Bradford City May 1937; Boston United 1938.
Powerfully built custodian whose bulk didn't prevent lively performances. Shared the senior spot with Geordie Maddison for much of his 6 years with City and, indeed, in 1929/30 and 1931/32, was first choice. Originally Fred worked as a miner at Dinnington Colliery. A 1930 comment: "Young in years but old in skill and courage".

GIBSON, John Rutherford (1922-1929)
Right-back: 210 apps.
1925: 5ft. 10¾ ins; 11st. 5lbs.
Born: Philadelphia, USA, 23 March 1898.
Died: July 1974.
Career: Netherburn; Blantyre Celtic; Sunderland November 1920; CITY May 1922; Sheffield United March 1929 (£5,000); Luton Town cs 1933; retired cs 1934.

A fine and well built defender who was the perfect foil to his partner, Matt Bell. Brought City a hefty fee at the age of 31. He left the States when 2 years of age when his family moved to Sheffield. When 13 they moved to Hamilton, Lanarkshire, where he learned his football and from this Scottish association came the nickname 'Jock'. He continued to live in Luton after leaving the game, working as an inspector for Vauxhall Motors and retired in 1964.

GIBSON, Robert H. (1949-1950)
Centre-forward: 12 apps; 4 goals.
1949: 5ft. 9½ins; 11st. 12lbs.
Born: Ashington, 5 August 1927.
Career: Ashington FC; Aberdeen January 1949; CITY October 1949; Ashington again August 1950; this time as player/manager; Lincoln City May 1951, Peterborough United cs 1955; Gateshead March 1957 – 1959.
Honours: (Lincoln City) Div. 3 (North) champions 1952.
A capable leader of the attack, unselfish and a consistent scorer (in his aggregate 90 League games with Lincoln and Gateshead, Bob scored 47 goals). Able to take the inside positions too.

GILBERTHORPE, Alfred Edward (1908-1909)
Inside-right: 18 apps; 4 goals.
Born: Bolsover, Derbyshire, 1886.
Died: 1960.
Career: Chesterfield Town 1906; CITY cs 1908.
A smart and clever forward but somewhat handicapped by lack of inches. Not altogether a tyro when he arrived at Anlaby Road, having experienced Second Division football during his 2 seasons at Saltergate.

GILHOOLEY, Michael (1920-1922)
Centre-half: 65 apps; 1 goal.
1921: 6ft; 12st. 11lbs.
Born: Edinburgh, 26 November 1896.
Career: Glencraig Celtic; Celtic professional when 16; Vale of Leven; Clydebank during WW1; CITY July 1920 (£2,500, a then club record); Sunderland March 1922 (£5,250: then a British record, but for a few days only!); Bradford City May 1925; Queen's Park Rangers May 1927 – 1928.
Honours: Scotland international vs. Wales 1922.
Dominating pivot superb in the air (Jimmy Lodge related that this ability earned him the name 'Rubberneck' among his colleagues). Dogged by bad injuries after leaving the Tigers, which undoubtedly prevented him enjoying longer success. A pithy contemporary summing-up ("... a strong, forceful player") seems a trifle inadequate.

GILL, Gary (1983/84)
Midfield: 1 substitution.
1983: 5ft. 10ins; 11st. 9lbs.
Born: Middlesbrough, 28 November 1964.
Career: Junior football to Middlesbrough as an apprentice professional, turning full professional December 1982 (CITY on a month's loan December 1983).
Promising young Teessider who spent a few weeks at Boothferry Park at the turn of the year.

GOLDSMITH, George (1928-1934)
Right-back: 171 apps.
1930: 5ft. 10½ins; 11st. 6lbs.
Born: Loftus, North Yorks, 11 March 1905.
Died: September 1974.
Career: Bishop Auckland; Loftus Albion; CITY December 1928; Tottenham Hotspur June 1934; Bolton Wanderers March 1935-1936.

Honours: (City) Div. 3 (North) champions 1933.
Master of the offside trap (not altogether unexpectedly being a Bill McCracken full-back signing!). Had but 1 senior game for Spurs although those for Bolton were nearly all in the top Division. A critic's verdict: "... lithe of build and fleet of foot; a clever and effective tackler".

GOODALL, Edward Ilderton (1937-1938)
Goalkeeper: 26 apps.
1938: 5ft. 10½ins; 11st. 5lbs.
Born: South Shields, 13 October 1913.
Died: 30 September 1978.
Career: Jarrow (Chesterfield on amateur forms 1936); North Shields 1936/37; CITY May 1937; Bolton Wanderers May 1938.
Highly promising 'keeper whose fine displays in 1937/38 brought the scouts to Anlaby Road. City, under some financial stress, accepted the offer of a 1st. Division club as at the same time they did for David Parker. Goodall didn't resume in the first-class game after the War.

GOODE, Herbert J. (1912-1913)
Inside-left: 28 apps; 10 goals.
1912: 5ft. 7½ins; 12st.
Born: Chester circa 1888.
Career: Chester FC; Wrexham; Aston Villa circa 1910 (£250); CITY May 1912 (£300); Wrexham again May 1913 – 1926.
Honours: (Wrexham) Welsh Cup winner 1914, 1915, 1921, 1925; finalist 1920. (Chester) Welsh Cup winner 1908.
It occasioned surprise in the local press when Goode's name did not appear in the Tigers' retained list for 1913/14, for he had enjoyed a successful season. Played inside-right for Wrexham, his long second run with the Welsh club taking in the club's initial Football League seasons. Notched 46 goals one season for Villa's reserves when they won a Birmingham League championship.

GOODIN, Walter (1905/06)
Forward: 1 app.
Born: Hull, 1883.
Career: Beverley Barracks prior to his association with CITY.
Amateur: Played against City before the club became a professional organisation in a Beverley Hospital Cup semi-final on March 7, 1903, so perhaps his form was noted then. Goodin's sole League outing was against Lincoln City in the last match of 1905/06 (April 28, 1906).

GORDON, Daniel (1910-1911)
Right-back: 11 apps.
1910: 5ft. 9¾ins; 12st. 7lbs.
Born: West Calder, Midlothian.
Career: Middlesbrough; Bradford 1908; CITY April 1910; Southampton cs 1911 – 1912.
Not related to the Gordon brothers, David and Ted of Hull City, although like them Dan was a Scot hailing from the Edinburgh locality. He possessed a useful physique and had experienced senior soccer at Park Avenue, but there weren't many chances in Dan's time with Tommy Nevins getting established. City debut – vs. Leicester Fosse, 14 April 1910.

GORDON, David S. (1905-1914)
Left-half: 275 apps; 17 goals.
1910: 5ft. 8½ins; 12st.
Born: Leith, Edinburgh, 1883.
Career: Leith Athletic; CITY June 1905; Leith Athletic again 1914. Hibernian secretary/manager 1919 to appointment as Hartlepools United manager July 1922 to the mid-1920's, after which he was secretary/manager of Edinburgh St. Bernard's to around 1930.
Easily takes the palm as the tiger with the greatest number of League appearances in the pre-WW1 period, only John McQuillan and Joe ('Stanley') Smith of the rest topping 200. David's style was well described by a contemporary writer: "a worrying type of half-back, being feared by many a forward for his grim never-say-die persistency. The Tigers have a no more consistent player". His brother Ted, was also on City's books but did not play in the League side. Another brother had been on the books of Middlesbrough Ironopolis and Preston North End.

GOULDEN, John Thomas (1924-1926)
Centre-forward: 2 apps.
1924: 5ft. 8½ins; 10st. 10lbs.
Born: Sunderland, 26 December 1903.
Died: 1981.
Career: Hull Schoolboy football; North Hull Liberals; Needler's FC (Hull); CITY 1924-1926.
Came to Hull with his parents when a child and learned his football at the Sidmouth Street School. Afterwards prominent in local junior circles, joining the Tigers from the Needler's works side, where he was employed. League debut: vs. Wolves away, 4 October 1924.

GOWDY, William Alexander (1929-1931)
Left-half: 65 apps; 1 goal.
1930: 5ft. 7½ins; 10st. 11lbs.
Born: Belfast.
Career: Ards; CITY June 1929 (originally on trial); Sheffield Wednesday December 1931; Gateshead 1932/33; Linfield cs 1933; Hibernian December 1935; Goole Town 1936; Altrincham July 1937; Aldershot cs 1938.

Honours: Northern Ireland international (6 apps). Irish League (3 apps).

A writer of the time said Gowdy was "... a bundle of restless activity. Preferred the ball on the ground and endeavoured to keep it there; daring in method and inclined to rove". Inclined to rove between clubs too, his journeyings taking him to three countries of the UK in a mere decade, to clubs of varying quality, even the non-League variety.

GRANGER, Michael (1962-63)
Goalkeeper: 2 apps.
1961: 5ft. 9½ins; 11st. 11lbs.
Born: Leeds, 7 October 1931.
Career: Cliftonville FC (York) to York City as an amateur August 1951, turning professional the following December; CITY July 1962; Halifax Town July 1963; Scarborough cs 1965.

Shared the goalkeepers' appearances in 1962/63 with Williams and Fisher, but the former was very much the man in possession that term. And Mike had no better luck at Halifax. However, he had proved a reliable performer in a long York City sojourn (for much of it understudying the ex-Tiger, Tommy Forgan) grossing 71 League appearances.

GREEN, Leslie (1960-1962)
Goalkeeper: 4 apps.
1962: 5ft. 9ins; 11st. 9lbs.
Born: Atherstone, Warwicks, 17 October 1941.
Career: Atherstone Town; CITY August 1960; Nuneaton Borough July 1962; Burton Albion; Hartlepools United November 1965; Rochdale April 1967 (originally on a month's trial); Derby County May 1968 (£8,000) – 1972.
Honours: (Derby County) Div. 2 champions 1969.

Achieved prominence some time after leaving City, more especially with Derby County. An ever-present in the Rams' 1969 championship side, Les had improved his goalkeeping technique greatly. And the next season, although the smallest 'keeper in Div. 1, he conceded only 37 goals, again as an ever-present. Was with Brian Clough at both Derby and Hartlepools.

GREEN, Melvin (1967-1974)
Half-back: 10 apps.
1972: 5ft. 11ins; 11st. 4lbs.
Born: Hull, 20 October 1951.
Career: East Riding schoolboy football; Yorkshire Schools; CITY as an apprentice professional September 1967, turning full professional July 1970; Cambridge United June 1974 – 1975.

Capable reserve who deputised in both the right-half and pivotal positions in seasons 1971/72 and '72/73. Shone as a schoolboy, graduating to county level.

GREENHALGH, James Radcliffe (1946-1950)
Right-half: 148 apps; 5 goals.
1947: 5ft. 8½ins; 11st. 4lbs.
Born: Manchester, 25 August 1923.
Career: Newton Heath Loco (Manchester); CITY August 1946; Bury November 1950 (£13,000); Wigan Athletic cs 1955; Gillingham as player/coach July 1956 until appointment as Lincoln City's trainer February 1959; Newcastle United trainer June 1962; Darlington manager July 1966 – February 1968; Middlesbrough trainer March 1968; Sunderland chief scout December 1979 – cs 1982.
Honours: (City) Div. 3 (North) champions 1949.

If Jimmy's distribution had been on a par with his devastating tackle, he could well have won representative honours. Justifiably popular, he always gave of his best, his sunny temperament seemed to transmit itself to the terraces.

GREENWOOD, Patrick G. ('Paddy') (1964-1971)
Right-half: 137 apps. plus 12 subs; 3 goals.
1972: 6ft; 11st. 6lbs.
Born: Hull, 17 October 1946.
Career: Hull Schools; CITY as an apprentice professional, turning full professional October 1964; Barnsley November 1971 (£12,000); Nottingham Forest September 1974 (£10,000) to January 1976, when he left by mutual agreement; player/assistant coach to Boston Minutemen, USA, cs 1976. On returning to England was out of action for some time, eventually joining Bridlington Trinity as a player December 1977.

An excellent local product – lithe in build and, in performance, both solid and fluent. A broken leg, sustained when with Forest, shortened his first-class career. As with City Paddy's Barnsley appearances topped the century.

GREENWOOD, Roy T. (1970-1976)
Outside-left: 118 apps. plus 6 subs; 24 goals.
1973: 5ft. 10ins; 11st.
Born: Leeds, 26 September 1952.
Career: Junior football to CITY as an apprentice professional turning full professional October 1970; Sunderland January 1976 (£141,600); Derby County January 1979 (£50,000); Swindon Town February 1980 (£30,000); Huddersfield Town cs 1982; Scarborough June 1984.
Honours: (Sunderland) Div. 2 champions 1976.

Extremely clever winger, elusive and possessed of adroit footwork and ball control. The fee paid by Sunderland is among the largest received by City, and justified because the player was an exciting prospect.

GRIMES, Vincent (1970-1978)
Midfield: 84 apps. plus 5 subs; 9 goals.
1976: 5ft. 8ins; 11st. 5lbs.
Born: Scunthorpe, 13 May 1954.
Career: Scunthorpe Schools; CITY on amateur forms before signing as an apprentice professional August 1970 and full professional May 1972 (Bradford City on a month's loan December 1977); Scunthorpe United January 1978 (£12,000) – 1982.

Mostly a first choice midfielder in the 2 seasons following his debut season (1973/74), turning in some accomplished displays. Had success with his home town club later, his aggregate League appearances numbering 143.

GUBBINS, Ralph Grayham (1959-1961)
Inside/outside-left: 45 apps; 10 goals.
1960: 5ft. 9ins; 11st. 3lbs.
Born: Ellesmere Port, 31 January 1932.
Career: Shell-Mex FC (Ellesmere Port); Ellesmere Port FC; Bolton Wanderers October 1952; CITY October 1959 (£4,000); Tranmere Rovers March 1961 (around £3,000); Wigan Athletic June 1964.

A workmanlike player of some adaptability – besides being able to make a showing anywhere in the attack, he switched to left-half for Tranmere. Was prominent in Bolton's successful FA Cup run in 1958 deputising for Nat Lofthouse, but didn't appear in the Final as that great player had recovered from injury.

GUYAN, George Wood (1926-1928)
Centre-forward: 19 apps; 9 goals.
1927: 5ft. 8ins; 12st. 12lbs.
Born: Aberdeen.
Career: Dundee 1922/23; South Shields August 1923; CITY December 1926, reputedly costing the club its highest fee up to then; Connah's Quay cs 1928; Exeter City June 1929; Swindon Town June 1930; Rochdale 1931.
Honours: (Connah's Quay) Welsh Cup Winner 1929.

Received his senior baptism with South Shields where his promise induced City's outlay. Yet the peak of George's career must be the season spent with non-Leaguers Connah's Quay. Not only did they soundly beat Cardiff City 3-0 in the Welsh Cup final but also won the Welsh National League championship, scoring 135 goals in a 34-match tourney.

HAIGH, Paul (1974-1980)
Defender: 179 apps. plus 1 sub; 8 goals.
1977: 5ft. 9¾ins; 11st. 6lbs.
Born: Scarborough, 4 May 1958.
Career: Hessle schoolboy football; Pudsey Juniors (Leeds United's nursery) 1971-73; Hessle Juventus (Hull Sunday League); Schultz Youth Club (Hull); CITY as apprentice professional July 1974, full professional June 1975; Carlisle United November 1980 (£102,000).
Honours: England Under-21 international vs. Norway (sub) 1977.

Though born in Scarborough moved to Hessle near Hull when 10, hence the association with local schools soccer. Highly promising as a youngster, making his League debut when 16 and selected for the England Under-21 squad at 18. This promise has been fulfilled, Paul's clever work at Hull being followed by excellent displays in Carlisle's strong Second Division side.

HALL, Ellis (1906-1907)
Centre-half: 8 apps.
1906: 5ft. 9½ins; 12st. 4lbs.
Born: Ecclesfield, nr. Sheffield, 1889.
Died: 1949.
Career: Junior football to CITY; Stoke circa 1907; Huddersfield Town cs 1910 – 1912; later with South Shields (Guest player for Goole Town during WW1); Hamilton Academicals 1919; Halifax Town June 1922 – 1926.

Very young when with City (certainly one of the youngest to appear in a Tigers' League side) and correctly described as "a centre-half of great promise". Also played for Huddersfield in their initial FL campaign. A consistent performer post-war; 117 top flight Scottish League appearances for Hamilton Acies and 115 Northern Section with Halifax. Younger brother of City's Harry Hall.

HALL, George (1922-1924)
Centre-forward: 12 apps; 4 goals.
1922: 5ft. 9ins; 10st. 9lbs.
Born: Errington, Northumberland.
Career: Junior football to CITY during season 1921/22, staying until 1924.
Played inside-forward too. Ten of his dozen League outings occurred in 1922/23 along with all the goals. Incidentally noting that George is yet another North-Easterner, it would appear more Tigers have hailed from this quarter than from Yorkshire! (That is without, of course, making a strict analysis).

HALL, Harry (1906-1907)
Outside-right: 2 apps.
1906: 5ft. 11st.
Born: Ecclesfield, nr. Sheffield, 1887.
Career: Junior football to CITY; Rotherham Town circa 1907; Huddersfield Town June 1910; Grimsby Town June 1911.
Chiefly noted for a tremendous turn of speed. Like brother Ellis, appeared in the initial League seasons of both City and Huddersfield Town. Another – and older – brother was Ben Hall, well known Derby County centre-half of the 1900's. And yet another was Fretwell, a Halifax colleague of Ellis's in the early 'Twenties. Quite a family!

HALLIGAN, William (1913-1919)
Inside-right: 64 apps; 28 goals.
1919: 5ft. 9ins; 11st.
Born: Athlone, circa 1886.
Career: Belfast Distillery; Leeds City cs 1909; Derby County 1909/10; Wolverhampton Wanderers June 1911 (£450); CITY May 1913 (guest player for Manchester United and Rochdale during WW1); Preston North End July 1919; Oldham Athletic January 1920 (£750); Nelson cs 1921 – 1922.
Honours: Irish international vs. Wales 1911 and England 1912. Ireland in the Victory internationals of 1919 vs. Scotland (2). Irish League vs. Scottish League 1909.
Was said to be City's most expensive signing when he put pen to paper in May 1913. Haligan played in all three inside positions with equal facility, a craftsman of the highest class and a fine marksman. Consisely summed up in his time as "... a typical Irish forward, full of dash", but there was a lot more to Halligan than that.

HAMILTON, Samuel (1924-1925)
Inside-right: 27 apps; 7 goals.
1924: 5ft. 8ins; 11st.
Born: Belfast, 1902.
Died: 6 August 1925.
Career: Ebbow Vale; CITY during the 1924/24 season.

An Irish junior international and a highly promising young centre and inside-forward whose death at such an early age was keenly felt. He died in a Hull nursing home following nose and throat operations. Not to be confused with Tommy Hamilton, the 1923/24 trialist.

HAMILTON, Thomas (1923/24)
Outside-right: 2 apps.
Born: Stevenston, Ayrshire.
Career: Falkirk 1920; Llanelly 1922; CITY (on trial) in the autumn of 1923, registration cancelled January 1924.
For 2 campaigns a regular in Falkirk's top flight Scottish League side (62 appearances, 5 goals) before going to Wales. While with City a commentator wrote "... he showed great promise at Sheffield last week, but is rather on the slow side". This referred to a match against Sheffield Wednesday on November 17, 1923. Shoi t but very stockily built.

HANNABY, CYRIL (1946-1948)
Goalkeeper: 17 apps.
1947: 5ft. 10¾ins; 12st. 4lbs.
Born: Doncaster, 11 October 1923.
Career: Doncaster schoolboy football; Woodlands OB (Doncaster); Doncaster LNER Plant & Loco Works; Wolverhampton Wanderers 1943; CITY August 1946; Halifax Town February 1948; Scarborough cs 1948.
Nicely built 'keeper. The Tigers fielded 4 players in that position during season 1946/47 and only Billy Bly played on more occasions than Hannaby.

HARDY, John Henry (1937-1939)
Left-half: 65 apps.
1938: 5ft. 8ins; 11st. 3lbs.
Born: Chesterfield, 15 June 1910.
Died: 1978.
Career: Chesterfield League football; Unstone (Sheffield); Chesterfield FC 1934; CITY July 1937; Lincoln City cs 1939 – 1947.
At the beginning of his senior career had shown plenty of ability in tackling and, when his distribution matched this, Jack became a valued half-back. Nephew of Sam Hardy, the celebrated England goalkeeper.

HARRIS, Albert (1930-1931)
Outside-right: 5 apps.
1930: 5ft. 8ins; 10st. 10lbs.
Born: Horden, Co Durham, 16 September 1912.
Career: Co Durham Schools; Hetton United; CITY cs 1930; Blackhall Colliery 1931; Newcastle United March 1935 (£100); Barnsley May 1936 (£200); Darlington January 1937 to the War.

Could play on the extreme left as well; a stocky, hard shooting wingman of infinite courage. Later in his career was known as Diddler, which seems to be self-explanatory.

HARRIS, William C. (1950-1954)
Wing-half: 131 apps; 6 goals.
1950: 5ft. 10½ins; 11st. 12lbs.
Born: Swansea, 31 October 1928.
Career: Swansea Town's third team as an amateur; Llanelly 1949; CITY March 1950 (about £2,000); Middlesbrough March 1954 (£15,000); Bradford City as player/manager March 1965, resigned March 1966; Stockton FC coach for 2½ seasons to May 1969.
Honours: Welsh international (6 apps).
One of City's best ever half-backs: lithe and lively, fast, and with one incisive pass able to split an enemy defence. On leaving the game in 1969 Bill worked for an insurance firm in Middlesbrough.

HARRISON, Francis John (1948-1960)
Right-back: 199 apps.
1957: 5ft. 11ins; 12st.
Born: Gateshead, 12 November 1931.
Died: November 1981.
Career: Hull schoolboy football; Ainthorpe Grove Youth Club (Hull); CITY as an amateur cs 1948, turning part-time professional May 1949 and full professional February 1952; Margate July 1960; retired through injury the following October and returned to the Hull area and had a brief spell in 1962 as Bridlington Trinity's manager/coach.
Honours: England Youth international (4 apps., captaining the side on 2 occasions).
Came to notice through an excellent record in local amateur soccer when his honours included selections for both the East Riding junior and senior teams. Developed into a mobile defender but his career was marred by a bad injury – a right leg broken in two places – and he was never the same player again. Held a bank appointment at the time of death.

HARRISON, Kenneth (1947-55)
Outside-right: 237 apps; 48 goals.
1950: 5ft. 5½ins; 10st. 4lbs.
Born: Stockton-on-Tees, 20 January 1926.
Career: Billingham FC and Army football; CITY March 1947; Derby County March 1955 (£6,600 including Alf Ackerman); Goole Town July 1956.
Honours: (City) Div. 3 (North) champions 1949.
Joined City as an inside-right but blossomed on the wing early in his professional career due in no small measure to the prompting of his partner, Raich Carter. Ken was notably fast, quite tireless and a formidable shot, his one weakness being an occasional lack of ball control. Suffered a bad injury in 1954, fracturing a knee in three places.

HARRON, Joseph (1920-1921)
Outside-left: 2 apps.
1929: 5ft. 8½ins; 11st. 9lbs.
Born: Langley Park, Co Durham 1901.
Died: 19 February 1961.
Career: Langley Park FC. CITY August 1920; Northampton Town June 1921; York City cs 1922; Sheffield Wednesday during season 1922/23; York City again 1925; Scarborough 1926; Barnsley December 1928 (£500); Dartford August 1930.
During the Twenties moved in and out of the Football League ambit in the way Alan Daley did in the post-WW2 era. (And both, coincidentally, were outside-lefts). Joe's best senior season was 1923/24 as the Wednesday's regular left-winger, making 38 Div. 2 appearances.

HART, James (1925-1927)
Centre-forward: 2 apps.
1925: 5ft. 10½ins; 11st.
Born: Glasgow, 2 January 1903.
Career: Vale of Clyde; CITY cs 1925; Bradford 1927; Crewe Alexandra 1928/29; Connah's Quay cs 1929; Charlton Athletic May 1930; Chester February 1931; East Stirlingshire cs 1931; Hibernian July 1932.
One of the roving kind, a much-travelled Scot to rival City's Allan Livingstone. Turned in his best figures at Crewe, scoring 13 goals in 19 League outings. Could turn in a useful show at inside-right also.

HASSALL, Wilfred (1946-1953)
Right-back: 142 apps; 3 goals.
1950: 5ft. 7½ins; 10st. 10lbs.
Born: Manchester, 23 September 1923.
Career: Junior football in the Prestwich and Whitefield districts of Manchester; Brindley Heath circa 1939; Royal Marines football; CITY August 1946; Worcester City July 1953.
An inside-right in junior days and joined the Tigers as an outside-right. Wilf was switched to full-back in his first term at Boothferry Park, developing into a neat, stylish and capable defender. An injury sustained early in 1948 kept him out of the senior side for the whole of the 1948/49 promotion campaign.

HAVELOCK, P(eter) Henry W. (1923-25 and 1931-32)
Centre-forward: 9 apps; 2 goals.
1925: 5ft. 8ins; 12st.
Born: Hull, 20 January 1901.
Died: 31 May 1973.

Career: Hull junior football; CITY 1923; Lincoln City August 1925; Portsmouth March 1926; Crystal Palace November 1927; CITY again May 1931; retired cs 1932 and became a coach.

After his senior baptism with City, Harry's 7-month sojourn at Lincoln, which brought a creditable 18 goals from 27 League outings, encouraged a rising Pompey to sign him as understudy to the redoubtable Billy Haines. At Palace, where he took inside berths too, the record was again excellent – 40 goals in 67 matches. Elder brother of John Havelock (Bristol Rovers). Latterly lived for many years in Hornsea.

HAWKER, David (1975-1980)
Midfield: 33 apps. plus 2 subs; 2 goals.
1978: 5ft. 7ins; 9st. 12lbs.
Born: Hull, 29 November 1958.
Career: Hull Schools; CITY as an apprentice professional July 1975, turning full professional August 1976; Darlington March 1980 (£5,000); Bishop Auckland 1982/83.

Had his best run with City in 1978/79, making 22 League appearances, mostly in the No. 4 shirt. No physical advantages so necessarily called on skills. A regular during all his Darlington sojourn.

HAWLEY, John E. (1972-78 and 1982-83)
Forward: 104 apps. plus 13 subs; 23 goals.
1978: 6ft. 0½in; 13st. 5lbs.
Born: Withernsea, 8 May 1954.
Career: East Riding junior football; CITY as an amateur April 1972, turning professional August 1976; Leeds United May 1978 (£81,000); Sunderland September 1979 (£200,000); Arsenal September 1981 (£50,000) (on loan to Orient October 1982 and CITY November 1982). Played for Happy Valley FC, Hong Kong, for a spell during 1983 before joining Bradford City in August of that year.

Played a fair amount of League football for City as an amateur before taking the professional ticket. And strictly on merit: a strike forward whose flair and physique commands respect in the opposition. An antique dealer by vocation.

HAWORTH, Ronald (1924-1926)
Inside-left: 36 apps; 10 goals.
1924: 5ft. 7ins; 11st.
Born: Lower Darwen, nr. Blackburn, 10 March 1901.
Died: 1973.
Career: Blackburn Sunday school football to Blackburn Rovers 1921/22; CITY June 1924; Manchester United cs 1926 – 1927.

Experienced a rapid rise from minor soccer to the 1st. Division in the 1921/22 campaign and did well, doubtless profiting from association with international forwards, Dicky Bond and Jock McKay. He was first choice in his first Anlaby Road season but appeared infrequently in 1925/26. A confident-sounding critic of the time said Haworth was "... a clever schemer but inclined to be selfish. Had strong left foot and could shoot as hard as anyone".

HEAD, Michael (1953-1955)
Outside-left: 3 apps.
Born: Hull, 13 April 1933.
Career: Bridlington Central United; CITY on amateur forms before signing as a professional December 1953; Wisbech Town July 1955.

Some positive performances on the wing in junior football brought him to City's notice. However, with the two promising Brians available (Cripsey and Bulless) the management obviously thought Head could find pastures new.

HEATH, R(ichard) Terence (1964-1968)
Outside-right/inside-forward: 27 apps. plus 6 subs; 1 goal.
1968: 5ft. 8ins; 11st.
Born: Leicester, 17 November 1943.
Career: Leicester City as an apprentice before signing as full professional November 1961; CITY May 1964 (£8,000); Scunthorpe United March 1968 (£5,000); Lincoln City May 1973 after being on loan from the previous February; retired through injury circa 1974.

Did best at Scunthorpe where he enjoyed regular first team football, totting up 174 appearances in which he netted 50 goals. A good worker holding progressive ideas. On leaving football was employed as a stores foreman and then in a steelworks before taking a guest house in Newquay.

HEDLEY, Foster (1928-1929)
Outside-left: 2 apps.
1928: 5ft. 5½ins; 10st.
Born: Monkseaton, Northumberland, 6 January 1908.
Died: 22 December 1983.
Career: Jarrow; CITY cs 1928; Nelson June 1929; Manchester City March 1930; Chester July 1931; Tottenham Hotspur November 1933; Millwall June 1937.
Honours: (Chester) Welsh Cup winner 1933.
A diminutive winger highly dangerous on his day. Had his best spell at Chester, netting 29 goals in 88 League outings. Another of the game's wanderers.

HEDLEY, George Thomas ('Tot') (1906-1908).
Right-back: 78 apps; 1 goal.
1907: 5ft. 8½ins; 11st. 8lbs.
Born: Co. Durham, 1882.
Died: 1937.
Career: West Stanley; Middlesbrough; Chester; Heart of Midlothian (on trial) January 1906; CITY March 1906; Leicester Fosse April 1908; Luton Town cs 1909 – 1910.
A high commendation from a critic of the time read "... he kicked with admirable judgment, headed like an old-styler, while his coolness under difficulties was a thing to wonder at". Played for Brandesburton in 1924 when over 40 – he was currently working on East Riding roads when employed by a Middlesbrough-based company. City debut: vs. Blackpool, March 14, 1906.

HEDLEY, Ralph Bickerton (1923-1924)
Right/left-back: 9 apps.
1924: 5ft. 9ins; 12st.
Born: Byker, Newcastle-on-Tyne. 1897.
Died: 1969.
Career: Newburn; CITY 1923/24; Crystal Palace December 1924 (£50); Durham City August 1926 – 1927.
A reserve defender with each of his three senior clubs, the 9 League outings for City his best return. Made 4 for both Crystal Palace and Durham, the time with the latter being that club's penultimate season as a member of the Football League.

HEDLEY, Thomas (1912)
Centre-forward: 2 apps.
Born: Jarrow, 1890.
Career: Woolwich Arsenal 1910/11; Jarrow Caledonians 1911; CITY January 1912, leaving later that year.
Hedley's association with Woolwich Arsenal was confined to run-outs in reserve sides and he did not play for their League team. He did well enough in a short spell at Jarrow to awaken City's interest and he had a taste of the first-class game while at Anlaby Road.

HELSBY, Thomas (1934-1935)
Wing-half: 22 apps.
1930: 5ft. 7½ins; 11st. 10lbs.
Born: Runcorn, Cheshire, 1904.
Died: 1961.
Career: Rhyl Athletic; Wigan Borough cs 1925; Runcorn FC 1927; Cardiff City April 1928; Bradford City May 1931; Swindon Town June 1933; CITY cs 1934; Newport County June 1935.
Honours: (Cardiff City) Welsh Cup winner 1930.
Usually at right-half (although no stranger to the left-half and inside-forward berths) and usually knocking on the first team door wherever he went. Tom, substantially built, was both capable and reliable. When with Bradford City told he would never play again because of heart trouble, but a local doctor got him fit again.

HEMMERMAN, Jeffrey L. (1969-1977)
Forward: 45 apps. plus 14 subs; 10 goals.
1975: 5ft. 11ins; 11st.
Born: Hull, 25 February 1955.
Career: Hull Schools; CITY on amateur forms during the 1968/69 season, apprentice professional July 1971, full professional February 1973 (Scunthorpe United on loan September – October 1975); Port Vale June 1977; Portsmouth July 1978; Cardiff City cs 1982; retired through injury 1984.
Moved around on free transfers but with a fair degree of success. Particularly latterly, missing only 2 games in Cardiff's Div. 3 runners-up side in 1982/3 and netting 22 goals in so doing. Mostly first choice in his Portsmouth years too.

HENDERSON, Raymond (1961-1968)
Outside-right/inside-forward: 226 apps. plus 3 subs; 54 goals.
1965: 5ft. 9ins; 11st. 6lbs.
Born: Wallsend, 31 March 1937.
Career: Wallsend Schools; Willington Quay & Howden Boys Club (Co Durham); NE marine engineering works team; Ashington; Middlesbrough May 1957; CITY June 1961 (£2,000); Reading as player/coach October 1968; Halifax Town manager August 1971 – May 1972; Everton reserve team coach July 1973 – May 1976 on appointment as Southport manager, leaving this latter post March 1977.
Honours: (City) Div. 3 champions 1966.
Mostly on the extreme right for the Tigers, a progressive forward who linked up well with Ken Wagstaff on his arrival from Mansfield in '64. Ray's best season for scoring was the promotion winning 1965/66 when he netted a dozen.

HENDRY, C(onal) Nicholson ('Nick') (1910-1921)
Goalkeeper: 140 apps.
1910: 5ft. 11ins; 11st. 3lbs.
Born: York, 1887.
Died: 9 April 1949.
Career: North-Eastern Railway FC (York); Middlesbrough (as an amateur) 1907; Darlington as a professional 1908; CITY March 1910 – cs 1921; York City 1922.

HENZELL, William Henry (1920/21)
Inside-forward: 2 apps; 1 goal.
1920: 5ft. 8½ins; 10st. 8lbs.
Born: Newcastle-on-Tyne, 1897.
Career: Walker Celtic (Newcastle); CITY cs 1920; retired through injury 1921.

One of the unfortunates whose bad luck gets a brief mention in the sports pages from time to time. Henzell was badly injured in the match against Birmingham on the 30th August 1920. He spent some time in hospital, fears as to the chances of continuing a career in senior football were being voiced not long before season 1920/21 ended and he was not re-engaged. Henzell had been a prospect, going straight into the Tigers' League side.

HEWITSON, Robert (1913-1914)
Outside-left: 2 apps.
1913: 5ft. 6ins; 10st.
Born: Newburn, Northumberland, 1888
Died: 18 August 1957.
Career: Newburn FC (Northern Alliance); CITY early in 1913-1914.

Registered one senior appearance in each of his Anlaby Road seasons. Small and light, and one of the several stand-ins for Gordon Wright and Jack Lee.

HICKTON, John (1977)
Centre-forward: 6 apps; 1 goal.
1976: 6ft; 12st.
Born: Birmingham, 24 September 1944.
Career: Junior football to Sheffield Wednesday January 1962; Middlesbrough September 1966 (£20,000) (CITY on loan January – February 1977); Fort Lauderdale Strikers, USA, 1978, where he broke a leg on his debut and decided to retire.
Honours: (Middlesbrough) Div. 2 champions 1974.

Showed his mettle at Hillsborough with 21 goals in 51 Div. 1 outings and then proceeded to render magnificent service for Middlesbrough. John's figures for the Cleveland club were 395 League games, 20 substitutions and 159 goals, which reflect his consistency and constant endeavour.

HIGGINS, William (1934-1935)
Wing-half: 5 apps.
Born in Scotland.
Career: Rutherglen Glencairn; CITY May 1934; not retained April 1935.

A deservedly popular Tiger for over a decade. Very consistent, a measure of this consistency being the fact he missed only 1 League game in the 3 seasons 1912/13 – 1914/15 inclusive, that is 113 out of a possible 114.

Played on both flanks of the intermediate line. Only young when in his Anlaby Road season and one of four signings from the productive Scottish junior level to make their senior bow then. The others were Hugh Farquharson, John Mackie and Harry Pinkerton.

HILL, John Henry (1931-1934)

Centre-half: 94 apps; 2 goals.
1930: 6ft. 2½ins; 13st. 3lbs.
Born: Hetton-le-Hole, Co Durham, 2 March 1897.
Died: April 1972.
Career: Durham junior football to Durham City as a professional 1919/20; Plymouth Argyle September 1920; Burnley May 1923 (£5,450); Newcastle United October 1928 (£8,100); Bradford City June 1931 (£600); CITY November 1931; retired April 1934 on appointment as City's manager; resigned January 1936. Then he went into business but scouted for City 1948-55 and was in charge of the Scarborough FC Pools Scheme until retiring in August 1963.
Honours: England international (11 apps).
Football League (3 apps).
(City) Div. 3 (North) champions 1933.

Spent the tail-end of a distinguished career with the Tigers. Had the towering figure to make him a natural pivot. A great worker and a master of defence who wasn't averse to a solo attacking dash. Played right-half on occasion also.

HOLAH, Eric T. (1959-1961)
Centre-forward: 1 app; 1 goal.
1962: 5ft. 10ins; 11st. 6lbs.
Born: Hull, 3 August 1937.
Career: Junior football to CITY on amateur forms; Bradford City as a professional July 1961 – 1963.

As this one-time Tigers' amateur scored 2 goals in 4 outings for Bradford City, his aggregate League record reads 5 matches, 3 goals. Which is creditable by any standards, illustrating opportunism and maybe a failure in team selectors to give him more senior outings. Eric could also play half-back.

HOLBROOK, Stephen (1968-1972)
Outside-right: 2 apps. plus 1 sub.
1973: 5ft. 5¼ins; 10st. 13lbs.
Born: Richmond, Yorks, 16 September 1952.
Career: Yorkshire Schools; CITY as an apprentice professional May 1968, turning full professional September 1970; Darlington June 1972 – 1977.
Honours: England schoolboy international (8 apps).
Very much a schoolboy star – besides his 8 England caps, he captained Yorkshire Schools. Despite this, Steve didn't make an impact at Boothferry Park but won a regular first team berth with Darlington, making over a century of League appearances.

HOLLIFIELD, Michael (1983-)
Left-back: 33 apps; 1 goal.
1983: 5ft. 10½ins; 11st.
Born: Middlesbrough, 2 May 1961.
Career: Stockton-on-Tees junior football to Wolverhampton Wanderers as an apprentice professional, turning full professional April 1979; CITY August 1983.
Eventually joined City 8 days before season '83/4 started, after doubts that the transfer would take place, and proved an excellent capture. Aware of the modern full-back's duties in exploiting his wing in attacking moves without neglecting a primary defensive role.

HOLME, Philip C. (1972-1974)
Inside-forward: 29 apps. plus 9 subs; 11 goals.
1973: 6ft. 1in; 13st. 4lbs.
Born: Briton Ferry, Glam. 21 June 1947.
Career: Bridgend Thursday; Swansea City on amateur forms 1970, signing as a professional June 1971; CITY July 1972; retired through injury July 1974. City's first team coach August 1976 – April 1977.
Honours: Welsh amateur international.
Big and burly and enthusiastic, so a handful for any defence. It was unfortunate he was forced to retire at 27. An electrician by trade. Appointed a coach at the Afan Lido, Port Talbot, in August 1977.

HOLMES, Maxey Martin (1935-1937)
Centre-forward: 29 apps; 11 goals.
1937: 5ft. 8ins; 11st. 4lbs.
Born: Pinchbeck, nr. Spalding, Lincs. 1909.
Career: Spalding schoolboy football; Spalding United; Grimsby Town 1931/32; CITY May 1935; Mansfield Town July 1937; Lincoln City August 1938.
Honours: (Grimsby Town) Div. 2 champions 1934.
Fast and packing a fair shot, Max could take wing and inside berths too. In 1938/39 he further demonstrated his versatility by successfully moving to right-half. A schoolmaster by profession and a graduate of London University. He was a class rugger player too – a three-quarter who represented Midland Counties in the county championships.

HOOD, Derek (1977-1980)
Midfield: 20 apps. plus 4 subs.
1978: 5ft. 10½ins; 11st. 4lbs.
Born: Washington, Co. Durham, 17 December 1958.
Career: Junior football to West Bromwich Albion as an apprentice professional around the mid-1970's; CITY on a similar level cs 1977, turning full professional October 1977; York City February 1980 (£1,000).
Honours: (York City) Div. 4 champions 1984.
Released by Albion at 18, Derek commenced to build a career at Boothferry Park, where he had his League baptism. Has proved a bargain for York with consistently effective displays, and was an integral part of their '84 championship team.

HOOLICKIN, Stephen (1980-1982)
Right-back: 31 apps.
1981: 5ft. 11ins; 11st. 2lbs.
Born: Manchester, 13 December 1951.
Career: Junior football to Oldham Athletic as an apprentice professional, turning full professional December 1969; Bury July 1973 (originally on 2 months' trial); Carlisle United October 1976 (£20,000); CITY December 1980; retired on health grounds March 1982.
Signed to take Gordon Nisbet's place when the latter moved to Plymouth. Steve was a sound performer, well versed in the ramifications of senior soccer, and his enforced retirement came as a blow. His younger brother, Garry, has been an Oldham player since the mid-1970's.

HORNE, Alfred (1925-1927)
Outside-right 25 apps; 2 goals
1928: 5ft. 8½ins; 10st.
Born in the Birmingham district.
Career: Stafford Rangers; CITY May 1925; Southend United May 1927; Manchester City March 1928; Preston North End September 1929 (£2,000); Lincoln City June 1932; Mansfield Town December 1936 – cs 1938.

52

Regarded as a winger, right or left, in his earlier League seasons. Alf, though, played a fair amount in the inside berths and at Lincoln went to right-half, where many thought his constructive qualities were best employed.

HORSWILL, Michael F. (1979-1982)
Full-back/midfield: 82 apps. plus 2 subs; 6 goals.
1980: 5ft. 10½ins; 11st.
Born: Annfield Plain, Co Durham, 6 March 1953.
Career: Co Durham junior football to Sunderland as an apprentice professional, turning full professional March 1970; Manchester City March 1974 in a complicated deal – Horswill and Dennis Tueart exchanged for £25,000 and another player; Plymouth Argyle July 1975 (£30,000); CITY July 1978 (£15,000); Happy Valley FC, Hong Kong March 1982.
Honours: (Sunderland) FA Cup Winner 1973.
Primarily a half-back. Quickly came to the fore, winning a prized FA Cup medal when barely 20. Captained City at a time when fortunes were low but always the competent professional in defence as well as midfield.

HORTON, J. Kenneth (1952-1955)
Right-half/inside-right: 76 apps; 16 goals.
1955: 5ft. 7¼ins; 10st. 5lbs.
Born: Preston, Lancs. 26 August 1922.
Career: Preston junior football; Preston North End January 1942; CITY October 1952 (£8,000); Barrow July 1955; Morecambe cs 1956.
Honours: (PNE) Div. 2 champions 1951.
Partnered the great Tom Finney at school and repeated the process in Preston's first team. (And, for good measure, worked as a book-keeper for the Finney plumbing firm). Ken was a competent performer in both his positions; a hard worker, sound in distribution with a fair scoring tally.

HOUGHTON, John (1910-1913)
Full-back/centre-half: 28 apps; 3 goals.
1910: 5ft. 11ins; 11st. 8lbs.
Born: Wallsend 1888.
Died: August 1950.
Career: Wallsend Elm Villa; Wallsend Park Villa; CITY May 1910; Fulham May 1913 (£175) – 1921.
Mainly a back, his pivotal appearances being occasional, but it was beneficial to have a player around able to assume both roles. Jack figured at full-back in his Craven Cottage days as well.

HOUGHTON, Kenneth (1965-1973)
Inside-forward: 253 apps. plus 11 subs; 79 goals.
1966: 5ft. 10ins; 11st.
Born: Rotherham, 18 October 1939.
Career: Silverwood Colliery (on Sheffield United's books for a season); Rotherham United originally as an amateur, turning professional May 1960; CITY January 1965 (£40,000); Scunthorpe United June 1973 (in part exchange for Steve Deere); Scarborough May 1974 as player/manager; Bridlington player/coach July 1975. Appointed City's full time youth development officer May 1976, later serving as club manager April 1978, after being caretaker from the previous February, until December 1979.
Honours: (Rotherham) FL Cup finalist 1961. (City) Div. 3 champions 1966.
Usually at inside-left, where he early gained a reputation as a powerful left-foot shot. A stylish forward and a brainy one who brought the best out of his partner, Ian Butler, both at Millmoor and Boothferry Park.

HOULT, Alan J. (1978)
Forward: 3 apps; 1 goal.
1977: 5ft. 8ins; 10st. 8lbs.
Born: Burbage, Leics. 7 October 1957.
Career: Leicester Schools; Leicester City on schoolboy forms May 1971, turning professional September 1975 (CITY on loan January – March 1978) (Lincoln City on loan March – April 1978); Bristol Rovers July 1978 – 1979.
Honours: England schoolboy international (4 apps).
A notable schoolboy footballer. He was, however, unable to get into Leicester's Div. 1 side which then included forwards of the calibre of Frank Worthington and Keith Weller.

HOWE, Peter (1904-1906)
Centre-forward: 32 apps; 15 goals.
1905: 5ft. 7ins; 11st. 10lbs.
Born: Co. Durham circa 1884.
Career: Reading early in 1904; CITY cs 1904 – 1906.
Not very experienced when signed for the Tigers' initial professional season with just a couple of Southern League appearances to his name. On his debut for the first of these, against Plymouth Argyle on March 25, 1904, Peter received a favourable write-up: "The debut of Howe in the (Reading) first team was a most successful one. Despite his very short legs he gets over the ground pretty quickly and, not only has his passing accurately timed, but he upheld his position as a dead shot. What is more, he has plenty of pluck".

HOWIESON, James (1927-1928 and 1929-30)

Inside-left: 67 apps; 12 goals.
1927: 5ft. 8ins; 12 st.
Born: Rutherglen, Lanarkshire, 7 June 1900.
Died: 1974.
Career: Rutherglen Glencairn; Airdrieonians November 1921 (£5); St. Johnstone May 1924 (£250); Dundee United 1925; St. Mirren 1925/26; CITY March 1927 (approaching £4,000, then a City record); USA football May 1928 – August 1929 when he returned to City; Shelbourne June 1930; Clyde September 1932; Alloa Athletic cs 1934; Glenavon later in 1934.
Honours: Scottish international vs. Northern Ireland 1927. (Shelbourne) League of Ireland vs. Welsh League 1931. (St. Mirren) Scottish Cup winner 1926.
Nicely summed up in his playing days as " . . . a neat and powerful dribbler, a cute schemer, an opportunist and marksman". Jimmy was adaptable too and played at left-back during the Tigers' famous 1930 Cup run.

HUBBARD, Clifford (1933-1939)

Outside/inside-right and centre-forward: 182 apps. 52 goals.
1935: 5ft. 8ins; 11st.
Born: Worksop, 1911.
Died: November 1962.
Career: Worksop Schools; Notts Schools; Manton Colliery; Scunthorpe United 1932; CITY cs 1933; West Ham United May 1939 (£3,000). After WW2 played for Ransome & Marles (Newark); Goole Town and, finally Worksop Town. Was the last-named club's trainer/coach from 1960 to his death.
An assertive forward especially useful because of his utility value. Like so many, the War came at a vital point in Cliff's career.

Before it he had notched 3 goals in 4 League outings for the Hammers, which looked as if the Upton Park club had invested wisely.

HUGHES, Emlyn Walter (1983)

Right-back: 9 apps.
1983: 5ft. 10ins; 12st. 6lbs.
Born: Barrow-in-Furness, 28 August 1947.
Career: North Lancashire Schools; Roose FC (Blackpool); Blackpool September 1964; Liverpool February 1967 (£65,000); Wolverhampton Wanderers August 1979 (£90,000); Rotherham United as player/manager July 1981; CITY March 1983; Mansfield Town August 1983; Swansea City September – October 1983.
Honours: England international (62 apps. including 3 subs). England Under-23 international (8 apps). Football League. (Liverpool) European Cup winner 1977, 1978. EUFA Cup winner 1973, 1976. League champions 1973, 1976, 1977, 1979. FA Cup winner 1974; finalist 1971, 1977. FL Cup finalist 1978. (Wolves) FL Cup winner 1980.
A much honoured football celebrity, familiar to TV viewers as well as the soccer public, who gave City the benefit of his wide experience during the 1983 promotion run-in. Of sporting stock – son of Fred ('Ginger') Hughes, a Great Britain Rugby League international, while a brother and an uncle played Rugby League professionally and an aunt played hockey for England. Awarded the OBE in the 1980 New Year's honours.

HUGHES, Robert (1919-1922)

Outside-left: 66 apps; 10 goals.
1920: 5ft. 6ins; 10st. 7lbs.
Born: Pelaw, Newcastle-on-Tyne, 1892.
Died: September 1955.
Career: Pelaw FC (Tyneside League); Northampton Town cs 1910; CITY July 1919 (for the club's then record fee); Sheffield United May 1922; Brentford cs 1923; Rochdale July 1924; Wigan Borough cs 1928 – 1930.
Honours: Southern League vs. Football League 1915.
Small, dark and as tricky as they come, Bobby was equally adept on the other flank. Noted as a scorer and one of the first wingers to top a century of goals in senior league football.

HUTCHISON, Duncan (1934-1935)

Outside-right: 38 apps; 8 goals.
1935: 5ft. 7ins; 10st. 12lbs.
Born: Kelty, Fife, 3 March 1903.
Died: 1972.
Career: Rosewell (Edinburgh); Dunfermline Athletic; Dundee United 1925; Newcastle

United August 1929 (£4,050); Derby County March 1932 (£3,100); CITY July 1934; Dundee United again June 1935; retired 1939, later becoming a Dundee United director.
Honours: (Dundee United) Scottish League Div. 2 champions 1929.
A legend at Dundee where his all action style earned the soubriquet 'Hurricane Hutch' after Charles Hutchinson, a dare devil film star of the silent era. Duncan could play anywhere in the attack and made his reputation as a centre-forward, notching 35 in the Tannadice club's 1929 promotion season.

HUXFORD, Harold (1938-1939)
Forward: 10 apps; 2 goals.
1938: 5ft. 7ins; 10st. 8lbs.
Born: Grimsby, 2 February 1916.
Career: Grimsby YMCA; Grimsby Town 1936/37; CITY cs 1938; Boston United 1939 (guest player for Grimsby Town during WW2).
A utility forward – could take both right flank berths and centre-forward. The player himself preferred the latter, although on the small side, and scored many goals in local soccer aided by a natural quickness. Son of A. T. Huxford, a well-known Grimsby Town forward of pre-1914 days.

INWOOD, Gordon Frederick (1950-1952)
Outside-left: 3 apps.
1950: 5ft. 8ins; 11st.
Born: Kislingbury, Northants, 18 June 1928.
Career: Rushden Town; West Bromwich Albion January 1949; CITY May 1950; Kettering Town cs 1952.
Succeeded Ernie Shepherd as the Burbanks deputy and found it equally unrewarding. Gordon, nonetheless, was a left-winger of ability, lively and quick off the mark with a sure touch in ball control.

IREMONGER, James (1924-25)
Goalkeeper: 1 app.
Born: Wilford, Notts, 5 June 1901.
Died: 27 January 1980.
Career: Clifton Colliery (Notts); CITY late in 1924 – 1925.
Signed as cover for Geordie Maddison following Billy Mercer's departure to Huddersfield and made his solitary League appearance a few days before Christmas 1924. Member of a famous sporting family – son of James snr. (Forest and England back and Notts cricketer) and nephew of Albert Iremonger, Notts County's goalkeeper for 22 years. James jnr. was himself a useful cricketer and had a trial for Notts in 1921.

JACKETTS, George Arthur (1908-1920)
Wing-half: 2 apps.
1919: 5ft. 6ins; 10st. 10lbs.

Born: Hull, 1887.
Died: 1957.
Career: Hull junior football; CITY – started a long connection with his home club in 1908, eventually turning professional; Ebbw Vale cs 1920.
Serviceable local player capable of taking both flanks. Most prominent in wartime soccer: in the period's final season, 1918/19, for example, George was a regular, making 34 appearances. First team debut: vs. Huddersfield Town November 20, 1915, and his last: against Leeds City, September 20, 1919.

JARVIS, Alan Leslie (1964-1971)
Right-half: 148 apps. plus 11 subs; 12 goals.
1971: 5ft. 9ins; 11st.
Born: Wrexham, 4 August 1943.
Career: Wrexham Schools; Everton staff around the late 1950's, turning professional July 1961; CITY May 1964; Mansfield Town March 1971 (£10,000) – 1973.
Honours: Welsh international vs. Scotland, England and Northern Ireland 1967. Welsh Youth international. (City) Div. 3 champions 1966.
Fine wing-half outstanding in the pinpoint accuracy of his passing. Became Mansfield's most expensive signing but his service there was marred by a bad eye injury. Alan showed early promise, first appearing in Everton's Central League side at 16. A bit of an all-rounder too – a Welsh schoolboy rugger international – and a quantity surveyor by profession.

JENSEN, H(ans) Viggo (1948-1956)
Left-back/wing-half/inside-right: 308 apps; 50 goals.
1950: 5ft. 10ins; 12st.
Born: Skagen, Denmark, 29 March 1921.
Career: Esbjerg Forende (Denmark); CITY as an amateur October 1948, turning professional December 1950; returned to Denmark towards the end of 1956.
Honours: Danish international (at the time of signing for City had already won 15 caps besides representing his country at the 1948 Olympic Games). (City) Div. 3 (North) champions 1949.
Assuredly one of the most popular City players ever. Viggo was quite fearless, a full 90 minutes player because of superb physical fitness, and scrupulously fair. And, of course, magnificently versatile, giving class performances in whatever position he was selected.

JOBSON, John William (1930-1931)
Outside-left: 2 apps.
Born: Burradon, Northumberland, 29 July 1908.

55

Died: 1974.
Career: Hatfield Main; CITY November 1930. Also assisted Blyth Spartans.

North-Easterner, Dally Duncan's stand-in for the better part of a season. City down the years have had a number of players with a Blyth Spartans' connection (Newton, Middlemas and W.T. Bell among them) but few joined direct from that club. A recent exception is Les Mutrie.

JOHNSON, Samuel (1947-1948)
Right-back: 10 apps.
1947: 6ft; 12st. 12lbs.
Born: Barnton. nr. Northwich, Cheshire, 10 February 1919.
Career: Cheshire Schools; Northwich ICI; Northwich Victoria 1946; CITY April 1947; Scarborough cs 1948.

Full-back built on hefty lines, it naturally followed he could boot the ball a goodly distance. Though sound enough, Sam's style was plainly robust and largely innocent of subtlety.

JOHNSON, W. (1919-20)
Outside-right: 5 apps.
Career: Assisted the Beverley Barracks side before his short association with CITY.

Possessed a fair burst of speed and doubtless enjoyed linking up with the brilliant David Mercer. Johnson's League baptism was in the 5-1 annihilation of Leicester City at Anlaby Road on February 12, 1920. A noted boxer.

JOHNSON, William (1923-1926)
Wing-half: 46 apps.
1924: 5ft. 7ins; 11st. 8lbs.
Born: Seaton Delaval, Northumberland, 1900.
Career: Seaton Delaval FC; CITY cs 1923 – 1926.

Played in 33 League matches out of a possible 42 in his first season as a Tiger, straight from minor football and one of the youngest on the books. Effective on both flanks, and though on the short side was weighty. Messrs Bleakley and Collier monopolised the wing-half berths the following term and Bill didn't retain regular status.

JONES, Ellis (1925-1926)
Half-back: 8 apps; 1 goal.
1925: 5ft. 7½ins; 11st. 8lbs.
Born: Spennymoor, Co Durham, 5 April 1900.
Died: 1972.
Career: Spennymoor United; CITY May 1925; Annfield Plain 1926; Oldham Athletic February 1928 – cs 1929.

Energetic performer whose form after leaving Anlaby Road induced Oldham to seek his signature. Ellis was then playing at inside-left and occasionally centre-forward, and had scored 36 goals for Annfield Plain (24 in North-Eastern League matches, 12 in cup-ties) during 1927/28 up to joining in the February.

JONES, Glanville (1946-1947)
Outside-left: 7 apps.
Born: Merthyr Tydfil, 27 February 1921.
Career: Merthyr Tydfil FC; CITY June 1946; Bournemouth & Boscombe Athletic May 1947; Crewe Alexandra March 1949.

One of several wingers who appeared in the Tigers' first team in the initial post-WW2 season when a record 43 players represented the club in League matches. Glanville had a further 9 at Bournemouth but registered none with Crewe.

JONES, James M. (1947)
Inside-forward: 1 app.
(Possibly born Bolton, 1925).
Career: From Lancashire junior football briefly to CITY on amateur forms in the Spring of 1947.

Amateur from the Manchester area. His solitary League outing was against Oldham Athletic on May 24, 1947. The season was greatly extended that year due to a severe winter and the consequent backlog of fixtures.

JONES, Thomas (1904-1906)
Left-back: 27 apps; 2 goals.
1905: 5ft. 11ins; 12st. 8lbs.
Born: Newport, Salop, 1877.
Career: Shrewsbury Town; Belfast Celtic; West Bromwich Albion June 1901; Bristol Rovers May 1903; CITY cs 1904; Wigan County 1906; Heywood 1907/08; Wrockwardine Wood FC (Salop) 1909.

Finely built defender and a City original who captained the side during the very first League campaign. Tom was a reliable partner to Ambrose Langley and others at that historic time. (Curious that the romantic sounding Wrockwardine Wood should crop up twice in this Who's Who – see also Billy Price). A professional cricketer for the Golcar CC, Yorkshire.

JORDAN, Alfred R. (1924-1926)
Right-half: 9 apps.
1925: 5ft. 8½ins; 11st.
Born: Belfast.
Career: Junior football to Stoke late in 1923; CITY June 1924; Bristol Rovers cs 1926.

Elder brother of David Jordan, their respective arrivals at Anlaby Road separated by the best part of a decade. Alf could also take the left-half berth. Made a couple of League appearances for Stoke soon after joining the club, but thereafter wholly in the reserves.

JORDAN, David (1933-1936)

Inside-forward: 25 apps; 15 goals.
1935: 5ft. 9ins; 11st. 8lbs.
Born: Belfast.
Career: Ards; CITY 1933; Wolverhampton Wanderers June 1936; Crystal Palace May 1937 to the War.
Honours: Eire international vs. Switzerland and France 1937.

A Tigers' reserve who achieved a most satisfactory goal tally in his occasional League outings, a fact that no doubt led to his signing by First Division Wolves. However, David had only 3 senior games for Wolves and experienced equally hard going at Selhurst (7 in 2 seasons). Brother of City's Alf Jordan.

KAYE, John (1971-1974)

Wing-half: 71 apps. plus 1 sub; 9 goals.
1973: 5ft. 9ins; 12st. 6lbs.
Born: Goole, 3 March 1940.
Career: Goole Schools; Goole Town; Scunthorpe United September 1960 (£1,750); West Bromwich Albion May 1963 (£45,000); CITY November 1971 (£10,000) – August 1974, when appointed club coach, then manager September 1974 – October 1977; Scunthorpe United coach October 1977 – February 1981.
Honours: Football League (2 apps). (WBA) FA Cup winner 1968. FL Cup winner 1966; finalist 1967, 1970.

First an inside-right, moving to centre at Scunthorpe when Barrie Thomas left. Was immediately successful, his powerful, bustling style producing many goals for both the United and Albion. Moved to left-half during the late 'Sixties, proving equally strong as a midfielder. Was the Midlands' 'Player of the Year' in 1966 and 1970.

KEEN, James Frederick (1924-1925)

Outside-right: 17 apps.
1924: 5ft. 6½ins; 10st. 6lbs.
Born: Walker, Newcastle-on-Tyne, 25 November 1897.
Died: 1980.
Career: Walker Celtic; Bristol City 1920/21; Newcastle United May 1922 (£100); Queen's Park Rangers cs 1923; CITY July 1924; Darlington cs 1925; Wigan Borough 1925/26. Later returned to Tyneside and played in local junior football there.

Notably fast, as one would expect from a successful professional sprinter. A kinsman of the England international, Errington Kenn, who came briefly to Boothferry Park towards the end of his playing career during Buckley's reign but who didn't appear in the League side.

KEERS, John Mandell (1925-1926)

Inside-forward: 8 apps; 1 goal.
1925: 5ft. 8ins; 11st.
Born: Tow Law, Co. Durham, 1900.
Died: 5 January 1963.
Career: Tow Law FC; CITY cs 1925; Annfield Plain 1926; Nelson early in 1927; Boston July 1927.

Had two brief spells in senior soccer (Nelson were a Football League outfit until 1931 and he had a similar record with them – 8 matches, 3 goals).

KILGALLON, Mark C. (1980-1981)

Forward: 1 app. as a substitute.
Born: Glasgow, 20 December 1962.
Career: Junior football to Ipswich Town as an apprentice professional; CITY August 1980 after a 6-weeks' trial; contract cancelled March 1981 and he returned to Scotland.

His fleeting appearance in the No. 12 shirt was made in the second match of the 1980/81 campaign, at home against Barnsley on 19 August 1980.

KING, David John (1957-1963)

Inside-forward: 65 apps; 24 goals.
1960: 5ft. 8¼ins; 10st. 9lbs.
Born: Hull, 24 October 1940.
Career: Hull junior football to City on amateur forms August 1957, turning professional October 1958; King's Lynn July 1963 – 1965. Subsequently assisted Bridlington Town as a player, assistant manager (1975/76 season) and manager (appointed April 1976); City youth coach cs 1983.

Clever locally produced inside man, able in combination and one contributing a fair share of goals. Graduate of Hull University in economics and social history and also a qualified physical education teacher.

KING, George (1948-1949)
Centre-forward: 3 apps.
1950: 6ft; 13st.
Born: Warkworth, Northumberland, 5 January 1923.
Career: RAF football to Newcastle United August 1946; CITY March 1948 (£750); Port Vale April 1949; Barrow February 1950; Bradford City January 1952 (£3,000); Gillingham October 1952; King's Lynn cs 1954, later becoming Ely City's player/coach.
Dashing and enthusiastic centre who did not shine especially in his infrequent first team appearances but scored well enough for the reserves. And he put in some capable performances after leaving City. Elder brother of goalkeeper Ray King, a colleague at Newcastle and Port Vale and an England 'B' international.

KIRMAN, Harold (1948-52 and 1955-56)
Full-back: 2 apps.
Born: Hull, 3 December 1930.
Career: Francis Askew Youth Club (Hull) to CITY on amateur forms June 1948, turning professional December 1950; Gillingham July 1952; returned to Hull City January 1955.
Originally on loan to the Gills and stayed 2½ years. Was mostly a reserve at the Medway club too but made 8 League appearances for them in the old Div. 3 (South). A solid and robust defender.

KITCHEN, Joseph (1921-1923)

Inside-left: 30 apps; 5 goals.
1922: 5ft. 8ins; 12st.
Born: Brigg, Lincs, 1886.
Died: 2 April 1962.

Career: Gainsborough Trinity; Sheffield United 1908; Rotherham County August 1920; Sheffield United again December 1920; CITY September 1921; Scunthorpe United August 1923; Gainsborough Trinity again September 1924, during which spell he briefly assisted Shirebrook from September to November 1925.
Honours: (Sheffield Utd) FA Cup winner 1915.
Centre-forward in his Cup Final, Joe also shone in both the right-wing spots when at Bramall Lane, a proof of adaptability. Attracted attention in Gainsborough's Div. 2 side and the United secured his signature in face of stiff competition. A noted goal getter. Played cricket for Lincolnshire.

KITCHEN, Norman (1935-1936)
Outside-right/outside-left: 4 apps. 1 goal.
1936: 5ft. 7½ins; 10st. 12lbs.
Born: Sunderland, 26 July 1911.
Career: Sunderland Schools; Millfield FC; Ferryhill Athletic circa 1928; Eden Colliery circa 1932 (trial with Sheffield Wednesday); CITY 1935; Southport July 1936; Bristol Rovers July 1938; Workington 1939 (Southport again, as a guest player, during WW2, 1939-42).
Reckoned at Southport, where he had his best run, to be one of their cleverest players – a bold raider dangerous on either flank. Somewhat apt, though, to overdo the dribbling at times. Dogged by injury when at Bristol and underwent a cartilage operation. A joiner by trade.

KNIGHTON, Kenneth (1971-1973)

Left-half: 79 apps. plus 1 sub; 9 goals.
1972: 5ft. 9ins; 11st. 5lbs.
Born: Barnsley, 20 February 1944.
Career: Barnsley schoolboy football; Wath Wanderers; Wolverhampton Wanderers ground staff 1959 turning professional February 1961; Oldham Athletic November 1966 (approaching £12,000); Preston North End December 1967 (£30,000); Blackburn Rovers July 1969 (£45,000); CITY March 1971 (£60,000); Sheffield Wednesday August 1973 (£50,000); retired 1976 and joined Wednesday's coaching staff; Sunderland coach before appointment as their manager June 1979 – April 1981; Orient manager October 1981 – May 1983.
Originally a wing-half then played a number of his early games for Wolves at right-back before reverting to half-back for the rest of his career. Strong in all departments, his competence recognised by the transfer fees involved in each move.

KNOTT, Herbert (1945-1947)
Centre-forward: 6 apps; 1 goal.
Born: Goole, 5 December 1914.
Career: Junior football to Walsall during the 1937/38 season; assisted a number of clubs thereafter eventually joining CITY from Brierley Hill Alliance during the latter part of WW2.
Had a taste of League fare in 1937/38, scoring 2 goals in 9 matches in the old Div. 3 (South) competition. Walsall had to apply for re-election at that season's end and Bert was among those not re-engaged. Achieved a measure of fame for the number of clubs played for during the War.

KOFFMAN, S(idney) Jack (1946-1947)
Outside-left: 4 apps.
Born: Prestwich, Manchester, 3 August 1920.
Died: 24 May 1977.
Career: Junior football to Manchester United during WW2; CITY June 1946; Oldham Athletic June 1947.
Another of the immediate post-war contingent from Manchester, Jack came bearing a promising reputation. But he didn't solve a problem position which actually persisted until Eddie Burbanks' arrival in 1949. Jack is numbered among comparatively few Jewish players to have attained FL status.

KYNMAN, David J. (1978-1982)
Midfield: 11 apps.
1981: 5ft. 10ins; 9st. 12lbs.
Born: Hull, 20 May 1962.

Career: Orchard Park United (Hull); CITY as an apprentice professional July 1978, turning full professional May 1980; Bridlington Trinity October 1982.
Midfielder of slim build. Unusual in joining as an apprentice from a local junior club – for many years now City have almost invariably signed their youngsters from Hull and/or Yorkshire Schools.

LANGLEY, Ambrose (1905-1906)
Right-back: 13 apps.
1905: 5ft. 11½ins; 14st. 7lbs.
Born: Horncastle, Lincs, 10 March 1870.
Died: February 1937.
Career: Horncastle FC; Grimsby Town circa 1889; Middlesbrough Ironopolis 1891; Sheffield Wednesday 1893; CITY as player/manager 1905, did not play after season 1905/06 but remained in charge until 1912. Sheffield Wednesday assistant secretary 1913; Huddersfield Town manager after WW1 until 1920.
Honours: Football League vs. Scottish League 1898. (Wednesday) FA Cup Winner 1896. Div. 2 champions 1900. League champions 1903.
The first nationally known personality to join the Tigers. Won a fine reputation for consistency at Sheffield and in the decade 1893-1903 had appeared in 290 out of a possible 320 League matches. Agile for his size, he could, however, be vulnerable to a fleet winger. Ambrose was an excellent manager and laid the foundations of Huddersfield's great 1920's side.

LAVERY, Patrick (1905-1906)
Outside-right/outside-left: 2 apps.
1905: 5ft. 4ins; 11st. 4lbs.
Born in Northumberland, 1884.
Killed in action 1915.
Career: Gateshead; CITY cs 1905 – 1906.
Short though weighty winger. His League debut was against Burslem Port Vale on April 16, 1906, but he had actually made his senior debut in the Cup-tie at Denaby the previous October. Lost his life while serving with the Highland Light Infantry.

LAWRANCE, Raymond S. (1933-1936)
Centre-half: 34 apps; 1 goal.
1938: 6ft. 2¼ins; 13st. 6lbs.
Born: Gainsborough Lincs, 18 September 1911.
Career: Gainsborough, Trinity; CITY 1933; Newport County May 1936.
Massive in build – surely one of City's biggest ever – and so a veritable defensive sheet-anchor by physical presence alone. At Newport a useful reserve in the Welsh club's championship side of 1938/39.

LAWRENCE, Matthew (1937-1939)
Left-half: 25 apps; 1 goal.
1938: 5ft. 7ins; 11st. 3lbs.
Born: Cefn-yBedd, nr. Wrexham, 1909.
Career: North Wales junior football to Wrexham 1931; CITY September 1937.
Honours: (Wrexham) Welsh Cup finalist 1932 and 1933.
Compactly built, sturdy midfielder. Had a good run with his local club – around 150 senior appearances – and figured on the right flank also.

LEE, James (1948-1951)
Left-back: 3 apps; 1 goal.
1949: 6ft; 12st. 8lbs.
Born: Rotherham, 26 January 1926.
Career: Wath Wanderers; Wolverhampton Wanderers during WW2; CITY October 1948; Halifax Town February 1951; Chelsea October 1951; Leyton Orient July 1954; Swindon Town November 1956; Hereford United July 1959.
Strapping full-back crowded out at Boothferry Park by a sufficiency of defenders. Came into his own at Halifax and soon snapped up by Chelsea where his activities were likewise confined to the reserves. Jimmy also played on the right and, unusually, appeared in City's reserve side with his brothers Charlie and Alf, both half-backs.

LEE, John (1913-1920)
Outside-left; 74 apps; 18 goals.
1919: 5ft. 10¼; 11st. 2lbs.
Born: Sheffield, 1890.
Died: 10 August 1955.
Career: Bird in Hand FC (Sheffield); CITY cs 1913; Chelsea February 1920 (£1,500); Watford 1924; Rotherham United June 1925.
Tall and quite weighty for a winger (by 1925 he turned the scales at 12 stones), Jack Lee's ability to score goals no doubt induced Chelsea to part with a then hefty fee. He made 164 first team appearances for the Tigers and was top scorer in 1916/17 with 17. Playing days over, Jack returned to Hull to live and work.

LEE, Patrick Francis (1925-1927)
Left-half: 25 apps. 6 goals.
1927: 5ft. 9ins; 11st. 4lbs.
Born: Uddingston, Lanarkshire, 20 January 1903.
Died: 1 March 1981.
Career: Vale of Clyde; CITY cs 1925; Accrington Stanley cs 1927; Southport September 1930 (on trial); Ballymena October 1930; Dundee 1933 for a season.
Specialised in the close passing often associated with thoughtful Scottish play. Prospered when the wing in front of him responded to this prompting.

LEES, Norman (1966-1971)
Full-back: 4 apps. plus 1 sub.
1970: 5ft. 9ins; 11st. 12lbs.
Born: Newcastle-on-Tyne, 18 November 1948.
Career: Junior football to CITY as an apprentice professional turning full professional November 1966 (Hartlepool on loan November 1970 – May 1971); Darlington June 1971 – 1977.
During the longest stint, his 6 years with Darlington, Norman showed himself to be extremely adaptable. In his 100 plus League outings he appeared in every position except that of goalkeeper. A real utility man.

LESTER, A(braham) Benjamin (1946-1947)
Centre-forward: 27 apps. 18 goals.
1947: 5ft. 11¼ins; 11st.
Born: Sheffield, 10 February 1920.
Career: Sheffield schools and then works football before Army service; Selby Town; CITY September 1946; Lincoln City December 1947; Stockport County August 1949-1951.
Honours: (Lincoln City) Div. 3 (North) champions 1948.
The netting of 8 goals in 4 games for Selby at the outset of 1946/47 prompted his signing, and the scoring rate in Northern Section football remained good. Adept at keeping his forwards moving. Also played inside-right at Lincoln.

LEWIS, Harry (1923-1925)
Inside-forward: 36 apps; 5 goals.
1924: 5ft. 6ins; 11st. 12lbs.
Born: Birkenhead, 19 December 1893.
Died: 1976.
Career: The Comets FC (Liverpool); Liverpool FC September 1916; CITY late in 1923 – 1925.
Honours: (Liverpool) League champions 1922.
In the 3½ peace-time seasons Harry was associated with Liverpool, the club enjoyed its best inter-war League spell, finishing 4th twice, winning the championship and on the way to winning another. Such a pedigree rubs off on individuals and this short and chunky inside man's foraging and team work had a touch of class.

LILL, David A. (1963-1969)
Centre-forward: 16 apps. plus 2 subs; 2 goals.
1970: 6ft; 12st. 12lbs.
Born: Aldbrough, East Yorks, 17 February 1947.
Career: East Riding Schools; CITY ground staff 1963, turning professional February 1965; Rotherham United October 1969 (around £4,000); Cambridge United July 1971; King's Lynn cs 1976.

Handy reserve whose impressive physique stood him in good stead for a spearhead role. His best League run was at Cambridge, a regular for 5 seasons and chalking up 166 appearances plus 6 substitutions.

LINAKER, John E. (1951-1953)
Outside-right: 26 apps; 3 goals.
1951: 5ft. 5½ins; 10st. 4lbs.
Born: Southport, 14 January 1927.
Career: Was on Everton's books as an amateur before joining Manchester City during WW2; Southport November 1946; Nottingham Forest September 1947; York City June 1950; CITY October 1951 (£5,000); York City again June 1953; Scarborough March 1956; Crewe Alexandra June 1957 (originally on 2 months' trial); Ashington cs 1958.
Winger possessing a direct style and, somewhat belying his slight build, one who carried a hard shot. John also had a reputation as an exceptionally good swimmer.

LIVINGSTONE, Allan (1922-1924)
Inside-left: 1 app.
1922: 5ft. 7ins; 10st. 7lbs.
Born: Alexandria, Dunbartonshire.
Career: Dumbarton Harp; CITY 1922 – 1924; New Brighton November 1925 (after a month's trial with Crewe Alexandra); Clapton Orient 1926/27; Merthyr Town cs 1927; Swansea Town cs 1928; Ayr United late in 1929; East Fife 1930; Walsall September 1931; Colwyn Bay later in 1931/32; Chester March 1932; Mansfield Town August 1933; Stockport County 1934/35.
At the tail-end of his career Allan successfully moved to right-half and then centre-half where his constructive ability and accurate ground passing had greater scope. By then he was also a stone heavier than in his City days. Younger brother of the well-known Dugald Livingstone (1898-1981), Celtic and Everton back between the wars, and manager of Newcastle United, Fulham and Chesterfield in the 1950's.

LLEWELLYN, George L. (1936-1937)
Half-back: 4 apps.
Born: Abercwmboi, Glam. 1916.
Career: Caerphilly; CITY May 1936 – 1937. Assisted Scarborough later in the 1930's.
Established a good reputation in South Wales' amateur soccer. Stated in the press to be a Welsh amateur international but a careful investigation has shown the statement to be incorrect.

LLOYD, Charles Frederick (1926-1928)
Left-back: 8 apps.
1927: 5ft. 8½ins; 12st. 8lbs.

Born: North Shields, 27 September 1906.
Died: 1979.
Career: Percy Main Colliery, Northumberland; CITY cs 1926; Southend United cs 1928; Loughborough Corinthians 1929; Mansfield Town cs 1931 – 1933.
Very solidly built defender, one of the several alternatives to the Jock Gibson/Bell monopoly. Enjoyed his longest spell of first team football with non-Leaguers Loughborough, clocking up around 90 Midland League appearances with the Leicestershire side.

LLOYD, Edward Hugh (1933-1935)
Full-back: 1 app.
1935: 5ft. 9ins; 12st. 2lbs.
Born: Oldham, 25 July 1905.
Died: 1976.
Career: Junior football to Stockport County 1929/30; CITY cs 1933; Carlisle United August 1935 – 1936.
For 2 seasons a regular at Stockport, before his departure; Lloyd was unable to gain a similar spot for the Tigers. Curiously, though, in the Carlisle season his fortunes changed completely and he was an ever-present, making 42 League appearances.

LODGE, James William (1919-1924)

Right/left-back: 81 apps.
1921: 5ft. 8ins; 12st. 2lbs.
Born: Felling, Co Durham, 11 January 1895.
Died: 24 October 1971.
Career: Coxlodge FC (Newcastle); Scotswood (Northern Alliance); Newburn (as a part-time professional); CITY December 1919; Halifax Town July 1924; assisted Nuneaton Town and York City during season 1925/26. Retired on appointment as City's assistant trainer August 1926 and masseur on the removal to Boothferry Park, remaining with the club for almost the remainder of his life.

The Tigers' greatest servant with half a century of devotion to the cause as player and 'back room boy'. On the field, a gritty, brave defender. Had a fine eye for emerging talent. Served in WW1 with great distinction, being awarded the DCM and Bar, and the MM and Bar.

LONGDEN, Eric (1930-31 and 1932-35)
Right-half/inside-forward: 89 apps; 12 goals.
1932: 5ft. 11½ins; 12st. 10lbs.
Born: Goldthorpe, nr. Rotherham, 18 May 1904.
Career: Goldthorpe United; Doncaster Rovers 1925/26; Leeds United January 1929; CITY October 1930; Blackpool January 1931; CITY again December 1932; retired April 1935.
Honours: (City) Div. 3 (North) champions 1933.

It was easy to pick out Eric on the field – tall, hefty and prematurely balding. And for his keenness over the whole 90 minutes. Could, and did, play in most outfield positions during his career. Perhaps the outstanding quality was in notably deadly tackling.

LORD, Barry (1954-1961)
Goalkeeper: 5 apps.
1958: 6ft. 2½ins; 14st.
Born: Goole, 17 November 1937.
Career: Goole Buchanan FC to CITY as an amateur October 1954, turning professional April 1956; Goole Town September 1961.

Certainly possessed a custodian's physical qualifications for height and reach, and his weight matched these generous dimensions. Barry, however, was a Boothferry Park contemporary of Bly and Fisher who usually held down the senior team spot.

LORD, Malcolm (1964-1980)
Midfield: 271 apps. plus 32 subs; 24 goals.
1973: 5ft. 7½ins; 11st. 10lbs.
Born: Driffield, East Yorks, 25 October 1946.
Career: Junior football to CITY on amateur forms 1964, turning professional July 1965; retired through injury February 1980 but joined Scarborough during the following close season.

Associated with City over a decade and a half, a compactly build midfielder usually wearing the No. 7 or No. 8 shirt. His quiet style of play was not to the liking of all the City fans, one of the club managers defending him at an AGM as 'a professional's professional'. Certainly Malcolm was an excellent club man, his sheer length of service a pointer to the fact.

LOUGHRAN, James (1922-1924)
Wing-half: 4 apps.
1923: 5ft. 6½ins; 11st. 4lbs.
Born: Seaham Colliery, Co Durham, in the late 1890's.
Career: Easington Colliery; CITY cs 1922; Barrow July 1924 – 1925.

Half-back of chunky build who apparently favoured the left flank. In his Barrow season made 24 Northern Section appearances, the one in a succession of four when the Lancashire club did not have to apply for re-election.

LYALL, George (1975-1978)
Midfield: 42 apps; 5 goals.
1977: 5ft. 8ins; 11st. 2lbs.
Born: John o'Groats, 4 May 1947.
Career: Kingskettle Amateurs (Fife); Raith Rovers 1964; Preston North End March 1966 (£8,000); Nottingham Forest May 1972 (around £40,000); CITY November 1975 (£17,500); retired through injury January 1978 but joined Scarborough later that season; Goole Town cs 1979, appointed manager February 1980 – February 1981 when he signed for Grantham; Bridlington Town as a player August 1981, soon afterwards joining the Yorkshire League side, North Ferriby United, for a short spell.
Honours: (PNE) Div. 3 champions 1971.

A good scoring record with Raith Rovers attracted English attention and he continued to take the eye at Preston for another reason – a high work rate – as well as popping in goals. A good example of the typical Scottish craftsman. Settled in North Humberside.

LYON, John (1914-1920)

Inside-left: 27 apps. 5 goals.
1919: 5ft. 9ins; 11st. 10lbs.
Born: Prescot, Lancs, in the mid-1890's.
Career: Prescot FC; CITY 1913/14; Leeds United July 1920; Prescot for second spell during 1920/21 season; New Brighton August 1921; Mold cs 1924.

Much of his career was spent with non-League sides (including the 2 seasons immediately prior to New Brighton's obtaining admission to the Football League). An adaptable forward, Jack figured at centre-forward as well with New Brighton, and won a Welsh League championship medal at Mold in 1924/25. Brother of City's Sam (see below).

LYON, Samuel (1913-1914)
Centre-forward: 16 apps. 1 goal.
1913: 5ft. 9½ins; 10st.
Born: Prescot, Lancs. in the early 1890's.
Career: Prescot junior football to CITY during season 1912/13; Barnsley cs 1914.
Brother of City's John Lyon. On the light side for leading the attack, which probably contributed to a miniscule goal tally. This improved in his Barnsley season, 9 League games producing 3 goals.

McAINSH, James (1933-1934)
Outside-right: 7 apps.
1935: 5ft. 8ins; 11st. 10lbs.
Born: Clackmannan, 1914.
Career: Scottish junior football to CITY December 1933; Gateshead cs 1934 – 1936.
Signed when a teenager, the young Scot stayed at Anlaby Road only a matter of months. At Gateshead saw a fair amount of first team football, playing 45 League games in which he scored 6 times.

McCLAREN, Stephen (1977-)
Midfield: 131 apps. plus 7 subs; 12 goals.
1983: 5ft. 7½ins; 9st. 4lbs.
Born: Fulford, York, 3 May 1961.
Career: Yorkshire Schools; CITY as an apprentice professional, turning full professional April 1979.
An extremely skilled young player, skill being rather essential as he hasn't the physique for bustling tactics. Creative in manufacturing chances for colleagues and can take the scoring chance himself. A fine prospect.

McCORRY, Henry (1913-1914)
Inside-right: 10 apps; 4 goals.
1913: 5ft. 7½ins; 11st. 6lbs.
Born: Felling, Co Durham, 1888.
Career: Newburn; CITY cs 1913; Chesterfield Town 1914.
From the ever fruitful Tyneside area. Henry's season at Anlaby Road was his only one in senior football – Chesterfield's first team were in the Midland League at that time – and he performed capably in those 10 League outings.

McDONALD, KENNETH (1928-1930)
Centre-forward: 41 apps; 26 goals.
1929: 5ft. 9ins; 12st. 7lbs.
Born: Llanrwst, Denbighshire, 24 April 1898.
Career: Inverness Clachnacuddin; Aberdeen; Caerau (Welsh League); Cardiff City December 1921; Manchester United February 1923; Bradford 1923/24; CITY June 1928; Halifax Town March 1930, leaving at the season's end. Subsequently assisted Coleraine, (joined December 1930), Walker Celtic and Blyth Spartans.
Honours: (Bradford) Div. 3 (North) champions 1928.
A famous name in the mid-1920's, his sharpshooting in 1925/26 bringing a personal goal tally of 43, only one fewer than the Football League record established the same season by Jimmy Cookson. The 43 stood as a Park Avenue Club record for 40 years. This scoring ability wasn't confined to a single season either: in his aggregate 145 League matches in Bradford's colours Ken netted 136 – almost a goal a game. After leaving football he worked as a house and ship's painter on Tyneside.

McDONALD, Robert R. (1977-1980)
Defender: 17 apps. plus 8 subs; 2 goals.
1979: 6ft. 3ins; 13st. 5lbs.
Born: Hull, 22 January 1959.
Career: Hull junior football to CITY as an apprentice professional, turning full professional January 1977 (Sportclub Cambuur, Holland, on loan February – March 1980); Wageningen FC, Holland, August 1980 (£19,000) later joining Willem II before signing for Groningen FC (Holland) for £75,000 in June 1982.
Rob has had a good run in Dutch football, as evidenced by the hefty fee paid by Groningen, following limited opportunity as a Tiger. Massively built, certainly one of the biggest men on City's pay-roll in the 'Seventies.

McDONALD, William (1912-1919)
Outside-right: 69 apps; 5 goals.
1913: 5ft. 6ins; 10st. 10lbs.
Born: Quebec, Co Durham, 1892.
Career: Craghead United (Durham); CITY February 1912; Fulham 1919 – 1922/23.
Short but sturdy wingman. Went into City's League side pretty well straight from junior soccer and held his place up to the outbreak of war – he did not appear in the 1914/15 season. Billy's great strengths were his speed and the ability to centre with pinpoint accuracy.

McEWAN, Stanley (1984-)
Midfield: 16 apps; 1 goal.
1983: 5ft. 11ins; 12st. 8lbs.
Born: Cambuskenneth, nr. Stirling, 8 June 1957.
Career: Junior football to Blackpool as an apprentice professional, signing full professional July 1974; Exeter City 1982; CITY April 1984 (£5,000) after a month's loan.
Saw a lot of senior action at Blackpool, his League appearance aggregate topping the 200 mark. Usefully built for a half-back's role and has a professional approach.

McGEE, John (1922-1928)
Right or left-back: 70 apps.
1925: 5ft. 11½ins; 12st. 6lbs.
Born: Rothesay, Bute, 1902.
Career: Harrogate; CITY March 1922 (£200 including Harold Slater); retired through injury 1927.
A first-class deputy for either J. R. Gibson or Matt Bell, Jock McGee's fine defensive work would have earned him regular selection in clubs not so well served by full-backs. He belonged to a Scottish family which moved to the village of Grantley near Ripon when he was very young (hence the eventual connection with Harrogate FC). At one time Jock worked on the estate of Lord Furness. His career was ended by a broken leg sustained in a Cup-tie at Wolverhampton, February 19, 1927.

McGIFFORD, Grahame L. (1976-1977)
Full-back: 1 app.
1977: 5ft. 7ins; 10st. 7lbs.
Born: Carshalton, Surrey, 1 May 1955.
Career: Cheshire Schools; Huddersfield Town as an apprentice professional 1970, turning full professional July 1972; CITY May 1976; Port Vale June 1977; Northwich Victoria September 1978.
Found opportunities difficult to come by at Hull, with Peter Daniel and de Vries in such consistent form, following a fair amount of senior experience. So Grahame soon moved to the Potteries in company with local boy, Jeff Hemmerman.

McGILL, James M. (1971-1976)
Midfield: 141 apps. plus 6 subs; 2 goals.
1973: 5ft. 8ins; 11st. 2lbs.
Born: Partick, Glasgow, 27 November 1946.
Career: Possilpark YMCA, Glasgow; Arsenal July 1965; Huddersfield Town September 1967 (£10,000); CITY October 1971 (around £50,000); Halifax Town February 1976; George Cross FC (Melbourne, Australia) 1977 where he sustained an injury that virtually ended his career although playing a few games for Frickley Athletic after signing in December 1977.
Honours: (Huddersfield) Div. 2 champions 1970.
An ever-present in the above championship side at inside-left; a probing one, laying on chances for the dangerous Frank Worthington and that scoring winger, Colin Dobson. In other words, a half-back's ploys as well as an inside man's. A panel beater by trade.

McGORRIGHAN, Francis Owen (1946-47 and 1947-48)
Inside-forward: 26 apps; 2 goals.
1948: 5ft. 11ins; 12st. 3lbs.
Born: Easington, Co Durham, 20 November 1921.
Career: Durham Schools; Eppleton Colliery Welfare; Middlesbrough 1943; Carlisle United 1945/46; CITY August 1946; Blackburn Rovers February 1947 (£6,000); CITY again September 1947; Southport July 1948, this

contract being cancelled during the ensuing season; Scarborough August 1950; Wisbech Town 1952; retired through injury circa 1953.
Emerged as one of the successes of 1946/47, the initial post-war campaign. No great goal scorer but a constructive player able to feed and bring out the possibilities of his wingers and fellow inside-forwards.

McINTOSH, James Boyd (1910-1914)
Right-half: 91 apps; 2 goals.
1914: 5ft. 9ins. 12st. 7lbs.
Born: Glasgow, 25 May 1886.
Died: 1959.
Career: Petershill; Third Lanark; Aberdeen 1907; Celtic 1909; CITY May 1910 (£750) (guest player for Heart of Midlothian during WW1). Coached in Germany after the War.
An excellent half-back of great versatility. In his first senior season he made 32 Scottish League appearances for Aberdeen at centre-half, and he played in 5 different positions for Celtic. But it was tough going at Parkhead, the club then in a 6-season championship run, and City stepped in with a high bid to secure his transfer.

McINTOSH, James W. (1976-1977)
Midfield: 20 apps; 1 goal.
1976: 5ft. 8ins; 11st. 2lbs.
Born: Forfar, Angus, 19 August 1950.
Career: Arbroath Victoria; Montrose 1969/70; Nottingham Forest September 1970 (£15,000) (Chesterfield on loan January 1976); CITY March 1976 (£5,000); Dundee United July 1977; Montrose again November 1977.
Looked upon as an outside-left at Forest where he had, of course, an unenviable task in competing with Scotland's John Robertson. All the same Jim made 45 League appearances (plus 8 substitutions) for the Midland club. Showed some clever touches and a deal of skill without realising his full potential.

MACKAY, William (1937-1938)
Outside/inside-right: 12 apps.
(Probably born in Ireland).
Career: Linfield; Swansea Town June 1935; CITY May 1937 - 1938.
Honours: (Linfield) Irish Cup winner 1934.
Could perform usefully in both of the right flank forward positions. But was probably best on the wing and it was as Linfield's outside-right that he won his Irish Cup medal. Scored 3 goals in 13 Div. 2 outings for Swansea Town but was for the most part a reserve in his two terms at the Vetch Field.

McKECHNIE, Ian H. (1966-1974)
Goalkeeper: 255 apps.
1972: 6ft; 13st. 11lbs.
Born: Lenzie, Dunbartonshire, 4 October 1941.
Career: Dunbartonshire Schools to Arsenal's ground staff, turning professional April 1959; Southend United May 1964; CITY August 1966 (originally on a month's trial); Goole Town October 1974. Subsequently worked as a prison officer, leaving when appointed Nuneaton Borough manager March 1978 but left after only a fortnight. Appointed Sligo Rovers' manager cs 1979.
A really economical and worth-while signing. Ian was undisputed first choice custodian for most of his 8-year sojourn. A big, burly Scot and a quick mover with lots of personality. His mammoth left-foot clearances will long be remembered. Joined Arsenal as an out-side left but his goalkeeping potential was spotted before he signed pro forms.

McKENZIE, Dr George Duncan (1933-1934)
Outside-left: 9 apps; 4 goals.
1930: 5ft. 8ins; 10st. 7lbs.
Born: Buckie, Banffshire.
Career: Buckie Thistle; Aberdeen University; Queen's Park 1929; CITY autumn of 1933; Stockport County cs 1934. Also assisted Macclesfield in the mid-1930's.
Honours: Scottish amateur international (8 apps).
A medico and an amateur. Came to Hull to work, bringing a glittering reputation as one of his country's finest amateurs, earned in 4 seasons of Scottish League Div. 1 experience. Quickly snapped up by the Tigers but the Scot's stay was brief due to taking up a practice in Stockport shortly before season 1934/35 commenced.

MACKIE, John (1934-1935)
Inside-right: 14 apps; 2 goals.
1935: 5ft. 8ins; 11st. 11lbs.
Born: Baillieston, Glasgow.
Career: Bridgeton Waverley; CITY cs 1934; Bradford City October 1935; Chesterfield July 1938.
Turned out to be a utility player, becoming Bradford City's regular centre-half and then, at Chesterfield, reverting to the forward-line, but this time at inside-left. Perhaps best as an inside man, for John was a fine schemer of strong individualistic bent.

McKINNEY, Daniel (1920-1923)
Outside-right/centre-forward: 54 apps; 12 goals.
1921: 5ft. 7½ins; 10st. 7lbs.
Born: Belfast, 9 November 1898.
Career: Belfast Celtic; CITY 1920; Bradford City July 1923; Norwich City October 1924 – 1926.

Honours: Irish international vs. Scotland 1921 and 1924. Irish Victory international vs. Scotland 1919(2). (Belfast Celtic) Irish Cup winner 1918. Irish Cup finalist 1917.

Though primarily a right-winger, McKinney led the Tigers' attack during the memorable 1921 Cup-ties and was no stranger to the other forward berths either. Slight in physique but a clever and assertive performer.

McLOUGHLIN, George (1926-1927)
Inside-left: 8 apps; 2 goals.
1927: 5ft. 8½ins; 11st. 2lbs.
Born: Glasgow, circa 1903.
Career: Joined Celtic around 1923; CITY cs 1926; Accrington Stanley cs 1927; Nelson cs 1929 – 1930.

Introduced to senior football with a solitary Scottish League appearance for Celtic in 1923/24. Adjudged at Accrington to be their cleverest forward, where he took the other inside berth also, excelling in laying on chances for team-mates.

McMILLAN, Eric (1960-1965)
Wing-half: 150 apps; 3 goals.
1962: 5ft. 10½ins; 11st. 10lbs.
Born: Beverley, 2 November 1936.
Career: RAF football; Chelsea briefly as an amateur before turning professional April 1958; CITY June 1960 (£2,000); Halifax Town July 1965; Scarborough July 1967; Port Elizabeth, South Africa, January 1969, on a 2-year playing contract.

Tasted top flight soccer at Stamford Bridge prior to returning to his native heath and Third Division fare. Eric proved a bargain, his mobile and competent displays being much to the liking of Boothferry Park patrons. On leaving the game, he came back to the Hull area.

McMURRAY, Campbell (1920-1922)
Centre-half: 4 apps.
1921: 5ft. 10ins; 11st. 10lbs.
Born: Glasgow.
Career: Strathclyde; Glasgow Ashfield; CITY January 1920 - 1922; York City cs 1923. Later surfaced in FL circles again, playing in 2 Northern Section matches for New Brighton during season 1925/26.

Played for a couple of crack Glasgow junior sides – Ashfield, for example, reached the Scottish Junior cup final the season he joined City. But at Anlaby Road had the difficult task of competing with the inimitable Mick Gilhooley. Could also play full-back.

McNAUGHTON, William Frederick (1932-1934)
Centre-forward: 84 apps; 57 goals.
1935: 5ft. 9½ins; 11st. 10lbs.
Born: Poplar, London, 8 December 1905.
Died: 27 August 1980.
Career: Barking Town; Millwall May 1925; Peterborough & Fletton United cs 1926; Northampton Town May 1928; Gateshead cs 1930; CITY June 1932; Stockport County October 1934-1936.
Honours: (City) Div. 3 (North) champions 1933.

A major name in City's history as holder of the club's League scoring record (41 in the above championship season), which has stood for over half a century. After a rather uneven start to his professional career, Bill found his goal touch at Gateshead (46 in 63 senior outings) which reached its peak in 1932/33. Represented Essex county when with Barking Town. Also played at inside-right.

McNEIL, Robert M. (1979-)
Full-back: 111 apps. plus 3 subs; 3 goals.
1983: 5ft. 8½ins; 10st. 9lbs.
Born: Bellshill, Lanarkshire, 1 November 1962.
Career: Lanarkshire schools football to CITY as an apprentice professional 1979, turning full professional November 1980.

An ever-present in 1983/84, this young Scot's development has been one of continuing progress, exploiting his wing with growing assurance besides fine defensive work. Certainly among the best of the late 1970's apprentices.

McNEILL, Hamilton John (1937-1939)
Centre-forward: 52 apps; 28 goals.
1938: 5ft. 9½ins; 12st.
Born: Glasgow.
Career: Ayr United; CITY May 1937; Bury February 1939.

His senior involvement at Ayr was confined to season 1936/37, when that club had temporarily left the 1st Division of the Scottish League. The inexperienced Scot, however, displayed plenty of thrust on City's behalf as the above record shows, and for Bury he scored 7 goals in 18 League outings before the outbreak of war.

McPHEAT, John (1935-1936)
Inside-forward: 9 apps.
Born in Scotland.
Career: Rutherglen Glencairn; CITY September 1935; not retained cs 1936.
John made his League debut not long after arriving from Scotland. It was on the 5th October 1935 in the home game against Plymouth Argyle.

McQUILLAN, John (1906-1914)
Left-back: 239 apps; 3 goals.
1906: 5ft. 8½ins; 11st.
Born: Boldon, Co Durham, 1888.
Career: Jarrow Town; CITY October 1906; Leeds City cs 1914 (£100) (assisted Fulham and Hull City again during WW1).
A reliable and consistent defender who aggregated a formidable number of appearances before his migration to Leeds. To these can be added his City wartime quota: 28 in 1915/16 and 4 in 1916/17. Later scouted for the club in Wales. A mid-1900s commentator wrote that John "... filled Harry Davies's position and, although not so smart in heading, he was quick on his feet".

McSEVENEY, John H. (1961-1965)
Outside-right/inside-forward/outside-left: 161 apps. 60 goals.
1963: 5ft. 8ins; 10st. 4lbs.
Born: Shotts, Lanarkshire, 8 February 1931.
Career: Carluke Rovers; Hamilton Academicals 1948; Sunderland October 1951 (£5,000); Cardiff City May 1955; Newport County June 1957 in a player exchange; CITY June 1961 (£1,000); retired June 1965 and joined City's coaching staff. Home Farm (Dublin) coach February 1973; Nottingham Forest chief coach December 1973 – January 1975; Waterford manager late in 1975 – December 1977.
Saw a deal of senior soccer with all his FL clubs, the League outings with both City and Newport topping the 160 mark. John was a perky Scottish forward, two-footed and adaptable as to position, and a consistent scorer. An excellent coach too.

MADDISON, George ('Geordie') (1924-1938)
Goalkeeper: 430 apps.
1930: 6ft; 13st. 6lbs.
Born: Birtley, Co Durham, 14 August 1902.
Died: 18 May 1959.
Career: Birtley FC (Northern Alliance); Tottenham Hotspur November 1922; CITY June 1924; retired through injury 1937/38.
Honours: (City) Div. 3 (North) champions 1933.
One of the major names in City's history, a great character who put in some 14 seasons of service at Anlaby Road. Quite unorthodox – almost a third back, never hesitating to venture beyond the confines of his penalty area – Geordie was nonetheless safe. And consistent, too – an ever-present in 4 seasons. His appearances would have reached an even higher total but for injuries that included 2 broken collar-bones and a fractured wrist. His son, George junior, also a goalkeeper, played professionally for Aldershot and York City.

MAJOR, John L. (1946-47 and 1955-56)
Outside-right/outside-left: 13 apps.
1947: 5ft. 6ins; 10st. 7lbs.
Born: Islington, London, 12 March 1929.
Career: Watford schools and junior football, then assisted Watford FC reserves before moving north in 1945, when he played for Hull Amateurs; CITY on amateur forms 1946, left 1947 to join the Forces, signing for Sunderland and Romford as an amateur during the 1947/48 season, afterwards joining Bishop Auckland circa 1949; CITY again, this time as a professional, June 1955; Goole Town September 1956.
Honours: England amateur international vs. France 1948 and Scotland and Wales 1955. (Bishop Auckland) Amateur Cup winner 1955. Amateur Cup finalist 1950, 1954.
Had a distinguished career in top amateur soccer. Essentially an outside-right but his ebullient, tenacious play transferred easily to the opposite flank. Tasted the senior game at a very tender age. Sometimes played inside-right. An accountant by profession.

MANNING, John Tom (1905-1907)
Outside-right: 54 apps; 9 goals.
1905: 5ft. 9ins; 11st. 12lbs.
Born: Boston, Lincs. 1886.
Died: 1946.
Career: Boston FC; CITY cs 1905; Bradford August 1907; Rochdale July 1910; Lincoln City cs 1911-1915.
A power-house of a right-winger, hefty enough to brush aside the opposition, impervious to knocks. Had tremendous acceleration, a repertoire of tricks and a bullet shot. An automatic choice with all his clubs.

MANNION, Wilfred J. (1954-1955)
Inside-forward: 16 apps; 1 goal.
1955: 5ft. 5ins; 10st. 4lbs.

67

Born: South Bank, Middlesbrough, 16 May 1918.
Career: South Bank St. Peter's; Middlesbrough as an amateur September 1936, turning professional January 1937; retired June 1954 but joined CITY the following December (£5,000); Poole Town September 1955 – March 1956; Cambridge United August 1956; King's Lynn May 1958; Haverhill Rovers (Suffolk) October 1958 – cs 1959; Earlestown (Lancashire Combination) as player/manager October 1960 – October 1962.
Honours: England international (26 apps). England wartime international (4 apps). Football League (7 apps).

One of the greatest players of the late Thirties and the immediate post-war era, Mannion played an orthodox inside-forward game with quite exceptional brilliance in ball control and passing. Known as 'The Golden Boy of Soccer', a title due in equal parts to this brilliance and his fair hair. Returned to Teesside on leaving the game.

MARCH, Harold (1929-30)
Forward: 7 apps.
Born circa 1904.
Career: Army football; CITY 1929; Lincoln City 1930 – 1932.

An amateur and one of two brothers on City's playing strength at the same time, Harold had been a soldier and represented the British Army. Played in 10 Northern Section matches for Lincoln City, scoring 6 goals, all appearances being at inside-left.

MARSHALL, James Michael (1920-21)
Outside-left: 1 app.
Born: Auckland, Co. Durham, 1897.
Career: St. Peter's Albion (Newcastle); CITY on trial during 1920/21 season; Preston Colliery (Co Durham) cs 1921.

Trialist who was given a run in the Tigers' League side. 'Topical Times', in the issue for January 15, 1921, remarked on the club's liking for Tyneside recruits and made a reference to Marshall – 'sturdily built and knows his work'.

MARTIN, Frank (1904-1911)
Left-half: 29 apps; 1 goal.
1913: 5ft. 8½ins; 12st.
Born: Gateshead.
Career: Millwall Athletic; CITY cs 1904; Grimsby Town August 1911 (£85, fee fixed by a tribunal) — 1921.

Largeley engaged in skippering City's reserves during his 7-year Anlaby Road stint. Won favourable comments from the critics in the course of both City and Grimsby Town service, the following being typical " . . . most energetic, fast and strong, and never spared himself. Frank had no end of courage too".

MARTIN, George Scott (1922-1928)
Inside-forward: 204 apps. 56 goals.
1925: 5ft. 9ins; 11st. 6lbs.
Born: Bothwell, Lanarkshire, 14 July 1899.
Died: 1972.
Career: Cadzow St. Anne's (Motherwell); Hamilton Academicals 1920/21; Bathgate (on loan); CITY October 1922; Everton March 1928; Middlesbrough May 1932; Luton Town August 1933; retired 1937 thereupon becoming the latter club's coach. He took over the Luton managership in December 1944 to March 1947 and subsequently held the manager's position with Newcastle United March 1947-December 1950, Aston Villa December 1950-August 1953 and Luton again (as 'caretaker' and chief scout) February 1965-November 1966.

An excellent ball playing inside man who enjoyed a long career in the game. Had a pronounced artistic bent – a noted singer and possessor of a fine tenor voice, and a diploma-winning sculptor. A commentator wrote: "More successful at inside-right (than centre) and could shoot straight, but not often enough to suit his critics".

MARTIN, John Joseph (1935-1936)
Outside-left: 4 apps; 1 goal.
1935: 5ft. 11ins; 12st. 8lbs.
Born: Manchester, 28 November 1908.
Died: 1980.
Career: Bacup Borough; CITY May 1935 – cs 1936.

Singularly well proportioned for a winger, he must have caused problems for Lancashire Combination defences prior to his Anlaby Road days. Didn't, though, make an impact then, in an unhappy relegation season.

MARTIN, Thomas (1955-1957)
Right-half/inside-forward: 32 apps; 2 goals.
1955: 5ft. 8½ins; 10st. 10lbs.
Born: Glasgow: 21 December 1924.
Career: Shettleston Juniors; Heart of Midlothian; Stirling Albion 1949/50; Doncaster Rovers July 1950; Nottingham Forest October 1952 (£15,000, then Forest's record fee); CITY June 1955 (£7,000); Rothes FC (Highland League) as player/coach September 1957.

Something of a two-footed utility player capable of outstanding performance whether at wing-half or inside-forward, and a true Scottish stylist. But perhaps a touch of inconsistency caused Tommy's failure to attain representative honours.

MARTIN, William Thomas John (1904-1906)
Left-half: 4 apps.
1905: 5ft. 9ins; 11st. 8lbs.

Born: Poplar, London, 1883.
Died: 1954.
Career: Millwall Athletic; CITY August 1904; Clapton Orient cs 1906; Stockport County April 1908; Oldham Athletic February 1909.
A 'first professional season' pioneer not to be confused with Frank Martin, also ex-Millwall who arrived about the same time. William was conspicuous on the field because of his white/grey hair. Playing weaknesses remarked upon were tendencies to kick the ball too far ahead when dribbling, and to 'toe' the ball rather than use the instep. But, on the credit side, he was equally dexterous with both feet.

MARWOOD, Brian (1976-1984)
Midfield/forward: 154 apps. plus 4 subs; 51 goals.
1983: 5ft. 7ins; 9st. 13lbs.
Born: Easington, Co Durham, 5 February 1960.
Career: North-East junior football to CITY as an apprentice professional June 1976, turning full professional February 1978; Sheffield Wednesday June 1984 (£115,000).
Among the best of City's developments from apprentice level in recent times, an incisive little player quick to seize scoring opportunities and giving full value in other departments too. At the time of his transfer was the longest-serving Tiger.

MASON, Thomas Edwin ('Tich') (1920-1922)
Outside-right: 3 apps.
Born: Hull, 26 July 1893.
Died: 12 June 1969.
Career: Hull Schools; Hull Thursday League football; Army football (Life Guards); CITY cs 1920 (Rotherham Town for a spell November 1920); retired through injury 1922.
Outstandingly fast winger – not surprisingly for he was a noted sprinter, both as an amateur and a professional, and the British Services' 100 yards champion in 1919. Sustained a broken leg during a match against Lincoln City which affected his sporting activities. Commissioned in both World Wars (Army 1914/18 and RAF 1939/45) and was an Army welter-weight champion. By vocation a master decorator.

MASSEY, Stephen (1983-)
Forward: 11 apps. plus 2 subs; 4 goals.
1983. 5ft. 11ins; 11st. 5lbs.
Born: Denton, Manchester, 28 March 1958.
Career: Junior football to Stockport County as an apprentice professional turning full professional, July 1975: AFC Bournemouth July 1978; Peterborough United cs 1981; Northampton Town February 1982; CITY July 1983 (£20,000).

Has had a considerable amount of experience in the League's lower divisions and his form at Northampton brought him to City's notice. In and out of the City side in 1983/84, happier times may be ahead.

MAYSON, John Dunnett (1936-1937)
Outside-left: 23 apps; 8 goals.
1929: 5ft. 7ins; 9st. 7lbs.
Born: High Park, Southport, 24 October 1908.
Career: Southport schoolboy and then local league football; Southport FC as an amateur cs 1929; Burscough; Bolton Wanderers as a professional April 1932; Clapton Orient July 1933; CITY May 1936; Tranmere Rovers May 1937; Runcorn cs 1938. Did not play after the outbreak of war.
Generally to be found on the other flank elsewhere. Jack was an elusive customer, possessing a degree of craft and clever control, but could be variable in performance. On leaving football, worked as an engineer until his retirement.

MEENS, Harold (1936-1954)
Centre-half: 146 apps.
1947: 6ft. 0½ins; 12st. 1lb.
Born: Doncaster, 5 October 1919.
Career: Yorkshire Schools; Shepherd's Road Club (Bentley & District League); CITY as an amateur August 1936, turning professional April 1937; retired through injury 1953/54 season.
Honours: (City) Div. 3 (North) champions 1949.
Played full-back on occasion too. Quiet in disposition and unruffled on the field, Meens possessed excellent defensive qualities, a steadying influence not being the least of them. Served with the RAMC during WW2. After leaving Boothferry Park worked for many years as a plasterer. Was team manager of Hull Brunswick FC for 15 months to November 1965 and he also had a spell managing Ainthorpe Youth Club.

MELLOR, J(ohn) Allan (1947-1952)
Left-half: 104 apps; 5 goals.
1949: 5ft. 8ins; 11st. 8lbs.
Born: Droylsden, Manchester, 16 October 1921.
Career: Lancashire Schools; Manchester United 'A'; Army football during WW2; Audenshaw United; Ashton United as a professional February 1947; CITY June 1947; retired through injury October 1952.
Honours: (City) Div. 3 (North) champions 1949.
Tough wing-half with a blockbuster of a tackle and an ability to out-jump taller opponents for the high balls. Specialised too in long crossfield passes. Had also played inside-forward before joining the Tigers.

MELVILLE, David (1914-1915)
Centre-forward: 5 apps.
1914: 5ft. 9ins; 12st.
Born: Glasgow.
Career: Glasgow junior football to CITY 1914; Clyde March 1915.
His few League outings all occurred in the first Anlaby Road phase, i.e. during the 1913/14 season. A blank 1914/15 sheet was remedied with Clyde: following his move in March, David played in 8 Scottish League Div. 1 matches (1 goal) before the end of season 1914/15.

MELVILLE, James (1933-1934)
Centre or left-half: 14 apps; 1 goal.
1935: 6ft. 1in; 12st. 4lbs.
Born: Barrow-in-Furness, 15 March 1909.
Died: 2 August 1961.
Career: Vickerstown FC (Barrow); Barrow FC as an amateur 1926/27; Blackburn Rovers as a professional 1928; CITY December 1933; Northampton Town June 1934.
Originally an inside-left, moving back to the intermediate line around 1930 after which his game speeded up and his large physique was put to more advantageous use. An intelligent performer possessing subtle touches. An excellent cricketer too, Jim became a professional with Millom CC in 1932 and played for Warwickshire in 1946.

MERCER, David William (1914-1920)
Outside/inside-right: 91 apps; 26 goals.
1919: 5ft. 7ins; 10st. 10lbs.
Born: St. Helens, 20 March 1893.
Died: 4 June 1950.
Career: Prescot Athletic (Liverpool County Combination); Skelmersdale; CITY January 1914; Sheffield United December 1920 (£4,500: then a record); Shirebrook cs 1928; Torquay United June 1929; retired cs 1930.
Honours: England international (2 apps). Football League (1 app). FA tour of South Africa 1920 during which he played against their national team. (Sheffield U) FA Cup winner 1925.
Won his honours as a winger where his dazzling footwork was seen to best advantage. Came to the fore in wartime soccer with an unbroken run of some 200 games from his debut (18 April 1914) to 2 April 1920, and consistent scoring. No doubt his 6 goals against Sheffield United in January 1919 was at least a factor in that club's large outlay! Brother of Arthur Mercer, whom he partnered at Sheffield, and father of Arthur jnr. (Torquay United 1946-49).

MERCER, William Henry (1914-1924)
Goalkeeper: 193 apps.
1920: 5ft. 11ins; 11st. 7lbs.
Born: Prescot, Lancs. 1888.
Died: 5 June 1956.
Career: Prescot Athletic (Liverpool County Combination); CITY August 1914 (Stockport County as a guest player briefly in 1918/19); Huddersfield Town November 1924; Blackpool May 1928; retired cs 1929.
Honours: (Huddersfield) League champions 1925. (Huddersfield) FA Cup finalist 1928.
Rightly described on his move to Blackpool as "exceptionally able" for he was most competent without being in any way showy. Billy also excelled at cricket (for Hull CC while with City), billiards and tennis. He served with the Royal Engineers throughout the 1914/18 War.

METCALFE, J. T. (1914-15)
Outside-left: 3 apps.
Born: Newark, Notts.
Career: Had been on Notts County's books as an amateur before joining CITY in 1914.
Reserve winger who made his League debut for City, not having reached that level for Notts County. This was in the opening match of 1914/15, against Stockport County on 3 September 1914. A local commentator wrote, no doubt truly but perhaps a touch dismissively: "A stripling, and therefore lacked the physical qualification to cope with the robust style expected from the opposition".

METCALFE, Victor (1958-1960)
Outside-left: 6 apps; 2 goals.
Born: Barrow-in-Furness, 3 February 1922.
Career: West Riding schools football; Ravensthorpe Albion; Huddersfield Town as an amateur January 1940, turning professional December 1945; CITY June 1958; retired February 1960. Huddersfield Town youth coach 1961 – October 1964; Halifax Town coach/scout December 1964, then their manager June 1966 – November 1967.
Honours: England international vs. Argentina and Portugal 1951. Football League vs. Irish League 1950 and League of Ireland 1954.
Came to City towards the end of a distinguished playing career, retiring on his 38th birthday. Vic had made 434 League appearances for Huddersfield in which he had netted 87 goals – a skilled, tricky winger employing excellent ball control.

MIDDLEHURST, James Henry (1914-1920)
Full-back: 9 apps.
Born: Prescot, Lancs, 1892.
Died: 1954.

Career: St. Helens district junior football; CITY August 1914 - 1920 (guest player for Liverpool during WW1).

Four players were sent for trial in August 1914 by Billy Robinson from his home district and Middlehurst was one of the two engaged (the other was the estimable Billy Mercer). When guesting for Liverpool Middlehurst partnered Ephraim Longworth, of England fame and an all-time Anfield 'great', which must have been a beneficial experience. His League debut was an away match against Woolwich Arsenal, September 26, 1914.

MIDDLEMAS, John Robert (1922-1923)
Right-half: 10 apps.
1922: 5ft. 8ins; 11st.
Born: Easington, Co Durham, 1896.
Died: 24 April 1984.
Career: Herrington Swifts; CITY cs 1922; York City cs 1923. Also had spell with Blyth Spartans.

A capable second string to Jock Collier, as the reaching of appearance double figures in his Anlaby Road season shows. Moved to York along with another reserve Tiger, Campbell McMurray.

MILLER, Alforth Henry (1933-1935)
Wing-half: 4 apps.
1935: 5ft. 10ins; 11st. 9lbs.
Born: Gainsborough, Lincs, 1911.
Career: CITY 1933; Barrow May 1935 – 1936.

Reserve player of sturdy build. With City at the time of a championship side when the wing-half spots were harder than normal to win.

MILLS, Bertie Reginald ('Paddy') (1920-26 and 1929-33)
Centre/inside-forward, latterly wing-half. 270 apps; 102 goals.
1925: 5ft. 10ins; 11st. 5lbs.
Born: Multan, India, 23 February 1900.
Career: Barton Town (Lincs); CITY 1920/21; Notts County March 1926 (£3,750); Birmingham February 1929; CITY December 1929; Scunthorpe United cs 1933. Later with Gainsborough Trinity.
Honours: (City) Div. 3 (North) champions 1933.

One of 6 brothers, the 2 eldest being killed in WW1 and 2 others, Percy and Arthur, professionals with Notts County and Luton Town respectively. Great marksman – his aggregate League tally stood as a club record for over 30 years until surpassed by Chris Chilton – direct, good in distribution and tough. His nickname derived from a boyhood scrap in which he was said to have 'fought like a Paddy'. Employed as a works policeman at a Scunthorpe steelworks for 25 years until his retirement in 1965.

MILLS, James ('Smiler') (1946-1947)
Wing-half: 42 apps; 1 goal.
1947: 5ft. 8½ins; 12st. 3lbs.
Born: Dalton Brook, nr. Rotherham, 30 September 1915.
Career: Bramley Park Rangers; Dinnington Athletic; Rotherham United cs 1937; CITY October 1946; Halifax Town December 1947; Gainsborough Trinity cs 1948.

Captained City after arriving from Rotherham, a jovial character with his fair share of footballing know-how. Originally played centre-half and occasionally inside-forward but his activities at Boothferry Park were in the flank half-back positions.

MILNER, Michael (1955-1968)
Centre-half: 160 apps.
1962: 6ft; 11st. 9lbs.
Born: Hull, 21 September 1939.
Career: Hull Schools; CITY as an amateur August 1955, turning professional July 1957; Stockport County July 1968; Barrow September 1969; Bradford City December 1969; Goole Town May 1970.
Honours: (City) Div. 3 champions 1966.

Played inside-forward for his school team (West Dock Avenue) and later wing-half before finding an ultimate role as a pivot. Very strong defensively, his height mostly assuring mastery in the air. A sheet metal worker by trade.

MITCHELL, Andrew (1933-1934)
Outside-right: 8 apps.
1930: 5ft. 8ins; 11st. 3lbs.
Born: Coxhoe, nr. Sunderland, 20 April 1907.
Died: 3 December 1971.
Career: Crook Town; Sunderland December 1927; Notts County August 1928; Darlington cs 1929; Manchester United April 1932; CITY cs 1933.

Darlington gave Andrew his senior baptism and he had an excellent 3 seasons there, 99 League games and 32 goals. For a winger, an average of a goal every 3 games is good going in any era.

MITCHELL, Ronald (1924-1926)
Left-half/inside-forward: 26 apps; 1 goal.
1925: 5ft. 9½ins; 11st. 10lbs.
Born: Birkenhead, 1902.
Career: Liverpool 1922/23; CITY May 1924; Nelson cs 1926; Bristol Rovers cs 1927.

Basically a left-half although he played in the forward line at Anlaby Road too. So an adaptable player besides having a degree of skill. Made his League debut in a Tigers' jersey.

MONTGOMERY, Stanley W. J. (1944-1946)
Right-half/inside-right: 5 apps.
1949: 6ft; 12st.
Born: West Ham, 7 July 1920.
Career: Romford; CITY 1944 (guest player for Southend United 1945/46); Southend United September 1946; Cardiff City November 1948 (£6,000); Worcester City July 1955; Newport County November 1955; Llanelly October 1956.
Tall, powerful and a fine forager. A player City were reluctant to lose but he had strong ties in the South. Performed at centre-half with Cardiff. Stan was a first-class cricketer too — after assisting Essex Second XI in the Minor Counties, he qualified for Glamorgan, playing for the Welsh county 1949 – 1953. Son-in-law of the late Jimmy Nelson, Scottish international right-back.

MOONEY, Edward (1927-1928)

Right-half; 11 apps.
1927: 5ft. 8ins; 13st. 6lbs.
Born: Walker, Newcastle-on-Tyne, 22 March 1897.
Career: Walker Celtic; Newcastle United August 1919; CITY June 1927 (£500); Scunthorpe United cs 1928; Walker Celtic again 1930, subsequently assisting several Tyneside amateur clubs as a permit player.
Honours: (Newcastle) FA Cup winner 1924.
A cheery Geordie, unconventional in method, whose finest hour had been Newcastle's Wembley triumph in 1924. For some unexplained reason, known as Peter when at St. James Park.

MOORE, Alan (1951-1952)
Outside-right: 13 apps; 4 goals.
1952: 5ft. 8ins; 10st. 10lbs.
Born: Hebburn, Co Durham, 7 March 1927.
Career: Sunderland May 1946; Spennymoor United; Chesterfield December 1948; City June 1951 (£7,000); Nottingham Forest January 1952; Coventry December 1954 (£10-11,000); Swindon Town June 1957; Rochdale November 1958; Wisbech Town June 1959. Subsequently coached the Cambridge University team for 2 seasons, 1967/68 and 1968/69.
Moved around the 2nd Division and North and South sections of the 3rd in the initial post-war era, a speedy winger with a liking for cutting in on goal. Possessed a full repertoire of tricks.

MOORE, John E. (1934-1935)
Inside-forward: 5 apps.
1935: 5ft. 9ins; 10st. 7lbs.
Born: Newcastle-on-Tyne, 1912.
Career: Hebburn Colliery; CITY cs 1934; Gateshead June 1935 – 1937.
There has been a lot of traffic between City and Gateshead from the former's earliest days, McAinsh as well as Moore moving north in the 1935 close season. Moore played 24 League games for the Redheugh Park club, scoring 4 goals.

MOORE, Norman Woodliffe (1947-1950)
Centre-forward: 81 apps; 45 goals.
1949: 5ft. 10½ins; 11st. 7lbs.
Born: Grimsby, 15 October 1919.
Career: Grimsby Schools; Grimsby Town as a professional 1936 after development in the club's nursery side (guest player during WW2 with Wrexham, Chester, Charlton Athletic and Norwich City, and also played in Army representative football); CITY April 1947; Blackburn Rovers March 1950; Bury August 1951; Goole Town July 1952; Wisbech Town 1953.
Honours: (City) Div. 3 (North) champions 1949.
Previously a wing-half, Norman took the centre-forward spot at Boothferry Park with marked success – a willing worker highly skilled in the art of heading goals. After leaving football worked as a representative for a Grimsby firm of paper merchants, subsequently becoming a director and then left to set up his own business. Also engaged in farming near North Kelsey, Lincs. His brother, Tom, and nephews, Kevin and David Moore, have served Grimsby Town too.

MORDUE, Thomas ('Tucker') (1923-1924)
Outside-right: 6 apps.
1927: 5ft. 6½ins; 10st. 7lbs.
Born: Horden, Co Durham, 22 July 1905.
Career: Herrington Swifts; CITY 1923; Horden Athletic 1924/25; Newcastle United November 1925 (£100); Sheffield United September

1926 (£500); Hartlepools United September 1928; Horden Colliery circa 1931.
After leaving the Tigers earned a reputation as an aggressive little centre-forward and a terror for his size. Played inside-left for Hartlepools, who fielded 3 other members of the Mordue clan in the 1920's. Nephew of John Mordue, a famous Sunderland and England forward of pre-1914 days.

MORGAN, Douglas (1913-1915)
Left-back: 52 apps.
1913: 5ft. 9ins; 11st. 9lbs.
Born: Inverkeithing, Fife, circa 1890.
Killed in action, 1 January 1917.
Career: Inverkeithing United; CITY cs 1913.
Stepped up from Scottish junior soccer to the English Second Division in fine style, taking over from the long serving McQuillan who moved on to Leeds City during the following close season. In 1914/15 Doug was undisputed first team left-back and could have been on the threshold of a notable career.

MORRALL, George Alfred (1919-1920)
Inside-left: 37 apps; 17 goals.
1919: 5ft. 5ins; 11st.
Born: Birmingham, 1893.
Died: 1964.
Career: Sparkhill Avon FC (Birmingham); Redditch as a professional 1910; Nuneaton 1914/11; Blackheath Town (Staffs) 1918/19; CITY cs 1919; Grimsby Town September 1920 – 1922.
Won a fine clutch of medals with his earlier clubs which included Birmingham Combination championships for both Redditch and Nuneaton. And he was a junior internationalist for the Birmingham FA against the Scottish Junior FA. An aggressive little forward, George had a good League season in 1919/20, scoring 17 goals in his 35 appearances.

MORRIS, Christopher Joseph (1957-1961)
Outside-right/centre-forward: 17 apps; 4 goals.
1959: 5ft. 9ins; 11st. 6lbs.
Born: Hull, 12 October 1939.
Career: Junior football to CITY as an amateur January 1957, signing as a professional the following October; York City June 1961.
Reserve forward. Of his 17 League outings, 11 were in the 1959/60 campaign when he also netted 3 goals. No League appearances for York City.

MORRIS, John (1926-1927)
Centre-half: 1 app.
1927: 6ft; 12st. 2lbs.
Born: Newarthill, Lanarkshire.
Career: Newarthill FC; CITY cs 1926; Bradford City cs 1927 – 1928.
Finely built Scot whose solitary League appearance for City was his only one – he made none in his Valley Parade season, having to contend with the Scottish international, Willie Summers. At Anlaby Road, of course, the man in charge was that consistent pivot, Stan Dixon.

MORRISON, John (1908-1910)
Centre-half: 4 apps.
1909: 5ft. 9ins; 11st. 10lbs.
Born: Jarrow, 1886.
Career: Jarrow FC; CITY March 1908; Swindon Town cs 1910 – 1911.
Didn't get much of a look-in with City, Andy Browell and W. S. Robinson then also being in contention for the pivotal berth. Morrison, though, had the reputation of being equally good in attack and defence and was a sound reserve.

MORTENSEN, Stanley Harding (1955-1957)
Centre-forward: 42 apps; 18 goals.
1957: 5ft. 8ins; 12st.
Born: South Shields, 26 May 1921.
Career: South Shields Ex-Schoolboys after starting in local schools soccer; Blackpool April 1937 (guest player for Aberdeen during WW2); CITY November 1955 (£2,000); Southport February 1957; Bath City July 1958; retired May 1959 but came out of retirement to join Lancaster City November 1960, finally retiring March 1962. Blackpool manager February 1967 – April 1969.
Honours: England international (25 apps). England 'B' international vs. Switzerland 1948. England wartime international vs. Scotland and Wales 1945. Football League (5 apps). (Blackpool) FA Cup winner 1953. FA Cup finalist 1948, 1951.
A great personality of the post-WW2 decade, an electrifying performer at centre and inside-forward with a tremendous burst of speed, the ability to rise astonishingly high to head and a fine marksman. Played as a substitute for Wales in a 1944 wartime international. Became a business man in Blackpool.

MOSS, Paul M. (1979-1981)
Midfield: 53 apps. plus 1 sub; 7 goals.
1980: 5ft. 7ins; 10st. 2lbs.
Born: Birmingham, 2 August 1957.
Career: Northfield FC (Birmingham); Wolverhampton Wanderers July 1976; CITY October 1979 (£47,300) after a month's loan; Scunthorpe United September 1981; retired May 1982 but assisted Worcester City the following season.

City paid a substantial fee for this player although he hadn't appeared for Wolves in League football. A clever player – as he demonstrated in the loan period – with youth on his side, and his Boothferry Park stay would perhaps have been longer had the club then been on an upward trend.

MUNNINGS, C(harles) Edward (1931-1932)
Outside-right: 31 apps; 7 goals.
1930: 5ft. 9½ins; 11st.
Born: Boston, Lincs, 1906.
Career: Boston FC; Grimsby Town September 1927; Swindon Town cs 1930; CITY cs 1931; Swindon Town again June 1932; Mansfield Town cs 1933 – cs 1934.
Big for a winger and made his presence felt accordingly, contributing to the score-sheet fairly regularly. Didn't make the Mariners' first team in 3 years at Blundell Park but enjoyed a regular place with his Div. 3 clubs.

MURPHY, George (1947-1948)
Centre-forward: 15 apps; 9 goals.
1949: 5ft. 9ins; 12st. 7lbs.
Born: Cwmfelinfach, 22 July 1915.
Died: December 1983.
Career: Monmouthshire Schools; Cwmfelinfach Colts; Bradford City November 1934; CITY December 1947; Scunthorpe United August 1948; Scarborough 1949; Goole Town cs 1951, his last club before retirement.
Honours: Welsh wartime international vs. England 1943 and 1944.
A super utility man who during his career occupied every position including goalkeeper, and a strong performer possessed of a hard shot. Assisted many clubs as a guest when in the wartime RAF including a record 8 in 9 weeks. Settled in Morley, Leeds, first working as a licensee and then as a club steward.

MURRAY, Joseph (1926-1931)
Left-half, inside or outside-left: 17 apps; 1 goal.
1929: 5ft. 7½ins; 10st. 6lbs.
Born: Hull, 28 August 1908.
Career: Hull schoolboy football; Dairycoates FC (Hull); CITY as an amateur 1925/6, turning professional April 1926; Lincoln City cs 1931; retired through injury cs 1932.
As will be gathered, a most adaptable player to have in reserve, being able to take three different left-flank positions. Had made a reputation in local junior soccer, joining City when only 17. Originally a member of a noted Hull school side of the early Twenties (Estcourt Street).

MURRAY, Terence (1951-1954)
Outside/inside-right: 32 apps; 6 goals.
Born: Dublin, 22 May 1928.
Career: Dundalk; CITY September 1951 (£5000); Bournemouth & Boscombe Athletic March 1954 (around £3000); King's Lynn July 1955.
Honours: Eire international vs. Belgium 1950. League of Ireland (6 apps).
Arrived bringing an excellent reputation from senior Republic of Ireland soccer, as his representative honours emphasised. Took the right flank positions with equal facility, and was generally sound in combined movements, but at Boothferry Park competition for forward places was particularly keen.

MURRAY, Thomas (1914)
Forward: 2 apps.
1913: 5ft. 9ins; 11st.
Born: Middlesbrough, 7 April 1889.
Died: 1976.
Career: Bradford City to CITY February 1914 (£500).
Then a First Division outfit, Bradford City were able to rope in a substantial fee (by pre-WW1 standards) for their reserve attacker. As it happened, the Tigers got little return for the outlay.

MUSGRAVE, Archibald (1909-1911)
Inside-forward: 7 apps.
1910: 5ft. 9ins; 11st.
Born: Carlisle, 1883.
Died: 22 February 1964.
Career: Workington; CITY May 1909; not retained May 1911.
Attracted the scouts to Workington, scoring 30 goals (out of 69) in that club's Lancashire Combination Div. 1 campaign of 1908/09. A reserve during his 2 years at Anlaby Road, though, with the Smiths and Arthur Temple in full spate.

MUTRIE, Leslie A. M. (1980-1984)
Forward: 114 apps; plus 1 sub; 49 goals.
1982: 6ft. 1ins; 11st. 6lbs.
Born: Newcastle-on-Tyne, 1 April 1952.
Career: Gateshead; Carlisle United June 1977; Blyth Spartans 1978; CITY December 1980 (£30,000) (Doncaster Rovers on month's loan December 1983); Colchester United January 1984 (£10,000); Hartlepool United August 1984 (£2,000).
Honours: England non-League international.
Had his ups-and-downs with the City management but on the field demonstrated he was a dangerous striker with spirit and dash. Made a solid contribution in the 1982/83 promotion season, playing in 40 games and scoring 12 goals.

NEAL, John (1949-1956)
Right/Left-back: 60 apps; 1 goal.
1957: 5ft. 8ins; 10st. 10lbs.
Born: Silksworth, Co. Durham, 3 April 1932.
Career: Silksworth Colliery Welfare Juniors; CITY August 1949; King's Lynn July 1956; Swindon Town July 1957; Aston Villa July 1959 (£6,000); Southend United November 1962; retired cs 1967. Worked at Ford's of Dagenham before appointment as Wrexham trainer/coach cs 1968, the following September becoming manager until May 1977; Middlesbrough manager May 1977; Chelsea manager May 1981.
Honours: (Villa) Div. 2 champions 1960. FL Cup winner 1961 (played in 2nd Leg only). Represented the Div. 3 (South) when with Swindon.
Made League debut in 1949/50 when a teenager, then waited three seasons for a second outing. But he matured into an excellent back, keen in the tackle and quick in recovery. Has a good managerial record too, the high spot being steering Chelsea to the 1983/84 Div. 2 championship.

NEEDHAM, John (1920-1921)
Inside-left: 18 apps; 1 goal.
1920: 5ft. 9ins; 12st. 6lbs.
Born: Newstead, nr. Nottingham, 1891.
Career: Mansfield Town; Birmingham 1909; Wolverhampton Wanderers April 1910; CITY March 1920 – cs 1921.
A real 'Mr. Consistency' in his Wolves days, for the 5 years never falling below 32 League appearances (the maximum then was 38). In all, John's total for these seasons, and not including a solitary 1909/10 outing, is 172 out of a possible 190, and he scored 52 goals.

NEILL, W(illiam) John Terence (1970-1973)
Centre-half: 103 apps; 4 goals.
1971: 5ft. 10½ins; 12st. 8lbs.
Born: Belfast, 8 May 1942.
Career: Belfast schoolboy football; Bangor (Irish League); Arsenal December 1959 (£2,500); CITY as player/manager June 1970 (£44,000), retired from playing after season 1972/73; Tottenham Hotspur manager September 1974, then Arsenal manager July 1976–December 1983.
Honours: Northern Ireland international (59 apps). Northern Ireland Under-23 international (4 apps). Northern Ireland schoolboy international. (Arsenal) FA Cup finalist 1968 (sub).
Much capped Irishman who established a record for Northern Ireland appearances (since surpassed). Played a lot at wing-half for Arsenal, a stubborn and uncompromising defensive performer. In the public eye as a manager, eloquent and charming with the media but held responsible by many for a negative playing style that led to falling gates at Highbury. Ultimately this caused his departure from Arsenal.

NEISH, John (1935-1936)
Forward: 1 app.
1935: 5ft. 9ins; 10st. 11lbs.
Born: Elgin, Morayshire, circa 1910.
Career: Scottish junior football to Partick Thistle in the mid-1930s; CITY August 1935; returned to Scotland 1936.
Arrived at Anlaby Road after having 9 Scottish League Div. 1 appearances for Partick Thistle in 1934/35 in which he netted 2 goals. Not a particularly happy time for John in 1935/36, though: the Tigers couldn't find a winning combination despite calling on 32 players and finished the Second Division's wooden spoonists.

NELSON, Arthur (1927-1929)
Centre-forward: 20 apps; 8 goals.
1928: 5ft. 10ins; 11st. 9lbs.
Born: Sheffield 15 May 1909.
Died: 1977.
Career: Nottingham schoolboy football; junior football to CITY 1927; Scarborough cs 1929; Notts County May 1930; Stockport County cs 1931; Luton Town September 1932-1933.
Started his professional career at Anlaby Road, then drifted to non-League soccer but an excellent season at Scarborough (27 goals in 53 matches) brought him back to the big-time. An adaptable forward, Arthur also played inside and, at Luton, outside-right.

NEVE, Edwin (1906-1912)
Outside-left: 102 apps; 12 goals.
1906: 5ft. 8ins; 12st.
Born: Prescot, Lancs, 1885.
Died: August 1920.

Career: St. Helens Recreational; CITY May 1906; Derby County cs 1912; Nottingham Forest cs 1914; Chesterfield Town April 1916.
For 6 seasons an excellent alternative to the Tigers' amateur celebrity, Gordon Wright, whose other commitments militated against regular appearance. There are conflicting opinions about Neve's speed – some City critics thought him too slow while a Midlands' football annual of 1913 describes him as 'a speedy outside-left'. A sadly short life.

NEVINS, Thomas (1907-1914)
Right-back: 130 apps.
1910: 5ft. 6½ins; 12st.
Born: Washington, Co. Durham 1886.
Died: 1950.
Career: Washington Athletic; CITY April 1907; Blyth Spartans 1914.
Thickset defender, a first teamer for much of his City service. Commentators of the time said Tommy 'went for the ball like a bull at a gate. Plucky (but) kicking a bit weak and feeding of his forwards left much to be desired' and had 'a style peculiar to his own'.

NEWTON, William (1931-1932)
Right-half: 24 apps.
1930: 5ft. 9ins; 11st. 10lbs.
Born: Cramlington, Northumberland, 14 May 1893.
Died: 29 April 1973.
Career: Hartford Colliery, Northumberland; Newcastle United cs 1919; Cardiff City cs 1920; Leicester City May 1922; Grimsby Town May 1926; Stockport County cs 1927; CITY July 1931; returned to Stockport County as coach August 1932 and remained with that club in a backroom capacity of one kind and another into advanced age.
Honours: (Leicester City) Div. 2 champions 1925.
Strong, forceful and possessor of a keen tackle and a liking for going forward. Billy's span of service to Stockport County was quite remarkable.

NICHOLSON, Peter W. (1960-1961)
Centre-forward: 1 app.
Born: Hull, 11 December 1936.
Career: Hull junior football to City on amateur forms; Barton Town of the Lincolnshire League as a professional February 1961.
Local amateur who had a run-out with the Tigers' League side in the 1960/61 season. Around this period the management seemed to have a liking for amateur centre-forwards – Eric Holab was a contemporary and Norman Wilkinson had been on the books a few years previously. All of them left to become professionals elsewhere.

NICKLAS, Charles (1950-1953)
Centre-forward: 6 apps; 1 goal.
Born: Sunderland, 26 April 1930.
Career: Silksworth Colliery Welfare; CITY December 1950; Darlington May 1953; Headington United July 1954.
Originally spotted by Raich Carter in Services football and eventually came to Boothferry Park after demobilisation. Charlie had a major asset in his speed – he had run professionally as a sprinter – and could also play inside-forward. Moved to Darlington on the same day as Les Robson.

NICOL, John C. (1936)
Centre-forward: 6 apps; 2 goals.
1931: 5ft. 11ins; 11st. 12lbs.
Born: Edinburgh, 26 January 1911.
Career: Leith Athletic; Portsmouth March 1932; Aldershot August 1933; Burton Town cs 1934; CITY February 1936; York City cs 1936; Scarborough cs 1937.
Honours: (Leith) Scottish League Div. 2 champions 1930.
Brought an excellent record from over the border – scored 37 goals (out of 92) in the above Leith championship campaign, and 25 in 49 Div. 1 games for the club during the succeeding two. Unable to displace the consistent Weddle at Pompey, though, and largely involved with non-league soccer thereafter.

NIELSON, Norman Fred (1957-1958)
Centre-half: 25 apps.
1957: 6ft. 3ins; 13st. 5lbs.
Born: Johannesburg, South Africa, 6 November 1928.
Career: Pretoria Athletic (South Africa); Charlton Athletic July 1949; Derby County September 1951 (£7,000); Bury May 1954 (in part exchange for another player); CITY April 1957; Corby Town July 1958; Gresley Rovers August 1959; Hinckley Athletic December 1959; Long Eaton United June 1960.
Towering pivot surprisingly fast for one of his bulk and, not so surprisingly, able to kick a ball with exceptional power. Played elsewhere at Derby, including centre-forward, but Norman's forte really was as a 'stopper' centre-half.

NISBET, Gordon James Mackay (1976-1980)
Right-back: 190 apps. plus 3 subs; 1 goal.
1978: 5ft. 10ins; 12st. 2lbs.
Born: Wallsend, 18 September 1951.
Career: Wallsend Schools; Northumberland Schools; Willington Boys' Club; West Bromwich Albion August 1968; CITY September 1976 (£10,000); Plymouth Argyle December 1980 (£32,000).

Honours: England Under-23 international vs. East Germany 1972.

Started out as a goalkeeper and also played wing-half and forward in Albion's reserve side. But his true position is undoubtedly at full-back (where he made his England Under-23 appearance). Calm, thoughtful and a first-rate club man. Gordon and another ex-Tiger, Staniforth, were members of the Plymouth team that surprisingly reached the 1984 FA Cup semi-finals.

NORMAN, Anthony J. (1980-)
Goalkeeper: 177 apps.
1983: 6ft. 1½ins; 12st. 8lbs.
Born: Mancot, Flintshire, 24 February 1958.
Career: To Burnley ground staff from schoolboy football, turning full professional during season 1976/77; CITY February 1980 (£30,000).
Honours: Welsh schoolboy international.

A splendid 'keeper, first choice since his arrival. Made no League appearances for Burnley but took to the senior game like a veteran on getting to Boothferry Park. One of Mike Smith's best imports.

NORRIE, Craig T. (1976-1982)
Forward: 22 apps. plus 9 subs; 4 goals.
1980: 5ft. 10½ins; 10st. 11½lbs.
Born: Hull, 22 July 1960.
Career: Hull Schools; CITY as an apprentice professional 1976, turning professional August 1978; Wageningen FC (Holland) February 1982; Winterslag FC (Belgium) May 1983 (£30,000).

Followed the example of fellow Hull-born Tiger, Rob McDonald, in joining Wageningen, but did so some 18 months later. Was at Boothferry Park nearly 6 years and found opportunities limited – Craig's professional career coincided with Keith Edwards's reign, for instance.

O'BRIEN, Michael Terence (1924-1926)
Centre-half: 74 apps.
1925: 6ft. 1½ins; 13st. 7lbs.
Born: Kilcock, County Dublin, 1893.
Died: 21 September 1940.
Career: Played no soccer until he was 18 when his family moved to South Shields. Then before WW1 had short spells with Walker Celtic (Newcastle), Wallsend, Blyth Spartans, Newcastle East End, Celtic and a 2-months' trial with Alloa Athletic. In 1919-20 assisted Brentford, Norwich City and South Shields. Queen's Park Rangers cs 1920; Leicester City March 1922; CITY June 1924 (£750); Brooklyn Wanderers (USA), May 1926; Derby County December 1926; Walsall June 1928; Norwich City again cs 1929; Watford June 1931-April 1933, when he retired as a player. Queen's Park Rangers manager May 1933-April 1935; Ipswich Town manager May 1936-November 1937.
Honours: Irish international (10 apps). Eire international (4 apps).

Few players have sampled so many clubs as this wandering Irishman, who crammed much into a comparatively short life. (He also served in the Army before the 1914/18 War and the Navy and Royal Flying Corps during it). A fine pivot, ideally built for the position, having a flair for combining with his forwards.

O'CONNELL, Patrick (1912-1914)
Centre-half: 58 apps; 1 goal.
1912: 5ft. 10ins; 11st. 6lbs.
Born: Dublin, circa 1887.
Career: Belfast Celtic; Sheffield Wednesday cs 1909; CITY May 1912; Manchester United cs 1914; Dumbarton August 1919; Ashington as player/manager cs 1921.
Honours: Irish international (5 apps).
Irish 'Victory' international vs. Scotland 1919.

Splendid Irish half-back who played top-flight club soccer in three of the four home countries. Obviously not lacking in generalship either for he skippered Ireland to their first British championship win (1913/14) when a Tiger.

O'RILEY, Paul J. (1966-1974)
Forward: 19 apps. plus 11 subs; 2 goals.
1972: 5ft. 9¼ins; 11st. 1lbs.
Born: Liverpool, 17 October 1950.
Career: Junior football to CITY as an apprentice professional 1966, turning full professional November 1968 (Scunthorpe United on loan March-May 1971); Barnsley July 1974; Goole Town December 1974 (£250); Southport March 1975 (around £1,000 paid to Barnsley); Corby Town October 1976. Subsequently went to Australia.

Mainly took the role of a provider, his personal goal returns being modest. A capable reserve, all the same, and a good worker.

OWEN, George Laurence (1924-1925)
Centre-forward: 2 apps.
1924: 5ft. 7½ins; 10st. 12lbs.
Born: Liverpool, 28 July 1897.
Died: 1970.
Career: Junior football to Liverpool FC during the 1920/21 season; CITY cs 1924; Chester 1925; Rochdale cs 1926; Flint FC January 1927.

Centre of stocky build almost wholly in the reserve sides of his three FL clubs (Chester

HULL CITY A.F.C. SEASON 1910

Back row: T. Nevins, W. Wright, F. Martin, H. Simmon, E. Gordon, T. Browell.
Second row: A. Langley (manager), E. Roughley, Dan Gordon, J. Houghton, A. Browell, J. B. McIntosh, G. Browell, W. Leach (trainer).
Seated: Jos. E. Smith, G. A. Temple, T. H. Pearce, D. S. Gordon, John Smith, Wallace Smith, E. Neve.
Front: J. McQuillan, A. Musgrave, E. A. Smith, F. Taylor, C. N. Hendry.

were Cheshire County League champions in Owen's season there). In all he made 5 senior appearances – 2 for City and 3 for Rochdale.

PACE, Arthur (1907-1910)
Outside-left: 5 apps.
Born: Newcastle-on-Tyne, 1885.
Died: 1968.
Career: Hebburn Argyle; CITY November 1907; Rotherham Town cs 1910; Croydon Common September 1911. Assisted City again during WW1.
Reserve forward who, like so many of City's imports, settled in Hull. (And, like that interwar winger, Fred Forward, bore an appropriate surname). Moved to Rotherham Town around the same time as George Walden of City.

PARKER, W(illiam) David (1937-1938)
Left-back: 30 apps.
1938: 5ft. 9½ins; 11st. 2lbs.
Born: Liverpool, 27 May 1915.
Died: 1980.
Career: Liverpool Marine; CITY June 1937; Wolverhampton Wanderers August 1938.
Such was David's progress on gaining a place in City's first team that Wolves, high fliers in Division One at the time, snapped him up. Sadly, another highly promising career savaged by WW2.

PARKINSON, Keith J. (1981)
Defender: substitute's app.
1981: 6ft. 1ins; 12st. 6lbs.
Born: Preston, Lancs, 28 January 1956.
Career: Leeds United as an apprentice professional, turning full professional February 1973 (CITY on a month's loan November-December 1981).
Tall player with over a score of Div. 1 appearances to his name prior to the loan period at Boothferry Park.

PATTERSON, George T. (1952-1956)
Centre-forward: 7 apps; 1 goal.
1957: 5ft. 9ins; 10st. 11lbs.
Born: Castleton, North Yorks, 15 September 1934.
Career: Silksworth Juniors (Co. Durham); CITY October 1952; King's Lynn July 1956; South Shields 1956/57; York City May 1957; Hartlepools United June 1960-1961. Assisted Goole Town in the mid-1960s, signing for that club August 1964.
Changed from leading the attack when at York and moved to left-half. With York too, George had his most successful senior run, playing in 56 League games and scoring 4 goals during the 3 terms at Bootham Crescent.

PATTISON, John Mason (1911-1915)
Right-back: 48 apps.
1913: 5ft. 10ins; 12st.
Born: Bedlington, 3 May 1889.
Died: 2 January 1978.
Career: CITY early in 1913 from Bedlington Colliery, subsequently assisted Bridlington Town.
Proved himself to be a reliable full-back in the 2 years immediately before and after the outbreak of war. Almost a regular 1913/14 and '14/15, having 46 League matches out of a possible 76. Signed in competition from Falkirk, Aston Villa and Sheffield United.

PEACH, John (1946-1947)
Inside-right: 19 apps; 2 goals.
1947: 5ft. 8ins; 11st. 6lbs.
Born: Barnsley, 4 April 1923.
Career: Barnsley schoolboy football; assisted York City in wartime then signed as an amateur for Barnsley in 1945/46, playing for Selby Town also in the same season; CITY October 1946; Selby Town again 1947/48 after a month's trial with Queen's Park Rangers from September 1947.
Played some useful games for City in the first post-war season although injury limited his League outings to 18. An infrequent scorer, Jack's talent lay rather in the matter of foraging.

PEACOCK, Terence (1949-1956)
Centre-forward: 2 apps.
1957: 5ft. 9ins; 11st. 3lbs.
Born: Hull, 18 April 1935.
Career: Hull junior football to CITY as an amateur 1949, turning professional December 1952; Queen's Park Rangers August 1956; Scarborough cs 1958, retiring through injury the following season.
Joined City's ground staff at a very tender age and graduated to pro status when 17. A courageous player, whole-hearted and having plenty of tenacity, Terry would likely have gone further in the game but for enforced retirement in his early twenties.

PEARCE, T(homas) Herbert (1910-1912)
Full-back: 3 apps.
1911: 5ft. 9ins; 10st. 10lbs.
Born: Bethnal Green, London 1889.
Died: 19 January 1961.
Career: To CITY on amateur forms. Also assisted Portsmouth around 1912.
On the Tigers' books both sides of the Great War but the above 3 League outings were made in 1910/11 and 1911/12, 2 and 1 respectively.

PEARS, John (1937-1938)
Outside-left: 30 apps; 8 goals.
1934: 5ft. 9ins; 11st. 8lbs.
Born: Ormskirk, Lancs, 23 February 1904.
Career: Skelmersdale United; Burscough; Liverpool 1927/28; Rotherham United August 1928; Accrington Stanley May 1929; Oldham Athletic July 1930; Preston North End March 1934; Sheffield United November 1934; Swansea Town July 1935; CITY June 1937; Rochdale cs 1938.
One of soccer's wanderers, usually first choice wherever he went. Possessed a hard shot and a goodly turn of speed. John's League record for his longest senior sojourn (at Oldham) reads 91 matches, 33 goals.

PEARSON, Frank (1906-1907)
Centre-forward/inside-left: 13 apps. 6 goals.
1907: 5ft. 9½ ins; 12st. 7lbs.
Born: Manchester, 18 May 1884.
Career: Preston North End 1899; Manchester City cs 1903; Chelsea 1905 (£250); CITY October 1906; Luton Town May 1907; Rochdale September 1908; Eccles Borough February 1909.
Considered a capture when signed (Pearson had skippered Chelsea where his record read 29 League games, 18 goals) but departed after only 7 months. A disappointing outcome for he possessed youth and the physical requirements that, allied with increasing experience, could have brought stardom.

PEARSON, J(ames) Stuart (1968-1974)
Centre-forward: 126 apps. plus 3 subs. 46 goals.
1971: 5ft. 9ins; 12st. 7lbs.
Born: Hull, 21 June 1949.
Career: East Riding schools football and then in local junior circles (Cottingham FC, Hull Brunswick, Ainthorpe OB and Black Prince FC). Also played in the East Riding County FA's representative team. CITY on amateur forms May 1966, turning professional July 1968; Manchester United May 1974 (£170,000 plus Peter Fletcher valued at £30,000); West Ham United August 1979 (£220,000); retired through injury 1982.
Honours: England international (15 apps). England Under-23 international vs. Hungary 1976. (Man Utd) Div. 2 champions 1975. FA Cup winner 1977; finalist 1976. (WHU) FA Cup winner 1980. League Cup finalist (sub) 1981.
Among the most honoured of City's local products, both at international and club level. A highly skilled attacker, resolute and never lacking in endeavour. Owner of a ceramic business in Manchester.

PETIT, Raymond J. (1963-1972)
Right-half: 78 apps. plus 1 sub.
1972: 5ft. 9ins; 11st. 6lbs.
Born: Hull, 11 December 1946.
Career: Hull Schools; CITY as an apprentice professional July 1963, turning full professional December 1964; Barnsley September 1972; Scarborough July 1974; joined the Customs service at Southend in 1975 and played for Romford until 1978, when transferred by the Customs dept. to work in London.
Tenacious and efficient half-back. His best term was 1968/69, missing only a couple of League engagements, and he appeared in exactly half of the following season's programme. First choice for most of his Barnsley service too.

PHILLIPS, Ernest (1951-1954)
Right/left-back: 42 apps.
1950: 5ft. 8¼ ins; 11st. 4lbs.
Born: North Shields, 29 November 1923.
Career: Ashington; Manchester City January 1947 (£1,650); CITY November 1951 (in part exchange for Don Revie, Phillips being valued at £12,000); York City June 1954 (£1,750); Ashington again cs 1958.
A back of some class, coming to Boothferry Park after a good measure of Div. 1 experience. Neat in style and effective without undue aggression, Ernie played most of his football on the right flank. Skippered York in their sensational 1955 FA Cup run.

PHILLIPS, Trevor (1979-1980)
Forward: 22 apps; 3 goals.
1979: 5ft. 6¾ ins; 10st. 3lbs.
Born: Rotherham, 18 September 1952.
Career: Barnsley Schools; Rotherham United as an apprentice professional 1968, turning full professional March 1970; CITY June 1979 (£75,000), equalling the then club record); Chester March 1980 (£51,000); Stockport County on loan March 1982, signing permanently July 1982.
Honours: England Youth international 1970, 1971.
Penetrative little inside-forward. He didn't reproduce his Rotherham form and consequently his Boothferry Park sojourn was short and the resulting transfer value diminished. But his Millmoor record had been good (289 League matches plus 33 appearances as substitute and 81 goals) with England Youth caps as proof of early potential.

PINKERTON, Henry (1933-1935)
Inside-left: 2 apps; 1 goal.
1935: 5ft. 9ins; 10st. 6lbs.
Born: Glasgow.

Career: Scottish junior football to CITY 1933/34; Port Vale May 1935; Burnley cs 1936; Falkirk 1938 (Dundee United during WW2). Subsequently reinstated as a junior and assisted Bo'ness United, playing in that club's Scottish Junior Cup winners' side of 1948. Later a coach in Toronto, Canada.
Honours: Scotland wartime international vs. England 1940.
Player of some versatility. By the time he reached Burnley, Pinkerton was a recognised right-half (and put on a stone in weight), and performed at inside-right in his Scottish Junior Cup final. It is also worthy of note that at the outbreak his number of League appearances totalled 19 only but he still made a Scotland wartime team.

PORTEOUS, Trevor (1949-1956)
Wing-half: 61 apps; 1 goal.
1950: 5ft. 10ins; 11st. 10lbs.
Born: Hull, 9 October 1933.
Career: Hull junior football to CITY as an amateur 1949, turning professional October 1950; Stockport County June 1956, player/manager from September 1963, retired from playing July 1965, remaining as manager until October of that year.
Showed tremendous promise in the Hull Schools' side and developed into a professional of grit, vision and no mean ability. Was first choice for City in only one season (1954/55) but at Stockport, to whom he gave devoted service, Trevor clocked up 336 League appearances.

POTTER, Cecil Bertram (1919-1920)
Inside-forward: 10 apps.
1919: 5ft. 9ins; 10st. 12lbs.
Born: West Hoathly, Sussex, 14 November 1888.
Died: 17 October 1975.
Career: Ipswich Town; Norwich City (originally on trial) 1911-1915; CITY cs 1919 after assisting the club in wartime football; Hartlepools United as player/sec. manager cs 1920 and, not long afterwards, on giving up playing, secretary/manager; appointed Derby County manager July 1922, holding post until appointment as Huddersfield Town manager July 1925 to become Norwich City manager December 1926-1929.
A player of adaptability filling most of the forward berths in his 4 years at Norwich when, in 131 Southern League and Cup matches, he scored 31 goals. But Potter was best known as a 1920s managerial figure, building a Derby County promotion side and steering Huddersfield to the last of 3 consecutive League championships.

POTTS, Joseph (1912-1914)
Right/left-back: 5 apps.
1913: 5ft. 10½ins; 12st. 7lbs.
Born: Newcastle-on-Tyne, 25 February 1889.
Career: Ashington; CITY March 1912; Portsmouth cs 1914; Leeds United cs 1921; Chesterfield cs 1923; Bradford cs 1925-1927.
Still a League player in 1926/27 at a venerable age in footballing terms. From the outset he showed a deal of promise, a sports journalist then writing Potts had '... all the qualifications for a class back. A strong kicker, good tackler, judicious placer and a non-believer in aerial flight'.

PRICE, A(lbert) J(ohn) William (1949)

Centre-forward: 8 apps; 5 goals.
1949: 5ft. 9¾ins; 11st. 4lbs.
Born: Hadley, Salop, 10 April 1917.
Career: Wrockwardine Wood Juniors (Wellington League); Huddersfield Town October 1937; Reading October 1947; CITY January 1949 (£5,000); Bradford City November 1949-1952.
Billy won golden opinions after becoming a Div. 1 regular for Huddersfield not long after joining, and was close to an England cap. Could shoot strongly with either foot, was deceptively fast and elusive, and a maker of opportunities. A pity the War interrupted such a promising career.

PRICE, T(homas) Dudley (1960-1963)
Inside-forward: 76 apps; 26 goals.
1961: 5ft. 6ins; 10st. 6lbs.
Born: Swansea, 17 November 1931.
Career: Junior football to Swansea Town April 1950; Southend United January 1958 (£3,000); CITY September 1960 (£2,500); Bradford City July 1963; Merthyr Tydfil cs 1965.

Despite his 8 years at the Vetch Field, Dudley's opportunities even in such a long period were extremely limited with the likes of Ivor Allchurch around. He blossomed afterwards, though, when his hard work and foraging abilities were given ample vent in senior football. Scored more freely as a Tiger than elsewhere.

PRINCE, Arthur (1928-1929)

Outside-left: 5 apps.
1928: 5ft. 10ins; 11st. 7lbs.
Born: Bucknell, Salop, 8 December 1902.
Died: 1980.
Career: Bucknell FC; Port Vale October 1922; Sheffield Wednesday May 1924; CITY cs 1928; Walsall cs 1929.
Honours: (Wednesday) Div. 2 champions 1926.
A rapid transition from minor to Second Division football culminating with a championship medal, but he fell out of prominence after leaving Hillsborough. At his best, though, Arthur had been an excellent winger – a fair shot, middling the ball in fine style and showing surprising stamina.

QUANTICK, John Henry (1933-1937)
Right-back: 88 apps; 1 goal.
1935: 6ft; 12st.
Born: Cwm, Mon., 7 July 1910.
Died: 24 January 1972.
Career: Ebbw Vale; West Bromwich Albion 1930/31; Dudley Town 1932/33; CITY June 1933; retired cs 1937 but joined Worcester City July 1938.
Made a couple of appearances in 1932/3 prior to permanent transfer and a 'regular' in his first full seasons with the Tigers, combining well with the ubiquitous Woodhead. Originally a half-back.

RAFFERTY, Ronald (1963-1966)

Centre/inside-forward: 16 apps; 6 goals.
1965: 6ft; 12st.
Born: Newcastle-on-Tyne, 6 May 1934.
Career: Wycombe Wanderers (also on Shrewsbury Town's books as an amateur); Portsmouth as a professional June 1954; Grimsby Town December 1956 (£3,500); CITY July 1963 (£10,000); Aldershot June 1966; Guildford City as player/coach July 1969; retired January 1970.
Crossed the Humber after a splendid 7 years at Blundell Park (145 goals from 263 League outings). Ron, however, had the misfortune to break an ankle in his third game as a Tiger and service to the club was accordingly limited. Finished his career as a centre-half. Became representative of a confectionery firm and retained his interest in soccer by running a junior side, Aldershot Athletic FC.

RAISBECK, Andrew (1904-1907)
Left-half/outside-left: 47 apps; 5 goals.
Born in Scotland.
Career: Associated with Queen's Park Rangers and Liverpool prior to joining CITY cs 1904, staying until 1907. Thought to have subsequently emigrated to Canada.
An original – in both the very first City professional line-up (1.9.1904) and League side (2.9.1905). Moreover he shares with Martin Spendiff the distinction of being the first Tiger League ever-present. Probably best on the left wing, and possibly a kinsman of the celebrated Liverpool and Scotland centre-half, Alex. Raisbeck.

RALEIGH, Simon (1930-1932)
Centre-forward: 31 apps; 20 goals.
1930: 5ft. 7½ins; 11st.
Born: Rotherham, 1909.
Died: 1 December 1934.

Career: Silverwood Colliery; Huddersfield Town as a professional 1929/30; CITY cs 1930; Gillingham cs 1932.
Stocky forward with a good eye for the scoring opportunity. Is in the record books because of his untimely demise occurring on the field of play, the result of a collision with a Brighton player when assisting Gillingham.

RANBY, Sam (1921)
Inside-right: 1 app.
Born: Hull, 1897.
Died: 20 January 1958.
Career: Gilberdyke FC (East Yorks); CITY January 1921; later played for Reckitt's FC, a Hull works side.
A recruit from local junior circles briefly at Anlaby Road. His solitary League outing was in the away game with Sheffield Wednesday on the 21 March 1921 which was lost 0-3. An electrician by trade.

REAGAN, C(harles) Martin (1947-1948)
Outside-right: 19 apps; 1 goal.
1947: 5ft. 7ins; 11st. 1lbs.
Born: York, 12 May 1924.
Career: York City as an amateur during WW2; CITY as a professional June 1947; Middlesbrough February 1948 (about £5,000); Shrewsbury Town August 1951 for a similar fee; Portsmouth December 1952 (£14,000); Norwich City June 1954; March Town as player/manager June 1956, later having 2 seasons with Goole Town.
Chiefly noted for his exceptional speed and whizzbang shooting. If Martin's other facets had been on their level, he would have been England material, and he had a tendency towards inconsistency. In 1950 scored Middlesbrough's 1000th League goal. Since 1954 a qualified FA coach and from October 1979 has been manager of the England women's team.

REVIE, Donald George (1949-1951)
Right-half/inside-right: 76 apps; 12 goals.
1950: 6ft; 12st.
Born: Middlesbrough, 10 July 1927.
Career: Middlesbrough schoolboy football; Newport Boys Club (Middlesbrough); Middlesbrough Swifts; Leicester City August 1944; CITY November 1949 (£20,000); Manchester City October 1951 (£13,000 plus Ernie Phillips); Sunderland November 1956 (£23,000); Leeds United November 1958 (£14,000), player/manager March 1961, retiring from playing cs 1963 then manager only to April 1974; England team manager April 1974-July 1977; Coach to the United Arab Emirates July 1977-May 1980.

Honours: Awarded the OBE January 1970. England international (6 apps). England 'B' international vs. Scotland 1954. Football League vs. League of Ireland 1954 and 1955. (Manchester City) FA Cup winner 1956. FA Cup finalist 1955. 'Footballer of the Year' 1955.
A famous footballing name for nearly four decades on and off the field. As a player he early demonstrated thrust and control far above the average, and was the main figure in 'The Revie Plan', a deep-lying centre-forward ploy that excited comment in the mid-1950s. As a manager he made a near-moribund Leeds United into a championship and cup-winning power, which led to the England job and his sensational departure from it that is now part of football history.

RICHARDS, Stephen C. (1978-1983)
Defender: 55 apps. plus 3 subs; 2 goals.
1983: 6ft; 12st.
Born: Dundee, 24 October 1961.
Career: Junior football to CITY as an apprentice professional July 1978, turning full professional October 1979.
Strapping young Scot with the right build for a centre-back. Fairly regular first teamer 1980/81 and '81/82 but latterly beset by injury.

RICHARDSON, George (1938-1948)
Inside-forward: 36 apps; 15 goals.
1938: 5ft. 10ins; 11st. 2lbs.
Born: Worksop, 12 December 1912.
Died: 1968.
Career: Manton Athletic; Huddersfield Town April 1933; Sheffield United cs 1934; CITY November 1938 (guest player for the Newark works side, Ransome & Marles, during WW2); Bangor City as player/manager cs 1948.

A useful attacker who had appeared pretty regularly in Sheffield United's League side in the season prior to joining the Tigers, notching 7 goals in 25 outings.

RICHARDSON, George Edward Holland (1923-1926)

Outside-right: 40 apps; 2 goals.
1925: 5ft. 7ins; 10st. 10lbs.
Born: Seaham Harbour, Co. Durham, 1891.
Died: 25 April 1969.
Career: Seaham Harbour FC; Huddersfield Town cs 1914. CITY December 1923 (£1,000); Bradford City cs 1926-1928. In 1946 rejoined Huddersfield Town as trainer to their Yorkshire League team, later promoted to assistant trainer.
Honours: (Huddersfield) FA Cup winner 1922, finalist 1920.
Played a full part in the first years of Huddersfield's rise to greatness – besides his two Cup finals, George was a regular member of the runners-up side that gained promotion to the top flight in 1919/20. Not a prolific goal scorer but fast and full of guile.

RINTANEN, Mauno (1956)

Goalkeeper: 4 apps.
Born in Finland.
Career: Finnish football to CITY in 1956, returning to his native land late that year.
Honours: A Finnish international.
An amateur. Showed himself to be a competent performer in his brief stay at Boothferry Park. Came from an unusual (and somewhat exotic) quarter but Mauno's spell did coincide with the 'Great Dane's' (Jensen's) last months on City's books. And elsewhere Arsenal had fielded an Icelandic international, in the 1940s and Scotland was to import many Scandinavian stars, particularly to Dundee United and Morton.

ROBERTS, David F. (1975-1978)

Central defender: 86 apps; 4 goals.
1977: 5ft. 11ins; 11st. 5lbs.
Born: Southampton, 26 January 1949.
Career: Hemel Hempstead Schools, Hertfordshire Schools; St. Albans City; Fulham as an apprentice professional 1964, turning full professional September 1967; Oxford United February 1971 (£4,000); CITY February 1975 (£60,000); Cardiff City August 1978 (£50,000) – cs 1981; assisted Kettering Town early in season 1981/82 before joining Taun Wan FC (Hong Kong) later in 1981.
Honours: Welsh international (17 apps. including 3 subs). Welsh Under-23 international (4 apps.).
One of the classiest players to wear a City shirt since the War, a talented half-back skilled in defence and attack. Unfortunately during his latter League years was plagued with back trouble. Qualified for Wales through his father, who was born in Anglesey.

ROBERTS, Garreth W. (1978-)

Midfield: 192 apps. plus 2 subs; 29 goals.
1983: 5ft. 4ins; 10st. 2lbs.
Born: Hull, 15 November 1960.
Career: Hull district schools football to CITY as an apprentice professional, turning full professional November 1978.
A gem of a local product, small in stature but dynamic in effect. To sound defensive work and precision passing has now added the valuable quality of popping in goals. Certainly a captain who sets the right example. An excellent tennis player.

ROBERTS, J(ames) Dale (1980-)

Central defender: 138 apps. plus 4 subs; 6 goals.
1983: 5ft. 10½ins; 11st. 5lbs.
Born: Newcastle-on-Tyne, 8 October 1956.
Career: Junior football to Ipswich Town as an apprentice professional in the early 1970s, signing full professional September 1974; CITY February 1980 (£60,000).
Honours: England Youth international 1975.

One of the three February 1980 signings that cost City in total over £180,000, made in a successful bid to avoid relegation that year. Dale has proved a good investment, being a sound defender and a first-rate club man.

ROBERTS, John G. (1980-1981)

Centre-half: 26 apps; 1 goal.
1980: 6ft; 12st. 2lbs.
Born: Swansea, 11 September 1946.
Career: Abercynon Athletic; Swansea Town July 1964; Northampton Town November 1967 (around £15,000); Arsenal April 1969 (around £35,000); Birmingham City October 1972 (£115,000); Wrexham July 1976 (£30,000); CITY August 1980 (£17,500); retired through injury June 1981.
Honours: Welsh international (23 apps). Welsh Under-23 international (5 apps). Welsh Under-21 international vs. England 1977. (Arsenal) League champions 1971. (Wrexham) Welsh Cup winner 1978; finalist 1979 (1st Leg only).

Around a long time and a veteran of some 16 League campaigns by the time he reached Boothferry Park. John was a strong defensive player, his physique ideal for a central defender. Appeared at wing-half as well in his Arsenal days.

ROBERTSON, Leonard V. (1947-1948)

Inside-forward: 8 apps; 2 goals.
1947: 5ft. 9ins; 11st. 2lbs.
Born: South Bank, Middlesbrough, 1 March 1916.
Career: Newcastle Schools; Stockton FC as an amateur; Hartlepools United during WW2, in which period he assisted Grimsby Town as a guest player for 2 seasons; Watford June 1946; CITY April 1947; Accrington Stanley July 1948.

A star as a schoolboy with his neat style and eye for openings. Like a myriad of others, Len suffered by having his best footballing years and the War coinciding and he was turned 30 when the normal peacetime order returned.

ROBINSON, Charles (1937-1939)

Right-half: 68 apps; 4 goals.
1938: 5ft. 9½ins; 11st. 7lbs.
Born: Rotherham, 20 August 1905.
Died: 1972.
Career: Stockport County 1932/33; Plymouth Argyle June 1936; CITY June 1937.

A regular first-teamer at Stockport – 115 League matches in 3 and a bit seasons – Charlie wasn't given a single opportunity with Plymouth. The Tigers used this handy wing-half to advantage, however. Had something of an attacking bent and well able to take a scoring opportunity.

ROBINSON, Joseph (1949-1953)

Goalkeeper: 70 apps.
1950: 5ft. 10ins; 11st. 10lbs.
Born: Ashington, Northumberland, 4 March 1919.
Career: Northumberland Schools, Hexham (North-Eastern League); Hartlepools United May 1938; Blackpool July 1946; CITY February 1949; Wisbech Town (as player/manager) July 1953.
Honours: (Blackpool) FA Cup finalist 1948.

Spent much of his Boothferry Park career as a reserve but was first choice in 1950/51 and played more League games in his final season than did Billy Bly. An upstanding and efficient 'keeper, Joe had some grim War experiences, being captured at Dunkirk and held as a prisoner of war for 5½ years.

ROBINSON, William Samuel (1905-1909)

Centre-half: 119 apps; 6 goals.
1905: 5ft. 9ins; 11st. 10lbs.
Born: Prescott, Lancs, 1880.
Died: 1926.
Career: Bolton Wanderers; Manchester City November 1902; CITY cs 1905; Bolton Wanderers again February 1909-1911.

A reserve right-half for Manchester City, he was the undisputed regular pivot for the Tigers, missing but 9 out of a possible 114 League games in his 3 full seasons. Scouted for City in his native locality after WW1, maintaining the flow of young talent that had so enriched the club's resources right from the earliest days. Married a sister of a fellow Tiger, Walter Dagnall.

ROBSON, C(harles) Leslie (1948-1953)
Inside-forward: 3 apps; 1 goal.
1950: 5ft. 7ins; 10st.
Born: South Shields, 1 November 1931.
Career: North Hull Juniors; CITY as an amateur during the 1948/49 season, turning professional May 1950; Darlington May 1953; Liverpool July 1955 (£750); Crewe Alexandra January 1956; Goole Town August 1956.
Developed into a winger, right or left, and put on a stone after leaving City. Played a useful couple of years at Darlington, mostly on the left flank, when he notched 19 goals in 68 League games. Clever and assertive.

ROBSON, John Cecil (1923-1925)
Outside-left: 1 app.
1924: 5ft. 10½ins; 11st. 2lbs.
Born: Birtley, Co. Durham, 24 March 1906.
Died: October 1966.
Career: Co. Durham junior football; CITY April 1923; Reading August 1925; Derby County June 1928; Southend United June 1932; Rochdale November 1933; Oldham Athletic June 1934; retired 1936.
Honours: (Reading) Div. 3 (South) champions 1926.
Bill McCracken's first signing. Powerfully built for a winger (by 1927 his weight was recorded as 12st. 6lbs.), his left foot shooting could be devastating but ball control was not a strong point. For many years a licensee in Hull, North Ferriby and Derby.

ROBSON, W. (1911-1912)
Left-back: 8 apps.
1911: 5ft. 7ins; 11st. 13lbs.
(Probably born in the North-East).
Career: Hebburn Argyle; CITY during season 1910/11-1912.
John McQuillan's deputy, on the short side though distinctly weighty and capable of the ultra-powerful clearance. First pulled on a Tigers' jersey for the reserves in January 1911. Must have felt at home – of the 23 others on the playing list at the outset of the 1911/12 campaign, 8 had been secured from Geordieland clubs.

RODGERS, Arthur (1929-1933)
Right/left-back: 67 apps.
1930: 5ft. 9½ins; 11st. 7lbs.

Born: Frickley, Yorks, 8 February 1907.
Career: Frickley Colliery; Denaby United; CITY 1928/29; Merthyr Town September 1932; Doncaster Rovers cs 1933; retired 1939.
Honours: (Doncaster) Div. 3 (North) champions 1935.
Sturdy, reliable defender. At Anlaby Road Arthur enjoyed a regular first team spot only in his last season, but was first choice for most of the 6 campaigns with Doncaster Rovers, grossing 175 League appearances.

ROUGHLEY, Edward (1906-1914)
Goalkeeper: 157 apps.
1906: 5ft. 9½ins; 11st.
Born: Prescot, Lancs, 1880.
Died: 1948.
Career: St. Helens Recreational; CITY May 1906; Chesterfield Town 1914; Rugby Town January 1920.
First choice custodian for half of his 8 seasons at Anlaby Road: 1908/09-1911/12, when he missed only 5 League games out of a possible 152. An agile and alert performer, Ed. remarkably saved 16 out of 21 conceded penalty kicks in his last season with St. Helens Recs.

ROUND, Leonard F. (1957-1958)
Goalkeeper: 17 apps.
1955: 5ft. 9½ins; 11st.
Born: Wallheath, Staffs, 21 May 1928.
Career: Army football (Royal Scots Fusiliers); Ayr United October 1946; CITY June 1957; Sittingbourne July 1958.
Englishmen playing in senior Scottish football have never been all that numerous, and for one to put in over a decade with a single club, as Len did, is unusual. This length of service illustrates his soundness and consistency.

RUMNEY, John (1922-1924)
Centre-forward: 13 apps; 4 goals.
1924: 5ft. 10½ins; 12st. 6lbs.
Born: Dipton, Co. Durham, 1901.
Career: Preston Colliery (Co. Durham); CITY 1922; Chesterfield May 1924; Merthyr Town May 1925; Bristol Rovers cs 1926.
The Tigers' management beat Chelsea for this two-footed leader's signature. Scored a lot of goals for the reserves before going to Chesterfield. John's best senior season was at Merthyr, scoring 24 goals in 39 Southern Section outings.

RUSHTON, George (1904-1907)
Centre-forward: 29 apps; 15 goals.
1905: 5ft. 9ins; 11st.
Born: Stoke-on-Trent, 1880.

Career: Leek FC; Burslem Port Vale cs 1901; CITY cs 1904; Swindon Town May 1907; Brentford cs 1909; Goole Town circa 1911.

One of the original Tigers and among the most notable of these pioneers. Led the attack in lively fashion, was dangerous when in sight of the enemy goal and had the capacity to keep his forwards on the move.

RYLEY, Henry Seymour (1921)
Outside-left: 1 app.
Born: Hull, 1894.
Career: Barrow to CITY on trial during season 1920/21. Not offered an engagement for 1921/22.

His one and only league game was the last one of the season: against Fulham at home on the 7 May 1921 when a goalless draw resulted.

SALVIDGE, George B. (1936-1941)
Outside-right: 4 apps; 1 goal.
Born: Hull, 1912.
Killed in action: 1941.
Career: Southcoates Lane Old Boys (Hull); CITY during season 1935/36.

A product of City's then nursery side who made his League debut in the last full season before WW2. Lost his life while serving with the Yorks & Lancs Rgt.

SARGEANT, Charles (1932-1934)
Outside-left: 60 apps; 16 goals.
1930: 5ft. 9ins; 11st. 2lbs.
Born: Cornsay, nr. Darlington, 1909.
Career: Esh Winning Juniors; Washington Colliery; Bishop Auckland; White-le-Head Rangers; Ushaw Moor; Norwich City 1930; Bristol City cs 1931; CITY May 1932; Chester March 1934 (£75); Stockport County March 1938; Plymouth Argyle May 1939.
Honours: (City) Div. 3 (North) champions 1933. (Chester) Welsh Cup finalist 1935, 1936.

Played no football at all until he reached the age of 17 then, in the space of 4 years, made a tour of good class County Durham sides before joining Norwich City. Charlie was a prominent figure in the Tigers' 1933 championship line-up, making a fine wing with the veteran Wainscoat. Had a good run at Chester, too, clocking up over 150 League games.

SARGEAUNT, Harry (1920-1922)
Inside-left: 19 apps; 8 goals.
1921: 5ft. 7ins; 10st. 7lbs.
Born: Newcastle-on-Tyne.
Career: Felling Colliery; CITY October 1920; Brighton & Hove Albion July 1922.

Quickly came into prominence by reason of his scoring feats – 8 goals in 12 matches before sustaining a bad injury. This occurred in an away match against Notts County on the 19 March 1921 when he fractured a leg below the knee. Made only 7 League appearances the following season and none for Brighton.

SAVAGE, John Alfred (1950-1952)
Goalkeeper: 4 apps.
1950: 6ft. 4ins; 14st.
Born: Bromley, Kent, 14 December 1929.
Career: RAF football; CITY September 1950; Halifax Town March 1952; Manchester City November 1953 (£4,000); Walsall January 1958 (£1,000); Wigan Athletic July 1959.

Possessor of exceptional physical attributes in height and weight and these did not adversely affect the capacity to move quickly or get down to low shots. John played for the Southern Section against the Northern Section in a Div. 3 representative match a couple of months after joining Walsall.

SAVILLE, Andrew (1980-)
Midfield: 1 app.
Born: Hull, 12 December 1964.
Career: Hull schoolboy football to City Minors circa 1979/80 and then the Juniors before becoming a CITY non-contract player.

Product of Malet Lambert School in Hull. A promising young player plucked from the Juniors to play against Port Vale on December 31, 1983.

SCORER, Robert (1922-1924)
Centre-half: 5 apps.
1922: 5ft. 10ins; 11st. 7lbs.
Born: Felling, Co. Durham, circa 1898.
Died: 1971.
Career: North-Eastern junior football; CITY April 1922; Bristol Rovers 1923/24-1925.

The season was nearly over when Bob became a Tiger (25 April, 1922) and he went straight into the first team and played in the final couple of matches. This heady start wasn't maintained, however, with only 3 League outings in 1922/23. Made 36 Div. 3 (South) appearances for Bristol Rovers in his 2 years at Eastville.

SCOTT, Henry (1926-1928)

Inside-right: 29 apps; 8 goals.
1927: 6ft; 13st.
Born: Newburn, Northumberland, circa 1897.
Career: Newburn Grange; Sunderland January 1922; Wolverhampton Wanderers cs 1925; CITY November 1926; Bradford June 1928; Swansea Town July 1932; Watford June 1933.
Made 14 Div, 1 appearances in his first half-season on joining Sunderland, thereafter getting a deal of Div. 2 football with his other clubs up to the Watford season. Tall and weighty and so could make opponents realise his presence.

SEDDON, Frank Owen (1947-1951)

Centre-half: 3 apps.
1949: 6ft; 12st. 7lbs.
Born: Stockton-on-Tees, 1 May 1928.
Career: Was in the County Durham junior team in 1945/46 and signed for Notts County in May 1946, a month later started his Army service; CITY May 1947; Halifax Town January 1951; Stockton August 1952.
Found opportunities rationed with Berry and Bowler on the playing strength, but this well proportioned youngster gave good service to the Midland League side. Played for the AA Command and the RA XI while on military service.

SEWELL, John (1959-1961)

Inside-forward: 44 apps; 8 goals.
1960: 5ft. 8ins; 11st. 7lbs.
Born: Kells, Whitehaven, 24 January 1927.
Career: Whitehaven Schools; Kells Miners' Welfare Under-18; Whitehaven Town (guest player for Workington and Carlisle United during WW2); Notts County as amateur 1942, professional October 1944; Sheffield Wednesday March 1951 (£34,500, then a record); Aston Villa December 1955 (about £18,000); CITY October 1959 (£5,000); Lusaka City (Zambia) as player/coach September 1961, also became Zambia's national coach until his return to England in May 1973.
Honours: England international (6 apps). Football League (5 apps). Toured Canada with FA team in 1950. (Notts Co.) Div. 3 (South) champions 1950. (Wednesday) Div. 2 champions 1952 and 1956. (Villa) FA Cup winner 1957.
Hit the headlines when Sheffield Wednesday forked out an astronomical fee in 1950s terms, but Jackie had been the subject of much transfer talk for some time when it happened. A skilful, enterprising player, quick on the ball and a regular scorer. Usually at inside-right.

SHARP, Alexander (1935-1936)

Inside-left: 18 apps; 4 goals.
1935: 5ft. 7ins; 11st.
Born: Dundee.
Career: East Fife; Blackburn Rovers November 1934; CITY October 1935; Raith Rovers cs 1936; Falkirk 1936/37; Raith Rovers again cs 1938.
A Scot built on stocky, sturdy lines. Had a neat style and was a forager and provider rather than a goal scorer. This is demonstrated by his Falkirk figures – in 61 Scottish League Div. 1 outings, Alex. found the net on 5 occasions.

SHARPE, Leonard T. (1962-1966)

Left-back/wing-half: 58 apps; 4 goals.
1964: 5ft. 9ins; 12st.
Born: Scunthorpe, 29 November 1932.
Career: Ashby Institute (Scunthorpe); Scunthorpe United May 1950; CITY May 1962 (£750); Goole Town September 1966; Scunthorpe United again as player/coach March 1967 until released to become Ashby Institute's player/manager for 1968/69.
Honours: (Scunthorpe United) Div. 3 (North) champions 1958.
A solid, reliable performer who arrived at Boothferry Park with 186 League outings under his belt. Equally good as a back or wing-half, and an excellent club man.

SHAW, Alan (1961-1964)
Outside-left: 15 apps; 1 goal.
1963: 5ft. 2ins; 9st.
Born: Preston, Lancs, 9 October 1943.
Career: Preston junior football to Preston North End October 1960; CITY August 1961 (originally on trial); Goole Town August 1964.
This diminutive winger must have been the shortest player of his time in the whole of the League. But Alan had a cleverness that discounted much of an apparent handicap and he was a useful stand-in for the regular outside-lefts.

SHAW, Frederick Elliott (1911-1913)
Outside-left 9 apps; 1 goal.
1913: 5ft. 9½ins; 11st. 7lbs.
Born: Newcastle-on-Tyne, 1891.
Career: Wallsend; CITY 1911/12; Portsmouth May 1913-1914.
A later Gordon Wright understudy, handily built for causing trouble to opposing defences. Made 19 Southern League appearances for Portsmouth in 1913/14 and scored 2 goals. Not to be confused with the earlier Shaw, who was also a forward and a North-Easterner.

SHAW, Joseph F. (1907-1909)
Centre-forward: 46 apps; 20 goals.
1907: 5ft. 9ins; 11st. 7lbs.
Born: Durham, 1882.
Career: Sunderland Schools; St. Mark's (Sunderland) circa 1898; Sunderland West End; Armstrong College (Newcastle); Bishop Auckland; Darlington for 3 months; Sunderland FC circa 1905; CITY April 1907; Grimsby Town October 1909.
Described as a veritable terrier and "...not a showy player. Fearless in front of posts. Custodian had to be alert or else he would find himself bundled in the net". A teacher by profession, some of the above changes in location dictated by moves to different schools.

SHEEN, John (1946-1947)
Inside-forward: 5 apps; 1 goal.
Born: Airdrie, 30 August 1920.
Career: Airdrie schoolboy football; Baillieston Juniors; Sheffield United (originally on the ground staff) May 1937; during WW2 had 2 seasons with Linfield and assisted Queen's Park Rangers 1945/46; CITY July 1946; Shrewsbury Town 1947.
Honours: (Linfield) Irish Cup finalist 1941. He also assisted this club when they won a wartime Irish League championship.
Came with a good reputation to Boothferry Park and appointed skipper for the initial post-war campaign. Did not, however, find his form, soon leaving the League scene.

SHELTON, Thomas (1932-1934)
Centre-forward: 6 apps; 1 goal.
1932: 5ft. 9½ins; 11st. 12lbs.
Born: Nottingham, 1907.
Career: Mansfield junior football to CITY early in 1932 on amateur forms, a little later signing as a professional; not retained cs 1934.
Soon made a senior bow (April 9, 1932) and his League appearances totalled 4 at the season's end. However, Tom had but a single outing in each of his two full terms at Anlaby Road, the redoubtable Bill McNaughton being an automatic choice as leader of the Tigers' attack.

SHEPHERD, Ernest (1949-1950)
Outside-left: 15 apps; 3 goals.
1949: 5ft. 6½ins; 10st. 12lbs.
Born: Wombwell, Yorks, 14 August 1919.
Career: Dearne Valley Schools; Bradford City ground staff circa 1933; Fulham ground staff 1935, turning professional 1936 (guest player for Huddersfield Town and Bradford City and represented the RAF during WW2); West Bromwich Albion December 1948; CITY March 1949; Queen's Park Rangers July 1950; Hastings United cs 1956. Subsequently Bradford (Park Avenue) trainer; Southend United trainer/assistant manager and then manager (April 1967) and general manager (October 1969 - 1972); Orient trainer/coach 1973-76.
Ernie's most notable asset was his speed – he had won prizes as a sprinter while in the RAF and afterwards in 'civvy street'. A bouncy, thrustful little winger, he was unable to displace an evergreen Eddie Burbanks. Established a unique record in 1948/49 by assisting 3 promotion-winning sides.

SHERWOOD, Charles (1938-1939)
Half-back: 4 apps; 1 goal.
Born: Wolverhampton, 1914.
Career: Wolverhampton Wanderers 1937/38; CITY cs 1938 – 1939.
Had no first team outings in a brief spell at Molineux and so made his League debut in a Tigers' shirt. This was in an away match against Carlisle United on September 10, 1938. Besides half-back, Sherwood played at outside-right for City too.

SHINER, Roy Albert James (1959-1961)
Centre-forward: 22 apps; 8 goals.
1959: 5ft. 8½ins; 12st. 1¾lbs.
Born: Seaview, Isle of Wight, 15 November 1924.
Career: Ryde Sports (IOW); Cheltenham Town February 1948; Huddersfield Town December 1951; Sheffield Wednesday July 1955 (together with the England international Ron Staniforth, exchanged for 2 other players

plus a small fee); CITY November 1959 (£5,000); Cheltenham Town again July 1961; retired cs 1962.
Honours: (Wednesday) Div. 2 champions 1956 and 1959.
Rumbustious leader whose wholehearted play responded to the promptings of England caps, Froggatt, Fantham and Quixall, in his Hillsborough days. By the time he reached Boothferry Park, however, Shiner was 35 and the club in a relegation season.

SIMMON, Henry (1905-1917)
Outside-right etc: 17 apps.
1910: 5ft. 8ins; 11st.
Born: Bearpark, Co Durham, 1879.
Died: 25 February 1951.
Career: Bearpark FC; Leadgate Park; CITY 1905; retired 1917.
Engaged as a right-winger but he turned out to be a super utility man, playing in every outfield position while wearing a Tigers' jersey. Harry's League outings all occurred in the club's first seasons in the competition, 1905/06 – 1907/08. His activities were then in the reserves' cause and he later coached City Juniors and managed the "A" team. Harry worked for a firm of Hull cargo superintendents, retiring in 1949. He was a founder member of the local National Dock Labour Board side and a member of the Sutton Trust FC (Hull) committee.

SIMMS, Sydney (1934-35)
Forward: 3 apps.
(Probably born in the West Riding).
Career: Thorne Colliery; CITY December 1934 - 1935.
Had attracted the scouts and been given a run-out with West Bromwich Albion's second string a few weeks before joining the Tigers. His League debut was in an away match against West Ham United on December 29, 1934.

SIMPKIN, Christopher J. (1959-1971)
Left-half: 284 apps. plus 1 sub; 19 goals.
1970: 5ft. 11½ins; 12st. 13lbs.
Born: Hull, 24 April 1944.
Career: Hull Schools; CITY as an amateur September 1959, apprentice professional May 1960 and full professional April 1962; Blackpool October 1971 (£30,000); Scunthorpe United October 1973 (£12,000); Huddersfield Town August 1975 (originally on trial); Hartlepool December 1976; Scarborough May 1978. Subsequently assisted a Hull junior side, Hall Road Rangers, retiring in 1980.
Honours: (City) Div. 3 champions 1966.
Looked upon as a forward in the early days but soon found his true bent in the middle line. An excellent wing-half, powerful in the tackle, strong in distribution and with an ideal physique for the role. One of the best of City's locals.

SKIPPER, Peter D. (1979-80 and 1982-)
Central defender: 114 apps. plus 1 sub; 7 goals.
1983: 5ft. 11ins; 12st. 6lbs.
Born: Hull, 11 April 1958.
Career: Hull schools football; Schultz Youth Club (Hull); CITY January 1979 (Scunthorpe United on a month's loan February 1980); Darlington May 1980; CITY again August 1982 (£10,000).
An ever-present in the two seasons following his return, this splendid local has developed convincingly since his early professional days. Perhaps the rigours of Div. 4 had something to do with it (he missed but 1 League match while at Darlington). A strong defender who loves to get involved in attacks.

SLATER, Harold (1922-1923)
Outside-right/outside-left: 3 apps.
1922: 5ft. 7ins; 10st.
Born: Bradford, circa 1900.
Career: Harrogate; CITY March 1922 (£200 including Jock McGee) – 1923.
One of 3 signings from the Harrogate club in the early spring of 1922 (besides the above-mentioned McGee there was an amateur, D. R. Fawcett). All had played against City reserves a few days previously, obviously impressing the Tigers' management. Harold played outside-right for Harrogate but his League debut (against Barnsley, April 24, 1922) was on the extreme left. He had been offered to City earlier but the asking price was considered too high.

SMALES, Kenneth (1953-1958)
Half-back: 1 app.
1957: 5ft. 10ins; 11st.
Born: Hull, 3 May 1932.
Career: Brunswick Institute (Hull); CITY May 1953; Scarborough cs 1958; Bridlington Town 1959, becoming that club's manager 1963 until cs 1969.
Served Bridlington Town for a decade: 4 years as a player and 6 as manager. Succeeded an ex-Tiger (the late Harry Brown) in the latter post and was followed by another in Bob Dennison.

SMITH, Alan (1946-47)
Forward: 1 app.
Career: Junior football to CITY September 1946.
One of the half-dozen players with a solitary League outing from the astonishingly large number (43) who represented the Tigers in that first post-war campaign. Alan replaced

his namesake, Dennis Smith. Incidentally, in the following season a still abnormal 35 were called upon – Major Buckley, as ever, in the throes of team-building.

SMITH, Dennis (1946-1948)
Centre-half etc: 15 apps.
1947: 5ft. 11¾ins; 12st. 3lbs.
Born: Nelson, Lancs, 22 August 1925.
Career: Nelson Schools; Sheffield Training College; Frickley Colliery; CITY July 1946; Accrington Stanley October 1947 – 1954.
Played in wing-half and both right-wing forward positions at Boothferry Park before going to centre-half. Not assertive enough for some City fans but his adaptability had value. Made over 150 League appearances for Accrington, scoring 17 goals, in his 7 years at Peel Park.

SMITH, Edwin Arthur (1910-1911)
Centre-forward: 9 apps.
1910: 5ft. 9ins; 12st.
Born: Birmingham, 1884.
Career: Brierley Hill Alliance 1908; CITY May 1910; Crystal Palace December 1911 – cs 1922.
Honours: (Crystal Palace) Div. 3 (South) champions 1921.
A good stint for Palace in spite of the lost war years. He topped the Southern League scoring list in 1913/14 with 26 goals, revealing splendid marksmanship, and when a postwar veteran notched 28 goals in 56 senior matches. City transferred two centre-forwards in December 1911, the other was the famed Boy Browell.

SMITH, E(dwin) Colin (1956-1960)
Centre-forward: 65 apps; 39 goals.
1958: 6ft. 1in; 12st.
Born: Doncaster, 3 March 1936.
Career: Hull junior football to CITY as an amateur December 1956, turning professional the following month; Rotherham United June 1960 (about £1,500); King's Lynn cs 1961.
Commandingly tall and a 12-stoner, Colin Smith's scoring record for the Tigers was excellent, averaging well over a goal every 2 games. In his best season, 1958/59, when promotion was won, he popped in 26 in 40 matches. Eventually returned to Hull and was involved in the local scene when appointed the Brunswick FC manager in April 1969 and with the Ex-Tigers' charity matches.

SMITH, Frederick, A. (1949-1951)
Inside-right: 17 apps; 1 goal.
1950: 5ft. 6ins; 11st.
Born: Aberdeen, 14 February 1926.
Career: Hall Russell's FC (Aberdeen); Aberdeen FC 1948; CITY October 1949; Sheffield United May 1951 (£4,000); Millwall January 1953; Chesterfield July 1956.
Experienced the inside-left spot too on occasion. Possessed the traditional ball control of a Scottish inside-forward and could plot a move ahead. Served in the Navy for 3 years before his junior football days.

SMITH, H(arold) Raymond (1951-1956)
Outside-right: 23 apps; 2 goals.
1955: 5ft. 7ins; 10st. 4lbs.
Born: Hull, 13 September 1934.
Career: Hull junior football to CITY on amateur forms May 1951, turning professional August 1952; Peterborough United July 1956 (£1,500 paid August 1960 on Peterborough's election to the FL); Northampton Town October 1962 (£4,000); Luton Town October 1963 (£5,000); retired cs 1964.
Honours: (Peterborough) Div. 4 champions 1961.
Played inside-forward in the decade following his departure from Boothferry Park, the first 4 years of which were in non-League soccer. A clever and effective attacker, Ray almost qualified for a medal at Northampton (14 appearances in their '62/3 Div. 3 championship side). On retirement came back to live in Hull.

SMITH, John (1905-1910)
Inside-forward: 156 apps; 91 goals.
1910: 5ft. 7ins; 11st.
Born: Wardley, nr. Newcastle-on-Tyne.
Killed in action during WW1.
Career: Hebburn Argyle; CITY June 1905; Sheffield United November 1910; Nottingham Forest March 1911 (£350); Nelson August 1911.
Honours: Football League vs. Scottish League 1908.
A great figure in City's early League campaigns, a prolific and noted goal scorer. Headed the Div. 2 list in 1907/08 with 30, the season that saw his Football League representative honour. John's best position was probably inside-right.

SMITH, Joseph Edward ('Stanley') (1905-1912)
Forward: 214 apps; 48 goals.
1912: 5ft. 7ins; 12st.
Born: Stanley, Co Durham, circa 1886.
Career: West Stanley; CITY September 1905 (£10); Everton February 1912; Belfast Distillery 1913; Bury December 1913; West Stanley again cs 1919.
Honours: Irish League vs. Football, Scottish and Southern Leagues 1914.

Known universally as Stanley – from his birth-place – to distinguish him the better from his contemporary, John Smith. An adaptable forward, thickset in build, he figured at outside-right, centre and inside-forward for City. Probably best on the right-wing (where he won inter-league honours) being especially good at middling the ball when going full tilt.

SMITH, Samuel James W. (1928-1929)
Inside-forward: 14 apps; 2 goals.
1928: 5ft. 10½ins; 10st. 12lbs.
Born: Stafford, 1904.
Career: Cradley Heath; Cardiff City February 1924; Port Vale cs 1927; CITY cs 1928: Millwall May 1929–1930.
In a comparatively short first-class career of 6 years Sam took in 4 clubs, making more first team appearances for City than anyone else. Had a good rangy build and mostly engaged in foraging and as a provider.

SMITH, T(homas) Potter (1923-1924)
Outside-right: 8 apps; 2 goals.
1923: 5ft. 7ins; 10st. 7lbs.
Born: Newcastle-on-Tyne, July 1901.
Died: 1 September 1978.
Career: Merthyr Town; CITY cs 1923; Hartlepools United 1924; Merthyr Town again cs 1925; Cardiff City March 1926 (£500); Brighton & Hove Albion May 1929; Crystal Palace September 1937.
Honours: (Cardiff) Welsh Cup winner 1928. Twice represented the Welsh League vs. The Irish League.
Made a reputation after leaving the Tigers when his clever play was given more scope as an inside-forward. The long stint at Brighton latterly saw a move to left-half, his experienced prompting a telling factor.

SMITH, Wallace (1909-1912)
Inside-left: 90 apps; 33 goals.
1910: 5ft. 10ins; 11st. 7lbs.
Born: Allerton, nr. Bradford.
Career: Kettering Town; Northampton Town cs 1904; Bradford City cs 1905; Leicester Fosse during the 1908/09 season (£750) but there only a matter of weeks before joining CITY in March 1909 at a much smaller fee; retired through injury cs 1912.
Honours: (Bradford City) Div. 2 champions 1908.
A forward of some versatility: besides inside-left, Wally occupied both right flank berths for Northampton and was outside-right in Bradford City's 1908 championship side. In the 'near miss' promotion bid side of 1909/10, the 3\Smiths\totalled 105 matches out of a possible 114, scoring 54 goals between them.

SMITH, William (1920-1921)
Half-back: 1 app.
1920: 5ft. 9ins; 12st.
Born: Langley Park, nr. Durham.
Career: Langley Park FC; CITY May 1920 – 1921.
His junior side was prominent in County Durham soccer in 1919/20, winning several trophies, and Smith accordingly prominent in it. City gave him trials at the end of that season, in which he acquitted himself so well as to lead to an engagement. But the highly accomplished Collier/Gilhooley/Bleakley triumvirate held down the half-back berths in 1920/21 with little scope accruing to likely reserves.

SPEED, Frederick (1931-1934)
Left-half: 49 apps; 15 goals.
1935: 5ft. 9ins; 11st.
Born: Newcastle-on-Tyne, 1909.
Career: Lincolnshire junior football; Newark Town; CITY February 1931; York City cs 1934; Mansfield Town June 1936; Exeter City July 1939.
Joined City as an opportunist centre-forward, then moved inside and finally to left-half. This versatility was notably continued at Mansfield, Fred occupying both full-back and inside-left berths as well as left-half in his 3 years at Field Mill. A two-footed performer, certain in his tackling, and employing a strong shot. Being a fast mover, possessed an unusually appropriate surname.

SPENCE, George (1904-1906)
Inside-forward: 19 apps; 3 goals.
1905: 5ft. 10½ins; 12st.
Born: Rothesay, Bute, 1876.
Career: St. Mirren; Derby County circa 1897; Reading 1900; Preston North End 1901; Reading again 1902; Southampton 1903; CITY cs 1904; Clyde cs 1906.
Honours: (Southampton) Southern League champions 1904.
Early into senior action, helping St Mirren win the Renfrewshire Cup as a teenager. Besides being one of the first Tigers, George scored the club's first League goal. Succinctly described as a "cautious and clever Scot: fast, tricky and a glutton for work".

SPENDIFF, Martin Nelson (1905-1908)
Goalkeeper: 104 apps.
1913: 5ft. 11½ins; 12st.
Born: North Shields, 1880.
Died: 18 October 1943.
Career: North-East junior football; Grimsby Town 1903; CITY May 1905; Bradford City April 1908; Millwall Athletic cs 1912; Grimsby Town again cs 1913.

A firm favourite on both sides of the Humber and the first chronologically in the long line of excellent City custodians. Consistent and assured, Martin missed but one League match in his first two seasons and was first choice in 1907/08 up to the Bradford City move.

SPIVEY, Richard (1934-1937)
Inside-forward: 21 apps; 5 goals.
1935: 5ft. 5ins; 10st. 5lbs.
Born: Hull, 18 August 1916.
Died: March 1973.
Career: Yorkshire Schools; Southcoates Lane Old Boys; CITY 1934/35; Torquay United July 1937; Bristol Rovers July 1938; Southport July 1939 where he finished his career at the outbreak of war.
A juvenile prodigy scoring an astonishing 400 goals in 5 seasons for his Hull school (Southcoates Lane) which led to his selection for the Yorkshire Schools in 1929/30.

STANIFORTH, Gordon (1970-1976)
Forward: 7 apps. plus 5 subs; 2 goals.
1974: 5ft. 6ins; 9st. 12½lbs.
Born: Hull, 23 March 1957.
Career: Hull Schools; Yorkshire Schools; CITY on schoolboy forms November 1970, apprentice professional July 1972, full professional March 1974; York City December 1976, originally on month's loan (£7,500); Carlisle United October 1979 (£120,000: York City record); Plymouth Argyle March 1983 (in exchange for another player).
Honours: England schoolboy international.
The eighth in line chronologically of the Hull-born schoolboy internationalists, a fine little forward, lively and dangerous. Proved a highly profitable investment for York, where his talents really blossomed. Helped Plymouth in their unexpected progress to the 1984 FA Cup semi-finals.

STANSFIELD, John (1922)
Outside-left: 12 apps; 1 goal.
Born: Bradford, 14 July 1896.
Died: 1980.
Career: Bradford FC during WW1; Bradford City cs 1919; Castleford Town 1920; CITY January 1922 (£400); Castleford Town cs 1922.
Stansfield's brief stay turned out an expensive one for City as he returned to Castleford on a free transfer. He had made a couple of Div. 1 appearances for Bradford City in 1919/20. Castleford Town, incidentally, were a useful Midland League outfit at the time and supplied several players to the first-class clubs.

STARLING, Ronald William (1925-1930)
Inside-forward: 78 apps; 15 goals.
1929: 5ft. 10ins; 11st. 4lbs.
Born: Pelaw, Newcastle-on-Tyne, 11 October 1909.
Career: Durham Schools; Washington Colliery; CITY as an amateur 1925, working in the club office until signing professional 1927; Newcastle United May 1930 (£3,750); Sheffield Wednesday June 1932 (£3,250); Aston Villa January 1937 (£7,500); retired July 1948 and became Nottingham Forest coach until June 1950.
Honours: England international vs. Scotland 1933 and 1937. (Wednesday) FA Cup winner 1935. (Villa) Div. 2 champions 1938.
A youthful prodigy – in his school team at 8 and scoring goals in men's soccer when 16 – his craft and scintillating ball jugglery delighted fans for a dozen inter-war seasons. On leaving the game ran a newsagency in Sheffield.

STEPHENS, W(illiam) John (1952-1958)
Outside-right: 94 apps; 20 goals.
1957: 5ft. 7ins; 10st.
Born: Cardiff, 26 June 1935.
Career: Cardiff junior football to CITY on amateur forms, signing professional June 1952; Swindon Town June 1958; Coventry City January 1960 – cs 1960.
Honours: Welsh Under-23 international vs. England 1958. Welsh schoolboy international.
Capital winger, on the light side but thrust and skill made up for any handicap on that account. Apparently John wasn't too enamoured with the professional game – City had difficulty in holding him as long as they did, and Coventry failed to re-sign him for the 1960/61 season.

STEPHENSON, William (1907-10 and 1919-20)
Right-back: 64 apps.
1907: 5ft. 8ins; 10st. 7lbs.
Born: Whitburn, Co Durham, 1888.
Career: Whitburn FC; CITY April 1907; Tottenham Hotspur August 1910; CITY again August 1919; Hartlepools United June 1920, leaving that club before they joined the Football League the following year.
Capable back, with City both sides of the Great War but only 9 of the above appearances relate to 1919/20. Hailed from a small Durham town that has produced many famous players down the years, including the English international brothers, Sep and Jack Smith.

STEVENS, Samuel (1911-1920)

Centre-forward: 150 apps; 87 goals.
1920: 5ft. 8ins; 12st. 7lbs.
Born: Netherton, nr. Cannock, Staffs, 18 November 1890.
Career: Cradley Heath St. Luke's; CITY January 1912 (guest player for Cradley Heath of the Birmingham League during WW1); Notts County July 1920; Coventry City March 1921 (£1,300).
A pre-1914 City celebrity, Sammy's scoring feats for the club brought him to the fringe of international honours (he was an England reserve for the '14/15 Scotland match). And induced Notts County to pay their record fee for his signature, estimated at a then hefty £1,750. Another record broken by this great opportunist was Jack Smith's goals total for the Tigers.

STEWART, David Charles (1974-1979)

Outside-left: 46 apps. plus 5 subs; 7 goals.
1977: 5ft. 8ins; 9st. 3lbs.
Born: Belfast, 20 May 1958.
Career: Bangor (Irish League); CITY as an apprentice professional cs 1974, turning full professional August 1975 (£20,000); Chelsea May 1979; Scunthorpe United November 1979; Bridlington Trinity cs 1982; Goole Town November 1982, later joining Grantham.
Honours: Northern Ireland international vs. Belgium 1978.
Secured by Terry Neill from his old club when a promising 16-year old. Development continued, culminating in the winning of a full cap. A clever enough player but perhaps handicapped somewhat by lack of weight when at Boothferry Park. This was remedied by the time he reached Scunthorpe.

STOCKS, Joseph Ronald (1956-1961)

Wing-half: 9 apps; 1 goal.
1960: 5ft. 7½ins; 10st. 4lbs.
Born: Hull, 27 November 1941.
Career: Hull schools football to CITY on amateur forms 1956, turning professional November 1958; Millwall September 1961 (after 2 months' trial); Romford 1964.
Played inside-forward for Millwall. Not very big but tenacious and enthusiastic. Eventually returned to his native city to live and work, and in the mid-1970's was coaching a local side, East Mount Youth Club.

STODDART, George G. (1920-1921)

Outside-right: 7 apps.
Born in Fife.
Career: Inverkeithing United; Raith Rovers 1919; CITY November 1920 – 1921.
Auburn-haired, stocky Scot, signed as a prospective successor to David Mercer who was poised to leave the club and, at the time, on the injured list anyway. Stoddart, however, although good in midfield work, was lacking in shooting power, and his connection with Anlaby Road was brief. Played at inside-right for much of his Raith Rovers spell.

STOKES, Archer (1937-1939)

Full-back: 1 app.
Born: West Ella, Hull, 1920.
Career: Hull Nomads to CITY on amateur forms during season 1936/37; turning professional cs 1937.
His solitary League appearance occurred in March 1939. Younger brother of Ernest Stokes, the Torquay and Southend left-back, who guested for the Tigers during WW2.

STOREY, Ernest (1908/09)

Goalkeeper: 3 apps.
Born: Birtley, Co. Durham, 1888.
Career: North-East junior football to CITY 1908; Spennymoor United cs 1910; Bradford City December 1911; Blyth Spartans 1912; Swansea Town August 1913 (£5).
Like Joe Harron and Alan Daley in subsequent eras, gets a pre-1914 palm for drifting in and out of senior soccer. Was unlikely to establish himself at Anlaby Road with Ed Roughley just starting a 4-year monopoly. If the above £5 transfer fee looks derisory, it still held good after WW1, being standard payment by Scottish League clubs for recruits from junior outfits for example.

STOTT, George Rae Burns (1932-1933)

Outside-right: 4 apps.
1930: 5ft. 6ins; 10st. 12lbs.
Born: North Shields, 1906.
Died: 15 February 1963.

Career: Monkton Athletic; Barnsley November 1926; Rochdale cs 1928; Bradford City cs 1931; CITY cs 1932.

Stocky winger who had a good run at Rochdale – a total of 108 League outings that produced a commendable tally of 30 goals. Thrustful and no slouch when moving down his touch-line.

SULLIVAN, Cornelius ('Neil')

Wing-half: 65 apps; 3 goals.
1928: 5ft. 9½ins; 12st. 10lbs.
Born: Tynemouth, 1903.
Career: Newburn; CITY cs 1926; Bradford cs 1929; Carlisle United July 1930.

Showed great promise on claiming a regular first team place in his very first League season, with powerful half-back play well abetted by natural physical attributes. Neil, however didn't fare very well after leaving the Tigers, making only spasmodic appearances at Park Avenue and Brunton Park.

SUMMERS, Gerald T. F. (1964-1965)

Left-half: 59 apps; 1 goal.
1964: 5ft. 9ins; 11st. 6lbs.
Born: Small Heath, Birmingham, 4 October 1933.
Career: Erdington Albion; West Bromwich Albion ground staff 1950, turning professional August 1951; Sheffield United May 1957 (£3,000); CITY April 1964 (£11,000); Walsall October 1965 (around £10,000); retired May 1967. Wolverhampton Wanderers coach July 1967 – 1969; Oxford United team manager July 1969 – September 1975; Gillingham manager October 1975 – May 1981; then briefly a Southampton scout until appointment as West Bromwich Albion's chief coach October 1981 – April 1982.
Honours: Toured the Far East with FA team 1962.

A cool, collected wing-half always showing professional competence. Had any amount of stamina, was a specialist in exact distribution and one who preferred a cerebral approach to the robust.

SUNLEY, David (1976-1978)

Centre-forward: 58 apps. plus 11 subs; 11 goals.
1977: 5ft. 9¼ins; 11st. 2lbs.
Born: Skelton, nr. Saltburn, 6 February 1952.
Career: North Riding & Cleveland Schools; Sheffield Wednesday as an apprentice professional cs 1968, turning full professional January 1970 (Nottingham Forest on month's loan October 1975); CITY January 1976 (£7,500); Lincoln City June 1978; Stockport County March 1980 – 1982.

Enjoyed a fair amount of senior soccer (121 League matches) for the Wednesday before coming to Boothferry Park. Neat and progressive in style though not a prolific scorer. Sought after as a schoolboy, having trials with Preston North End and Middlesbrough before going to Hillsborough.

SURREY, Thomas Hindmore (1929-1930)

Centre-forward: 1 app.
Born: Gateshead, 31 October 1907.
Died: 1976.
Career: Scotswood; CITY October 1929; not retained cs 1930.

Made his one and only League appearance on 29 March 1930 in a home game against Blackpool, deputising for an injured Paddy Mills. Hit the headlines on his debut for City reserves, scoring after only 2 minutes and then completing a hat-trick (vs. Boston on October 10, 1929).

SWAN, Christopher Samuel (1925-1929)

Right-half/inside-right: 73 apps; 8 goals.
1927: 5ft. 9ins; 11st. 3lbs.

Born: Byker, Newcastle-on-Tyne, 4 December 1900.
Died: 1979.
Career: Newcastle Schools, then in Tyneside junior football before joining Newcastle United May 1919; Stockport County cs 1923; CITY August 1925; Crystal Palace May 1929 – 1931. Later played for Scarborough.
Honours: England schoolboy international vs. Scotland and Wales 1915.
Early on a juvenile star, of course, developing into an adaptable senior. Although usually on the right, Chris could take the left-flank inside and wing-half positions. His best season was 1926/27 (39 League outings).

SWAN, Maurice M. G. (1963-1968)
Goalkeeper: 103 apps.
1965: 6ft; 10st. 13lbs.
Born: Drumcondra, Dublin, 25 February 1932.
Career: Schoolboy football to Drumcondra FC when 16; Cardiff City July 1960 (£3,000); CITY June 1963 (£5,000); returned to Ireland November 1968 and joined Dundalk the following month; retired cs 1973.
Honours: Eire international vs Sweden 1960 (sub). Eire schoolboy international vs. England and Wales. (City) Div. 3 champions 1966.
Tall, lithe 'keeper, the Irish element in the 1966 championship team that was otherwise made up of 8 Englishmen, a Welshman (Alan Jarvis) and a Scot (Andy Davidson). Maurice's other games were Gaelic football and hurling, and he was also an amateur boxer. An electrician by trade, with his own contracting business.

SWANN, Gary (1978-)
Defender: 99 apps. plus 7 subs; 4 goals.
1983: 5ft. 8½ins; 10st. 10lbs.
Born: York, 11 April 1962.
Career: Junior football to CITY as an apprentice professional July 1978, turning full professional May 1980.
Not the least of his qualities is versatility, having successfully played as a forward and in midfield as well as a defender. Latterly, though, has mostly partnered another excellent young prospect, Bobby McNeil, at full-back.

TABRAM, William David (1934-1937)
Centre-half: 106 apps; 5 goals.
1935: 5ft. 10½ins; 12st. 2lbs.
Born: Swansea, 19 January 1909.
Career: Cwm Athletic (Mon.); Swansea Town May 1928; Port Vale May 1933 (£400 including another player); CITY May 1934; South Shields cs 1937.
Understudying the evergreen Joe Sykes, Tabram didn't get much scope at Swansea, but immaculate displays after moving to the Potteries brought attention from the scouts. City were the lucky club and he gave 3 years consistent service. Elder brother of Phil Tabram, who also played for Swansea.

TAIT, Michael P. (1979-1980)
Midfield: 29 apps. plus 4 subs; 3 goals.
1980: 5ft. 11ins; 11st. 8lbs.
Born: Wallsend, 30 September 1956.
Career: Wallsend Boys' Club to Oxford United as an apprentice professional 1972, turning full professional October 1974; Carlisle United February 1977 (£60,000); CITY September 1979 (£150,000: a City record); Portsmouth May 1980 (around £100,000).
Honours: (Portsmouth) Div. 3 champions 1983.
A valuable player, as will be realised from the substantial fees involved on each transfer, able to perform in midfield or attack with like cogency. City had coveted him a while before actually securing his signature, expending their biggest-ever outlay in so doing, but in the event Mick's stay was brief.

TARRANT, J(ohn) Edward (1946-1953)
Wing-half/inside-forward: 30 apps; 2 goals.
1950: 5ft. 11ins; 11st.
Born: Stainforth, nr. Doncaster, 12 February 1932.
Career: Joined the CITY ground staff cs 1946 shortly after leaving school, turning professional February 1949; Walsall December 1953; Cambridge City July 1958.
Immensely promising as a boy, joining the Boothferry Park ground staff when only 14. Unfortunately Ted's subsequent career was marred by injury – he suffered a double fracture of an ankle in 1947 and underwent two cartilage operations during the 1955/56 season. The first choice left-half at Walsall.

TAYLOR, Alan David (1983-1984)
Forward: 13 apps. plus 1 sub; 3 goals.
1982: 5ft. 9ins; 10st. 6lbs.
Born: Lancaster, 14 November 1953.
Career: Lancaster City; Morecambe; Rochdale May 1973; West Ham United November 1974 (£40,000); Norwich City August 1979 (£90,000); Vancouver Whitecaps, Canada, July 1980 (£90,000) (Cambridge United on loan October 1980 – February 1981); CITY (originally on a month's trial) December 1983; Burnley June 1984.
Honours: (WHU) FA cup winner 1975. European Cup Winners' Cup finalist (sub) 1976.
Really came to the fore in the 1975 FA Cup final, scoring both West Ham's goals in their 2-0 win over Fulham. Taylor, a keen opportunist inside man, has been around since

then and gave City some useful service in the latter stages of the 1983/84 promotion battle.

TAYLOR, Arthur M. ('Archie') (1962-1963)
Outside-right: 1 app.
1962: 5ft. 8¾ins; 10st. 7lbs.
Born: Dunscroft, nr. Doncaster, 7 November 1939.
Career: Doncaster Rovers (where he was an amateur); Bristol City May 1958; Barnsley July 1961 (on trial); Mansfield Town November 1961; Goole Town January 1962; CITY May 1962; Halifax Town July 1963; Bradford City November 1967; York City October 1968; Gainsborough Trinity cs 1971.
Only 1 League outing for City but followed it with 173 at Halifax and 93 for York, and 10 for Bradford City sandwiched between. Archie, a fast and clever wingman, had had an up-and-down career marred by illness early on, when he also played inside-forward and outside-left.

TAYLOR, John (1907-1909)
Inside-forward: 9 apps; 3 goals.
Born in Scotland.
Career: Parkhead FC (Glasgow); CITY August 1907; not retained May 1909.
Signed from the ever fertile recruiting grounds of Scottish junior soccer, Jock made his League bow as a Tiger on February 29, 1908, the occasion an away fixture against Stockport County. Had to wait until the following season to repeat this elevation, playing 8 times and scoring 3 goals, and then appearing in both inside berths.

TAYLOR, John (1947-1950)
Right/left-back: 72 apps.
1949: 5ft. 9ins; 11st. 4lbs.
Born: Barnsley, 15 February 1914.
Died: 22 February 1978.
Career: Barnsley schoolboy football; Worsborough Bridge FC (Barnsley); Wolverhampton Wanderers ground staff 1931, turning professional January 1934; Norwich City June 1938 (guest player for Barnsley and Watford during the War); CITY July 1947; Weymouth as player/manager May 1950; Queen's Park Rangers manager June 1952 to appointment as Leeds United manager May 1959 – March 1961.
Honours: (City) Div. 3 (North) champions 1949.
A seasoned defender when he was signed by City and played an important role in the 1949 promotion success. Still covered his territory quickly, an aspect being a capacity to run backwards at speed. Elder brother of Frank Taylor, a wartime England cap and City's assistant manager under Major Buckley.

TAYLOR, William (1926-1931)
Outside-right/outside-left: 151 apps; 15 goals.
1928: 5ft. 8½ins; 10st. 11lbs.
Born: Langley Green, nr. Birmingham 1898.
Career: West Bromwich Albion as an amateur October 1920, turning professional the same month following a trial; Cardiff City cs 1922; Aberdare Athletic 1924/25; CITY June 1926; Norwich City cs 1931 – 1932.
Especially valuable because of a two-footed ability to play on both extreme flanks. Not a prolific scorer but gave excellent service to his inside partners. "A clever dribbler and quick on the ball" – so said a writer of the period.

TEASDALE, Thomas (1946-47)
Outside-left: 1 app.
An amateur and a late choice for the home game against Barrow on May 31, 1947. This was the season memorable for an arctic winter forcing rearranged fixtures into June, and a constant experimentation that resulted in 43 players being called upon by City. Teasdale disappeared into obscurity after the Barrow match.

TEECE, David A. (1952-1956)
Goalkeeper: 25 apps.
1955: 6ft; 12st. 7lbs.
Born: Middleton, nr. Manchester, 1 September 1927.
Career: Hyde United; CITY February 1952; Oldham Athletic June 1956; Buxton July 1959.
City paid what was described as a substantial fee for a non-League player for this well proportioned 'keeper. David turned out to be an able reserve while, at Boundary Park, he was first choice in his final two years.

TEMPLE, G(eorge) Arthur (1907-1914)
Centre/inside-forward: 173 apps; 77 goals.
1910: 5ft. 10ins; 11st. 2lbs.
Born: Newcastle-on-Tyne, 1887.
Died: 1959.
Career: Wallsend Park Villa; CITY July 1907; Blyth Spartans 1914/15.
One of the best and most serviceable inside men during City's first decade. An ever-present in his first League season and a regular for the next four. Summed up by a contemporary writer as a "very speedy and judicious player". Uncle of J. L. Temple, Fulham outside-right 1926-31.

THOM, Alexander (1922-1926)

Outside-left: 131 apps; 18 goals.
1924: 5ft. 7½ins; 10st. 10lbs.
Born: Stevenston, Ayrshire, circa 1895.
Career: Yoker Athletic and then Dumbarton before WW1; Morton cs 1920; Airdrieonians June 1921; CITY September 1922 (£250); Swindon Town cs 1926; retired cs 1930.
Invariably first choice with all his senior clubs until the very last season. An excellent little performer versed in all the arts of wing play, Alec's great popularlity at Anlaby Road was amply justified. Two 1920's verdicts: "...light on feet; quick into action; can centre quickly and score goals occasionally". And, "...speedy in the dribble and adept in getting in centres from a small area. A good shot".

THOMAS, Alfred Charles (1923-1925)
Outside-right: 36 apps; 3 goals.
1924: 5ft. 9ins; 11st. 6lbs.
Born: Hetton-le-Hole, Co Durham, 1895.
Career: Llanelly; Bradford City 1921/22; Merthyr Town 1922/23; CITY June 1923; South Shields cs 1925.

Quite hefty for a winger, Alf was the regular outside-right in the 1923/24 season, succeeding the transferred Jacky Crawford. But he only appeared 4 times in 1924/25, giving way to George Richardson and Jim Keen.

THOMPSON, Denis (1947-1948)
Centre/inside-forward; 9 apps; 8 goals.
1947: 5ft. 8½ins; 11st. 13lbs.
Born: Whitburn, nr. Sunderland, 10 April 1924.
Career: Whitburn Bankheads circa 1940; Bedewell FC (Jarrow) 1943/44; Whitburn Welfare 1945; CITY March 1947; returned to Co Durham cs 1948, subsequently playing in North-Eastern League football.
Hardly the most subtle of inside men, perhaps, but one who pulled his weight and let the opposition know he was on the field. And his League record of 8 goals in 9 outings indicated opportunism — so much so the thought occurs that possibly Denis should have had a longer stay.

THOMPSON, James William J. (1931-32)
Centre-forward: 1 app.
1930: 5ft. 11ins; 11st. 10lbs.
Born: West Ham, April 1898.
Career: Custom House; Charlton Athletic on amateur forms August 1921 and signed also for Wimbledon the following month; Millwall Athletic as a professional December 1921; Coventry City June 1923; Clapton Orient August 1924; Luton Town July 1925; Chelsea cs 1927; Norwich City cs 1929; Sunderland May 1930; Fulham October 1930; CITY October 1931; Tunbridge Wells Rangers January 1932. Later a scout for Chelsea and Southampton.
Actually came out of retirement to sign for City, a robust centre with a reputation for goal scoring. Did best at Luton, Chelsea and Norwich, his aggregate League figures for them being 88 goals in 135 matches. Of these totals the Chelsea return was an outstanding 33 in 37 games. This wanderer played on both wings for Coventry as well.

THOMPSON, Neil (1982-1983)
Left-back: 29 apps. plus 2 subs.
Born: Beverley, 2 October 1963.
Career: Junior football to Nottingham Forest as an apprentice professional; CITY 1981, signing as a contract player June 1982; Scarborough 1983.
After his apprenticeship in the Midlands this local youngster made his senior debut for City, playing the majority of his games in 1981/82. Usually appeared at either No. 3 or No. 5.

THOMSON, Robert (1934-1935)
Left-back: 4 apps.
1930: 5ft. 8½ins; 12st. 7lbs.
Born: Falkirk, 24 October 1905.
Career: Falkirk Amateurs; Falkirk FC 1925/26; Sunderland April 1927 (£5,000); Newcastle October 1928 (in exchange for another Scottish international, Bobby McKay); CITY July 1934 (£340); Racing Club de Paris 1935; Ipswich Town July 1936. Appointed the Ipswich assistant trainer after breaking a leg in 1937, then their head trainer 1938/39, taking up this appointment again following war service until around 1950.
Honours: Scottish international vs. England 1927. Scottish League vs. Football League 1927.
Originally a half-back, Bob's conversion to full-back in October 1926 brought an amazingly quick rise to fame, winning the highest Scottish representative honours and figuring in a costly transfer before the season's end. Did much to foster emerging talent during his Newcastle sojourn. During WW2 served with the RAF in the Middle East and was with the famous Eagle Squadron.

THORLEY, Ernest ('Cliff') (1934-1936)
Outside-left: 34 apps; 5 goals.
1935: 5ft. 10ins; 12st. 2lbs.
Born: Denaby, nr. Doncaster 12 November 1909.
Career: Denaby United; Frickley Colliery (for less than a week!); Sunderland September 1932; CITY November 1934 – 1936.
In the season of joining Sunderland had three 1st Division outings but only one more followed (in 1934/35), the class Scottish international winger, Jimmy Connor, being then at his considerable zenith. Things were better as a Tiger, Thorley's powerful raiding aided by a physique heftier than that of the average winger.

THORNTON, William (1905-1906)
Right-half: 1 app.
1905: 5ft. 4ins; 10st.
Born in the West Riding 1883.
Died: June 1966.
Career: Doncaster Rovers; CITY April 1905; Denaby United 1906.
Doncaster Rovers fielded 31 players in their dismal 1904/05 season (wooden spoonists with 8 points) but Billy wasn't among them. So his solitary League outing was as a Tiger: against Leeds City away, September 23, 1905. He also played in the FA Cup-tie against his future club, Denaby, the following month, when the reserves undertook the fixture.

TODD, Paul Raymond (1951-1953)
Inside-left: 27 apps; 3 goals.
1951: 5ft. 11½ins; 13st. 2lbs.
Born: Middlesbrough, 8 May 1920.
Career: RAF football; Doncaster Rovers cs 1945; Blackburn Rovers July 1950 (£10,000); CITY October 1951 (£6,500); King's Lynn as player/manager May 1953. Later managed Worksop Town.
Honours: (Doncaster Rovers) Div. 3 (North) champions 1947 and 1950.
Attracted much attention when wearing Doncaster's colours – a scheming, thrustful inside man whose fine play was backed by a powerful physique. Was at inside-right, to accommodate the great Peter Doherty, for his second championship medal. Recommended to Doncaster while on wartime service in Ceylon.

TOWARD, Alfred Vickers (1908-1909)
Centre-forward: 10 apps; 5 goals.
1908: 5ft. 8½ins; 11st. 8lbs.
Born: Castleside, Durham, 1882.
Died: 19 May 1962.
Career: Leadgate Park; CITY 1908; Oldham Athletic December 1909 (£350); Preston North End 1913; Darlington 1918/19-December 1920.
Speedy, scoring centre whose financially beneficial move to Oldham seemed a painful transaction to the Tigers later that season. For Alf netted one of the goals in a 3-0 victory against City that was instrumental in the Lancashire club gaining promotion to Div. 1 on goal average. The third-placed side was Hull City. Alf was one of several brothers in the Leadgate Park team of the mid-1900's.

TOWNEND, H(enry) Vincent ('Vinney')
Forward: 12 apps; 1 goal.
Born: Selby, Yorks, 1889.
Died: February 1958.
Career: Besides CITY he assisted two of his home town clubs – Selby Town and Selby Robins. Also played for Goole Town.
Vinney's dozen League outings were spread over 3 seasons, the most of which were in the second one, 1910/11, when he made 7 and scored a goal. Received high praise from one commentator of the period – "...fastest man on the City books, also one of the brainiest".

TREANOR, James Leslie (1936-1939)
Left-half: 44 apps; 1 goal.
1935: 6ft. 0½in; 11st. 2lbs.
Born: Heap, nr. Bury, Lancs, 1913.
Career: Winsford United; Bury 1933/34; Accrington Stanley September 1935; CITY 1936.
Blossomed at Accrington following a taste of Second Division fare with Bury, the former club rejecting overtures from elsewhere before City obtained his signature. Treanor was an able wing-half, his height a potent factor in the air.

TULLOCH, Roland ('Ron') (1953-1955)
Wing-half: 2 apps.
Born in South Africa, 15 July 1932.
Career: South African football to CITY December 1953; returned to his native land cs 1955.
One of a small contingent of South Africans which graced City's books in the 'Fifties – the most eminent, of course, was the two-spell Alf Ackerman. Ron could usefully play inside-forward in addition to half-back.

TURNER, Albert (1929-1931)
Outside-left: 21 apps; 2 goals.
1930: 5ft. 9ins; 12st.
Born: Sheffield, 3 September 1907.
Career: Denaby United 1926; CITY 1928/29; Walsall August 1931; Doncaster Rovers cs 1933; Cardiff City cs 1937; Bristol Rovers December 1938; Bath City July 1939.
Honours: (Doncaster) Div. 3 (North) champions 1935.
Powerful forward noted for fierce shooting – he netted 5 in a match against New Brighton in Doncaster's promotion season, a remarkable feat for a winger. A good cricketer who played in the Yorkshire Council and father of Gordon Turner (Luton Town and Football League).

TURNER, Henry (1914-1915)
Half-back/inside-forward: 6 apps; 3 goals.
Born: Wallsend.
Career: Junior football to CITY during season 1913/14.
The bald fact that Turner appeared for the Tigers in half a dozen League encounters hides a couple of noteworthy facets. Firstly, in them he occupied 4 different positions – centre and right-half and both inside-forward berths. Secondly, each and every match was away from home. Obviously an adaptable player. Senior debut: vs. Huddersfield Town on October 31, 1914.

VARNEY, John F. (1948-1951)
Left-back: 9 apps.
1950: 5ft. 11ins; 13st. 5lbs.
Born: Oxford, 27 November 1929.
Career: Oxford City; signed for CITY during season 1948/49 when serving in the RAF, turning professional December 1949; Lincoln City May 1951, retiring after 2 years with that club.
Honours: (Lincoln City) Div. 3 (North) champions 1952.
A brief span even in the terms of a career that is itself brief, yet John had the pleasure of playing in a championship side. A tall man and heavy, he could punt a long ball and was quick enough to take on most wingers.

VICKERS, John (1928-1929)
Right-half: 2 apps.
1928: 5ft. 9½ins; 12st.
Born: Auckland Park, Bishop Auckland, 7 August 1908.
Died: 1980.
Career: Bishop Auckland; CITY cs 1928; Darlington cs 1929; Doncaster Rovers cs 1930; Charlton Athletic June 1932 (£540); Port Vale May 1933 (£200); Newport County May 1936.
Moved to full-back during his Doncaster Rovers days and built a reputation for solid defensive work thereafter. John enjoyed a fair measure of first-team service with all his clubs on leaving Anlaby Road.

WADSWORTH, Eric Appleyard (1919-20)
Inside-right: 1 app.
Born: Goole, 1894.
Career: Yorkshire junior football to CITY on amateur forms.
Local amateur forward. His solitary League outing was in the drawn home game against West Ham United on the 17th April 1920. Two members of the unpaid brigade played for City that term, the other was W. Clark.

WAGSTAFF, Kenneth ('Waggy') (1964-1975)

Inside-forward: 374 apps. plus 4 subs; 173 goals.
1971: 5ft. 9¼ins; 13st. 11½lbs.
Born: Langwith, nr. Mansfield, 24 November 1942.
Career: Woodland Imperial (Langwith); Mansfield Town May 1960; CITY November 1964 (£40,000); retired through injury December 1975; George Cross FC, Australia as manager/coach May 1976 – 1977; on return-

ing played in Hull minor football and made 1 appearance for Goole Town before appointment as Bridlington Town manager September-December 1980.
Honours: (City) Div. 3 champions 1966.
A tremendous City favourite and deservedly so, a smiling roly-poly character with a penchant for goal scoring. The Waggy/Chris Chilton duo was feared and a prime feature of one of the club's best-ever sides. In 1982 became a licensee in the Hull area.

WAINSCOAT, W(illiam) Russell (1931-1934)

Inside-left: 79 apps; 41 goals.
1929: 5ft. 11ins; 12st. 7lbs.
Born: Maltby, nr. Rotherham, 28 July 1898.
Died: July 1967.
Career: Maltby Main; Barnsley March 1920; Middlesbrough December 1923 (£3,750); Leeds United March 1925; CITY October 1931 – 1934.
Honours: England international vs. Scotland 1929. FA touring team in Canada 1926. (City) Div. 3 (North) champions 1933.
Strength and intricate footwork were features of his play. And he certainly knew the way to goal (netted 5 in one of the 1926 Canadian tour matches). This befitted one who had had much experience as a centre-forward. Russell's jobs outside football included at different times railway clerk, licensee, running a shoe shop and a drapery store.

WALDEN, George (1909-1910)

Centre-forward: 2 apps; 1 goal.
1910: 5ft. 9ins.
Born: London circa 1889.
Career: London Sunday League football; CITY November 1909; Rotherham Town September 1910; Luton Town March 1912. Also assisted Scunthorpe United.
Scored on his League debut (against Bradford, an away game, on November 6, 1909). Appeared on 7 occasions in Luton Town's Southern League Div. 1 side and scored 2 goals in the short period up to the close of the 1911/12 season. The Hatters were then relegated to Div. 2 of that competition.

WALKER, J(ohn) William (1923-1924)

Inside-right: 5 apps; 1 goal.
1923: 5ft. 8ins; 11st. 2lbs.
Born: High Spen, Newcastle-on-Tyne, 1899.
Career: Langley Park FC (Co Durham); CITY July 1923; not retained cs 1924.
Joined the Anlaby Road brigade after shining as an inside-forward in Durham junior soccer. Soon made his League bow: in the 2-1 home win against Nelson on the 8 September 1923.

WALSH, James Arthur (1928-1931)

Right-half/inside-right: 82 apps; 10 goals.
1930: 5ft. 9ins; 11st. 6lbs.
Born: Stockport, 15 May 1901.
Died: 1971.
Career: Stockport junior football; Stockport County 1920, originally as an amateur; Liverpool June 1922; CITY June 1928; Colwyn Bay 1931.
Honours: Toured Australia with FA team 1925, during which time he played against Australia 3 times.
Scored all his City goals in his first season, afterwards making a successful transition to the half-back line in 1929/30. A clever performer who was tried at centre-forward by Liverpool but perhaps not robust enough for a 1920's leader. Summed up in his City days as "keen in tackling and could play his forwards. A ready wit and a ready kick".

WALTERS, Peter L. (1970-1973)

Goalkeeper: 2 apps.
1971: 5ft. 10ins; 11st.
Born: Whickham, Co Durham, 8 June 1952.
Career: North-East junior football to CITY July 1970 (Darlington on loan February – May 1972); Corby Town 1973 for a long spell, then to Bedford Town (£1,000) and, during the 1980 close season, Kettering Town; Scarborough July 1981 (£2,000).
Understudy to a then 'fixture' (Ian McKechnie) but first choice in his months on loan to Darlington. Peter did well too with his non-League clubs and represented the Southern League in 1978/79 when at Bedford.

WARBOYS, Alan (1977-1979)
Centre-forward: 44 apps. plus 5 subs; 9 goals.
1978: 6ft. 0½in; 13st. 7lbs.
Born: Goldthorpe, nr. Rotherham, 18 April 1949.
Career: West Riding junior football to Doncaster Rovers as an apprentice professional, turning full professional April 1967; Sheffield Wednesday May 1968 (around £12,000 plus another player); Cardiff City December 1970 (£40,000); Sheffield United September 1972 (£20,000 plus 2 players); Bristol Rovers March 1973 (£35,000); Fulham February 1977 (£30,000); CITY September 1977 (£25,000); Doncaster Rovers again July 1979 (£12,500); retired through injury October 1982.
A lot of cash and several players changed locations through the many moves of this burly centre. Was well in the public eye during his Bristol Rovers sojourn when his spearhead partnership with Bruce Bannister (also later a Tiger) brought the Eastville club umpteen goals. Certainly an attacking force to be reckoned with.

WASSELL, Kim D. (1983)
Forward: 1 app.
Born: Wolverhampton, 9 June 1957.
Career: West Bromwich Albion as an apprentice professional; Northampton Town September 1977; Aldershot November 1979, then played in Australia for some time before joining CITY on trial August 1983; Bradford City on trial September 1983.
Unable to agree terms with City, Wassell quickly moved on. Had been given his League baptism by Northampton, altogether playing 13 senior games plus 7 substitutions for the Midland club. Made no League appearances for Aldershot.

WATSON, Arthur E. (1939-1947)
Right-back: 35 apps.
1938: 6ft; 11st. 4lbs.
Born: South Hiendley, nr. Barnsley, 12 July 1913.
Career: Monkton Colliery; Lincoln City 1934; Chesterfield June 1936; CITY cs 1939 (£250); retired May 1947.
A popular figure in the initial post-war season with his timely tackling and clean kicking – though he could boot a ball a long way, Arthur endeavoured to place it. His younger brother, William, was also a right-back and on Lincoln's and Chesterfield's books in the 'Thirties.

WATSON, John Innes (1927-1931)
Right or centre-half: 47 apps.
1929: 5ft. 11ins; 11st. 10lbs.
Born: Aberdeen.
Career: Aberdeen Richmond; CITY cs 1927 – 1931.
From Dally Duncan's junior club, arriving a year prior to that celebrity. Could fill two of the three half-back berths very adequately, possessing the physique for the role. Jock's best season was 1929/30 when he had 22 senior outings.

WEALANDS, Jeffrey A. (1972-1979)
Goalkeeper: 240 apps.
1975: 6ft. 0½in; 12st.
Born: Darlington, 26 August 1951.
Career: Junior football to Wolverhampton Wanderers as an apprentice professional, turning full professional October 1968; Darlington July 1970; CITY February 1972 (about £10,000); Birmingham City July 1979 (£30,000) (Manchester United on loan February – May 1983).
Shared senior goalkeeping duties with a long-time incumbent, Ian McKechnie, in his first full season as a Tiger. Then himself an undisputed 'fixture' for 4 campaigns and an ever-present in 2 of them. Subsequently saw a lot of Div. 1 action in Birmingham's cause. Brisk in action and a clean handler.

WEAVER, Samuel (1928-1929)

Left-half: 48 apps; 5 goals.
1928: 5ft. 10ins; 11st. 7lbs.
Born: Pilsley, Derbyshire, 8 February 1909.
Career: Pilsley FC (Sutton Junction on trial); Sutton Town 1926; CITY March 1928 (£50); Newcastle United November 1929 (£2,500); Chelsea August 1936 (£4,166) (guest player for Leeds United 1942-43); Stockport County December 1945; retired cs 1947. Leeds United coach 1947-49; Millwall trainer/coach June 1949 – January 1954; Mansfield Town

coach September 1955 – June 1958 when he was appointed that club's manager to January 1960. Recalled by Raich Carter, the then Mansfield manager, to become assistant trainer February 1960 to 1967, when he became chief scout until his final retirement.
Honours: England international (3 apps). Football League (2 apps). (Newcastle United) FA Cup winner 1932.
Aggressive and progressive, Sam attained national fame by reason of his massive throws, judged to exceed 35 yards. (Curious the rival in the mighty throws' category, Tom Gardner, was likewise a Tiger). Also played at inside-left on occasion. Sam was a first-class cricketer too, for Derbyshire and Somerset, and the former club's masseur from 1956.

WELDON, Anthony (1930-1931)

Inside-left: 31 apps; 6 goals.
1930: 5ft. 8ins; 10st. 4lbs.
Born: Glasgow.
Career: Kilsyth Rangers; Airdrieonians December 1924 (£5); Everton March 1927 (£2,000); CITY June 1930 (£1,000); West Ham United June 1931; Lovell's Athletic (Newport, Mon.) cs 1932; Rochdale cs 1933; Dundalk as player/coach July 1934; Bangor (Northern Ireland) as player/manager late in 1934.
Honours: (Everton) League champions 1928.
A clever, ball playing Scot. At Airdrie had in turn succeeded two transferred internationals, Willie Russell (inside-right) and Hughie Gallacher (centre), before settling in the inside-left slot. Tony's link-up with compatriot Alec Troup was a factor in Everton's 1928 championship triumph. Father-in-law of Jim Storrie, the well-known Leeds United etc., centre-forward of the 1960's.

WEST, H. (1906-07)

Left-half: 1 app.
Born in the Hull district.
Career: Played in Army football prior to joining CITY circa 1906.
His appearance in the League side was occasioned by the absence of David Gordon, the latter's one and only non-participation that term. It was the home game against Gainsborough Trinity. West could play at centre-half too.

WHITE, Kenneth (1947-1949)

Right-half: 1 app.
1949: 5ft. 6ins; 11st.
Born: Selby, Yorks, 15 March 1922.
Career: Had a 6 months' spell with Huddersfield Town as an amateur and played in Army football before joining CITY in December 1947 from Selby Town; joined Scarborough cs 1949.
Stocky performer, usefully versatile – besides wing-half, he had led the attack and, at Scarborough, did some good work at inside-left. There Ken developed his marksmanship besides creating opportunities.

WHITE, William W. (1938-1939)

Inside-forward: 2 apps.
1937: 5ft. 8½ins; 11st. 6lbs.
Born: Kirkcaldy, 1911.
Career: Musselburgh Bruntonians; Charlton Athletic July 1930; Gillingham December 1930; Aldershot cs 1932; Carlisle United June 1934; Newport County 1934/35; Bristol City May 1935; Lincoln City 1936/37; CITY June 1938.
Another of the roving kind – and all points of the compass, as a glance at his clubs demonstrates. White was the enthusiastic kind as well, scoring goals by sheer dash and persistence. With Aldershot played right-half in addition to both the inside positions.

WHITEHURST, William (1980-)

Forward: 118 apps. plus 17 subs; 20 goals.
1983: 6ft; 13st.
Born: Thurnscoe, Rotherham, 10 June 1959.
Career: Mexborough Town; CITY October 1980 (£2,500).
As commentators keep saying, not the most subtle or clever of footballers, but no one can fault this wholehearted player for want of endeavour. And, of course, there is time for development. The enthusiasm is there, his physique is powerful, the scoring rate has improved.

WHITNALL, Brian (1948-1956)

Full-back: 2 apps.
1950: 5ft. 6ins; 10st.
Born: Doncaster, 25 May 1933.

103

Career: Junior football to CITY on amateur forms 1948, turning professional June 1950; Scunthorpe United May 1956; Exeter City July 1958; Bath City cs 1962.

Slightness in physique made Brian reliant on tenacity and judgement and he had his share of determination. His best League spell was with Exeter where he played in 37 4th Div. matches.

WHITWORTH, George (1925-1928)

Centre/inside-forward: 66 apps; 31 goals.
1927: 5ft. 9½ins; 11st. 4lbs.
Born: Northampton, 1896.
Career: Rushden Windmill; Northampton Town cs 1913; Crystal Palace March 1922; Sheffield Wednesday May 1925; CITY November 1925; Peterborough & Fletton United August 1928.

Admirably consistent scorer – his post-war record with Northampton and Palace was 114 from 219 games. George left the latter club through disagreement over a benefit and Wednesday faced competition in getting his transfer. Yet he stayed at Hillsborough only a few months. This attacking craftsman gave good service at Anlaby Road when it was said he was "...a clever dribbler and deadly shot".

WIENAND, George (1938-1939)

Outside-right: 15 apps; 3 goals.
1938: 5ft. 11ins; 11st.
Born: East London, Cape Province, South Africa.
Career: Transvaal FC (S. Africa); Huddersfield Town July 1937; CITY October 1938; returned to South Africa cs 1939.

Tall, slim, fast moving winger. Soon established himself on arriving in this country and made 28 Div. 1 appearances for Huddersfield in little over a season. The War interrupted a career that could have paralleled that of his famed compatriot, Berry Nieuwenhuys ('Nivvy') of Liverpool. Said to have cost Huddersfield £100 plus the boat fare to bring him from South Africa.

WIGGLESWORTH, Arthur (1919-20)

Right-back: 7 apps.
1919: 5ft. 8½ins; 12st.
Born: Hull, 26 October 1891.
Died: 15 June 1974.
Career: Turned professional with Goole Town in July 1912 and joined CITY before the resumption of peace-time soccer in 1919. With Doncaster Rovers 1920-26.

Powerful full-back. A tremendous favourite at Doncaster where he stayed long enough to earn (and receive) a benefit. For half of his Belle Vue service, Rovers were out of the League. On the club's return Arthur was an ever-present in the first season (1923/24), making 67 League appearances in total.

WILKINSON, Graham J. (1952-1960)

Wing-half: 3 apps.
1958: 5ft. 9ins; 11st.
Born: Hull, 21 October 1934.
Career: Hull Schools; played for the club's junior sides from 1951 before signing as a CITY professional September 1952; Bridlington Trinity cs 1960.

At Boothferry Park for approaching a decade but coinciding with the heyday of Bill Harris, Denis Durham etc. (the latter, incidentally, moving to Bridlington at the same time as Graham). A useful and efficient understudy.

WILKINSON, Jack (1936-1937)

Outside-left: 17 apps; 2 goals.
1935: 5ft. 6½ins; 10st. 7lbs.
Born: Wath-on-Dearne, nr. Rotherham, 13 June 1902.
Died: 1969.
Career: Yorkshire Schools; Dearne Valley Old Boys; Wath Athletic as a professional February 1925; Sheffield Wednesday October 1925; Newcastle United May 1930 (£3,000); Lincoln City September 1932 (£600); Sunderland January 1935; CITY 1936; Scunthorpe United August 1937.

Adroit little ginger wingman, slippery as could be but unfortunate in the way of injuries. Caught attention as a youngster by scoring over a century of goals from the wing in 5 seasons with Dearne Valley OB. Most of his League games were in the two top divisions.

WILKINSON, Norman F. (1952-1954)

Centre-forward: 8 apps; 3 goals.
1955: 5ft. 11ins; 12st.
Born: Alnwick, Northumberland, 16 February 1931.

Career: RAF football to CITY as an amateur November 1952; York City as a professional July 1954; retired cs 1966.
Chiefly known for his dozen years of meritorious service for York City. A star of the York side that sensationally reached the FA Cup semi-finals in 1955, Norman's thrustful play brought an aggregate League goals haul of 125 and established a club record. Also played inside-right at Bootham Crescent.

WILKINSON, Thomas (1924-1928)
Inside-left: 4 apps; 2 goals.
1925: 5ft. 8¾ins; 11st. 2lbs.
Born: Felling, Co Durham, 8 February 1904.
Career: Co Durham junior football; CITY 1924/25; Everton May 1927; Nelson cs 1928, leaving during the following season.
Able to play inside-right too. Never made the Everton League side due to the plethora of forward talent then at their disposal.

WILKINSON, William (1961-1972)
Right-half/inside-forward: 208 apps; plus 15 subs; 31 goals.
1966: 5ft. 8ins; 11st. 6lbs.
Born: Stockton-on-Tees, 24 March 1943.
Career: Stockton FC (also on Middlesbrough's books as an amateur); CITY as apprentice professional August 1961, becoming full professional May 1962; Rotherham United November 1972 (around £10,000); Durban City, South Africa, cs 1974; Bridlington Town December 1974; in cs 1975 went to USA and played for Boston Minutemen and then Tacoma Tides before returning to join Southport October 1976; joined George Cross FC (Melbourne, Australia) February 1977, later that year taking over the management of the club from Ken Wagstaff.
A sturdy player at both half-back and in the attack, Billy turned in many a telling performance and was maybe a touch better in the former role. Became quite a globe trotter after leaving Rotherham.

WILLIAMS, Emlyn (1929-1930)
Centre-forward: 1 app.
1929: 5ft. 8½ins; 11st. 2lbs.
Born: Aberaman, Glam., 1903.
Career: Clapton Orient 1926/27; CITY 1929; Merthyr Town 1930; Bournemouth & Boscombe Athletic December 1931 – 1932.
An understudy at each of his 3 League clubs (Merthyr, when he joined them, had just lost their first-class status). Emlyn's best return was in his half-season at Bournemouth: 6 League outings, scoring 2 goals.

WILLIAMS, Michael J. (1960-1966)
Goalkeeper: 88 apps.
1964: 5ft. 11ins; 11st. 4lbs.

Born: Hull, 23 October 1944.
Career: Hull Schools; signed amateur forms for CITY June 1960; became an apprentice professional August 1960 and a full professional October 1962; Aldershot July 1966; Workington July 1968; Scunthorpe United July 1970; Scarborough June 1974; Bridlington Trinity cs 1975.
Impressed in Schoolboy soccer and quickly snapped up by City. As a senior he enjoyed his best spell at Boothferry Park being first choice in 1962/63 and 1964/65, but only aggregated 43 League appearances elsewhere.

WILSON, David ('Soldier') (1905)
Inside-right: 10 apps; 4 goals.
1905: 5ft. 8ins; 11st. 6lbs.
Born: Hebburn, Co Durham, of Scottish parents, circa 1884.
Died: 27 October 1906.
Career: Heart of Midlothian; CITY cs 1905; Leeds City December 1905 (£120).
First choice during his brief spell with City but remembered, of course, because of his tragic passing. David collapsed and died in the dressing-room after playing for Leeds City against Burnley.

WILSON, Gordon Gill (1926-1931)
Left-back: 28 apps; 1 goal.
1928: 5ft. 9½ins; 12st. 7lbs.
Born: West Auckland, Co Durham, 1904.
Career: Scotswood; CITY April 1926; Luton Town cs 1931; Norwich City 1932; Barrow cs 1934.
Another of the capable young players kept in the background during the Jock Gibson/Matt Bell/Goldsmith monopoly of full-back berths. Wilson also performed on the right flank after leaving the Tigers.

WILSON, Henry (1920-1921)

Outside-left: 30 apps; 3 goals.
Born: Belfast, circa 1896.
Career: With Distillery 3 seasons and Belfast Celtic 1 season before joining the Army September 1914. Subsequently Dunmurry 1919; Glenavon cs 1920; CITY October 1920; Charlton Athletic July 1921; Aberaman June 1922.
Clever Irishman able to middle the ball in fine style and a first-teamer for the whole of his time with the Tigers. Was a prisoner of war towards the end of his Army Service. Early in his career represented the Irish Intermediate League and played for Ireland against Scotland in a junior international.

WILSON, Thomas (1967-1971)
Centre-half: 60 apps; 1 goal.
1967: 6ft. 0½in; 11st.
Born: Rosewell, Midlothian, 29 November 1940.
Career: Edina Hearts; Falkirk 1958; Millwall July 1961 (£750); CITY November 1967 (around £18,000); Goole Town July 1971 – October 1979; North Ferriby United (Yorkshire League) December 1979 for a short spell.
Scottish pivot of willowy build and commendable efficiency with plenty of experience at left-half also before his arrival at Boothferry Park. Gave Goole an extraordinary length of service for a League veteran venturing into non-League circles. Made 367 Northern Premier and cup appearances in his 8 years there.

WOOD, Alfred E. H. (1974-1976)
Centre-forward: 51 apps. plus 2 subs; 10 goals.
1975: 5ft. 11½ins; 12st. 2lbs.
Born: Macclesfield, 25 October 1945.
Career: Junior football to Manchester City's ground staff 1962, turning professional June 1963; Shrewsbury Town June 1966 (£5,000); Millwall May 1972 (£35,000); CITY November 1974 (£75,000): Middlesbrough October 1976; Walsall June 1977; Stafford Rangers August 1978.
Honours: England Youth international 1964.
A centre-half who took on the role of centre-forward with success when at Shrewsbury, and his scoring rate continued to impress with Millwall (38 in 99 League outings). This caused City to part with their then record fee but Alf didn't do especially well at Boothferry Park.

WOOD, James Linsley (1921-1923)
Inside-right: 2 apps; 1 goal.
1922: 5ft. 9ins; 12st.
Born: Byker, Newcastle-on-Tyne, 1901.
Career: Methley FC (Leeds); CITY December 1921.

A spirited performer believing attack is the best form of defence. This aggression, though, could get somewhat excessive and Wood received a caution from the ruling body in 1922.

WOODHEAD, Clifford (1930-1941)
Right/left-back: 305 apps.
1935: 5ft. 8ins; 11st. 3lbs.
Born: Darfield, nr. Barnsley, 1908.
Career: Ardsley Athletic (trial for Southport in the late 1920's); Denaby United; CITY May 1930; Goole Town 1945/46. City's assistant trainer for a spell during the 1950's.
Honours: (City) Div. 3 (North) champions 1933.
If the Twenties can be termed the Matt Bell era then the Thirties surely belong to Cliff Woodhead. Essentially a left-back, his run of League appearances from 1931/32 included 2 ever-presents and 3 more campaigns where only 1 match was missed. And he continued his consistent displays until the wartime shut-down in 1941. Sought after by many clubs but City was his sole senior one. Sturdy, reliable and a great Tiger.

WOOF, William (1982-1983)
Forward: 9 apps. plus 2 subs; 3 goals.
1983: 5ft. 10ins; 11st. 9lbs.
Born: Gateshead, 16 August 1956.
Career: Junior football to Middlesbrough as an apprentice professional, turning full professional August 1974 (Brighton & Hove Albion on loan December 1975, Peterborough United on loan March 1977) to cs 1982; at the commencement of season 1982/83 briefly assisted Blyth Spartans and Cardiff City before joining CITY October 1982 (Happy Valley FC, Hong Kong, November 1982 – January 1983) to cs 1983.
Signed for City about the same time that a former Middlesbrough clubmate, Billy Askew, received his permanent engagement. A capable strike forward, Woof has become widely travelled in pursuit of his profession.

WRACK, Charles (1931-1932)
Centre-half: 3 apps.
1930: 5ft. 9ins; 11st.
Born: Boston, Lincs. 28 December 1899.
Died: 13 April 1979.
Career: Cleethorpes Town; Grimsby Town cs 1925; CITY cs 1931; Boston FC cs 1932.
Charlie had given the Mariners good service and figured in two of their promotion sides: Div. 3 (North) champions in his first senior campaign (13 apps) and as a regular in the Div. 2 runners-up team of 1928/29 (38 apps). He lost his place, however, to Harry Swaby the following season.

WRIGHT, David (1934-1935)
Inside-left: 32 apps; 11 goals.
1935: 5ft. 9ins; 12st. 7lbs.
Born: Kirkcaldy, 5 October (year not known).
Career: East Fife; Cowdenbeath 1926; Sunderland April 1927 (£8,000 including another player); Liverpool March 1930; CITY July 1934; Bradford May 1935 – 1936.
Equally at home in the other inside position, David had sampled a great deal of top flight soccer before his arrival at Anlaby Road. Played a typical Scottish inside man's game, able to subtly prompt colleagues as well as take scoring chances himself.

WRIGHT, E(dward) Gordon D(undas) (1905-1913)
Outside-left: 152 apps; 13 goals.
1906: 5ft. 11ins; 11st. 6lbs.
Born: Earlsfield Green, Surrey, 3 October 1884.
Died: 5 June 1947.
Career: Besides his 8-year association with CITY, he assisted Cambridge University, the Corinthians (1904/5 – 1906/7), Portsmouth (1905/6), Leyton (1909/10), Worthing and Reigate Priory.
Honours: England international vs. Wales 1906. England amateur international (20 apps). Cambridge Blue 1904-5-6.
City's first international, a gifted amateur and thorough sportsman immensely popular everywhere. Could centre from any angle at high speed, and had immaculate ball control and first-rate tactical knowledge. Son of an East Riding clergyman, Gordon Wright was educated at St Lawrence School, Ramsgate, and Queen's College, Cambridge. After working as a master at Hymer's College, Hull, he went to South Africa as a mining engineer (graduated at the Royal College of Mines). Then worked in the States for a time before returning to South Africa, where he died.

WRIGHT, Frederick (1930-1931)
Left-back: 2 apps.
1929: 5ft. 8ins; 11st.
Born: Ruddington, nr. Nottingham, 1908.
Career: Nottingham junior football to Notts County 1926/27; Grantham Town 1930; CITY November 1930 – 1931.
Going to Meadow Lane as a teenager, he was adjudged to be one of County's most promising young backs "for a long time". Fred, however, made their League side only once (in 1928/29), having to contend with an even younger left-back of greater potential in Alf Feebery, who returned from a loan period at Newark to chalk up 220 League appearances before WW2.

WRIGHT, George Albert (1946-1947)
Inside-forward: 4 apps; 1 goal.
Born: Sheffield, 1920.
Career: Cardiff City, CITY June 1946 - 1947.
Played professionally for Cardiff in wartime football, his displays at that time attracting scouts from southern clubs. An accountant by vocation.

WRIGHT, John Bryant (1947-1949)
Centre-half: 1 app.
1949: 5ft. 10½ins; 12st. 10lbs.
Born: South Shields, 16 November 1922.
Career: Royal Marines football in WW2 during which he made a guest appearance for Albion Rovers; Tyne Dock United; CITY September 1947 as a professional; Dartford cs 1949.
Hefty reserve pivot. Had to operate in the shadow of Berry and Meens so his activities were confined almost entirely to the Midland League side. Could also play at left-back.

WRIGHT, William ('Tim') (1908-1921)
Wing-half: 152 apps; 6 goals.
1914: 5ft. 8ins; 11st. 11lbs.
Born: Patrington, East Yorks, 1891.
Died: 21 December 1951.
Career: Spring Bank School, Hull; Patrington FC; Withernsea FC circa 1905; CITY 1908; retired 1921.
Certainly among the best of the early locals, quite dependable and adaptable – he could play a fair game on the right-wing, for instance. Tim was a noted runner too. For many years employed by the Withernsea Urban District Council and later became a licensee at Ottringham.

WYPER, Henry Thomas (1927-1928)

Outside-right: 41 apps: 2 goals.
1927: 5ft. 7ins; 10st. 3lbs.
Born: Coatbridge, Lanarkshire, 8 October (year not known).
Career: Glengarnock Vale; Southport January 1922; Motherwell cs 1922; Southport again October 1922; Wallasey United September 1923; Accrington Stanley cs 1925; CITY February 1927; Charlton Athletic September 1928; Queen's Park Rangers June 1931; Chester February 1932; Bristol Rovers January 1933; Accrington Stanley again cs 1933; Crewe Alexandra 1934/35; Rossendale United 1935/36.
Honours: (Charlton) Div. 3 (South) champions 1929.
Speedy little Scot who liked to cut in and have a pop at goal himself. Fast too in moving around the soccer circuit, making 13 moves in as many years after leaving his junior club. After leaving the game had a boarding house at Bournemouth and later emigrated to Australia.

YORKE, Robert J. (1935-1937)
Left-half: 9 apps.
1935: 5ft. 9½ins; 11st. 7lbs.
Born: Dunfermline.
Career: Ayr United 1929/30; Aldershot cs 1932; Dundee United circa 1934; CITY cs 1935.
Played at right-half also for Ayr United, for whom he made 47 top flight appearances. Signed by City after being an ever-present in Dundee United's Scottish League side the previous term. A capable reserve at Anlaby Road.

YOUNG, Ronald (1963-1968)
Outside-left: 24 apps. plus 2 subs; 5 goals.
1966: 5ft. 10ins; 11st. 2lbs.
Born: Dunstan, Northumberland, 31 August 1945.
Career: North-East junior football to CITY August 1963; Hartlepool September 1968 (around £4,000); South Shields August 1973. Later played for Bishop Auckland.
A capital City stand-in for several years and a progressive forward keen to take scoring chances. Ron did well at Hartlepool, making 176 League appearances and notching a creditable 40 goals in them.

A TIGERS' MISCELLANY

THE MANAGERS
Of City's 20 managers up to the end of season 1983/84, 7 played for the club and so their biographical details appear on previous pages. They are:
    Ambrose Langley 1905-1912.
    Harry Chapman 1913-1915,
        whose appointment was given as 'secretary' on being made in March 1913.
    Jack Hill 1934-1936.
    Raich Carter 1948-1951.
    Terry Neill 1970-74.
    John Kaye 1974-1977.
    Ken Houghton 1978-1979.
Here are some notes on the others.

F. G. STRINGER (1915)
A stop-gap appointment between Harry Chapman's enforced retirement and the arrival of:

DAVID MENZIES
(1915-1921, also February-October 1936)
A Scot born at Kirkcaldy. Manager of Bradford City and Doncaster Rovers too between the wars, and in charge of the latter when they won promotion in 1935. His second spell as City's Chief was brief because he died in office.

H. PERCY LEWIS (1921-1923)
Hailed from Rotherham. Versed in football government and a one-time member of the Sheffield and Hallamshire FA.

BILL McCRACKEN (1923-1931)
One of the great soccer celebrities. An Irish International (15 caps) and famous (notorious?) with Newcastle United for his exploitation of the offside trap that eventually forced change in the game's rules. Also managed Millwall, Gateshead and Aldershot. Had a long life (born Belfast 1883, died 1979) and was still scouting for Watford when in his 80s.

HAYDN GREEN (1931-1934)
Held a number of managerial appointments extending over a long period. He was at Lincoln in the 1920's for instance, Swansea Town 1939-47 and Watford 1951-52. He died during February 1957.

ERNEST BLACKBURN (1936-1946)
A full-back for Aston Villa and Bradford City immediately after World War One until his retirement through injury in 1923. Later in the inter-war period managed Accrington Stanley, Wrexham and Tranmere Rovers besides City. Born at Crawshaw Booth near Rawtenstall in 1897, died 1964.

MAJOR FRANK BUCKLEY (1946-1948)
It is sometimes forgotten that this famous manager was also a class centre-half capped by England in 1914. Managed Blackpool and then Wolves from 1927. In the latter post always in the news through his continuous blooding of young talent and a skilful projection in the media. After leaving City was in charge of Leeds United and Walsall. Born Manchester 1883, died 1964.

BOB JACKSON (1952-1955)
Born Farnworth, Lancs. Played inside-forward for Tranmere Rovers and a number of non-League clubs before being forced to retire because of injury. Bolton Wanderers' chief scout for 11 years, then briefly Worcester City's sec/manager before an appointment as Portsmouth's chief scout and promotion to manager. Steered Pompey to successive League championships (1949 and 1950). Died May 1968 aged 72.

BOB BROCKLEBANK (1955-1961)
Played inside-right for Aston Villa and Burnley in the 1930's. After the war was manager of Chesterfield and Birmingham City before joining the Tigers, and Bradford City afterwards (1961-64). Born London, died September 1981 aged 73.

CLIFF BRITTON (1961-1969)
Renowned as a player, a polished right-half who won 9 England caps and a Cup winners' medal when at Everton in the 'Thirties. Also manager of that club (1948-56), Burnley and Preston North End before his last engagement at Boothferry Park. Born Bristol 1909, died 1975.

BOBBY COLLINS (1977-1978)
Played 31 times for Scotland, a dynamic little forward prominent throughout a senior playing career stretching over two decades. Won winners' medals in all of his country's main competitions with Celtic, later skippering Leeds United into the 1st Division. In charge of City for only 4 months but has managed Huddersfield and, currently, Barnsley. Born Govanhill, Glasgow, 1931.

MIKE SMITH (1980-1982)
Born Hendon, London, 1936. Never played professionally but did in top-class amateur football for Corinthian-Casuals. Represented British Universities and gained county honours for Middlesex, Leicestershire and Cornwall. A schoolmaster until appointment as the Welsh FA coach. In 1974 became the Wales team manager and was highly successful, but his first essay into club managership, with City, was a troubled one.

COLIN APPLETON (1982-1984)
For long Leicester City's left-half and captain, spending a dozen years at Filbert Street. In this time he appeared in two FA Cup and two League Cup finals, and represented the Football League. Subsequently assisted Charlton Athletic and was player/manager of Barrow 1967-69. In charge of Scarborough FC, where he was born in 1936, before coming to Boothferry Park. Left to take over the Swansea City managership in May 1984.

The latest and 21st City manager is:

BRIAN HORTON
Appointed in June 1984, his first managerial job. It follows meritorious spells of service as a midfield player for Port Vale, Brighton & Hove Albion and Luton Town. Has proved an inspiring captain at Brighton and Luton, a quality of leadership that should contribute towards success in administration. Is City's player/manager and his wide experience in the top flight will be a factor on the field of play. Born Hednesford 1949.

THE ABANDONED 1939/40 SEASON

Unlike its WW1 equivalent, 1914/15, the Football League did not keep going on a peacetime format after the outbreak of war. The season was but a week old and the following 12 players had represented Hull City in the 2 Northern Section fixtures fulfilled:

Cunliffe, A	2	Quigley, D	2
Curnow, J	2	Richardson, G	2
Davies, D D	2(1)	Robinson, C	1
Gilmore, H P	1	Smith, T F	2
Lowe, R E	2	Watson, A E	2
Meens, H	2	Woodhead, C	2

(Goals in brackets)

Five of the above, all signings of that fateful summer, do not appear in the main body of this Who's Who. They are:

JACK CURNOW
Goalkeeper born Lingdale, North Yorks in 1910. A burly 'keeper (6ft. 2ins. and 13st. 4lbs) who joined the Wolves in the 1935/36 season when he made half a dozen Div. 1 appearances. Transferred to Blackpool the following term, soon moving to Tranmere Rovers in the summer of 1937. A regular member of Tranmere's Div. 3 (North) championship side in 1937/38.

HENRY P. GILMORE
Right-half born Hartlepool 1913. 1938: 5ft. 11ins; 11st. 6lbs. Actually this was Gilmore's second spell at Anlaby Road. He had joined from Shotton Colliery of the Wearside League in 1934 but didn't make the League side before transferring to Mansfield Town in July 1935. Then moved to Bournemouth a year later and QPR in the summer of 1937.

RICHARD E. LOWE
Centre-forward born Cannock, Staffs. in 1915. Joined Leeds United as an inside-left in 1934/35 when a teenager. Moved to Sheffield United in the 1937 close season, the Blades giving him his League baptism the following campaign. 1939: 5ft. 10ins; 12st. 4lbs.

DENNIS QUIGLEY
Outside-right born in the Scottish university town of St Andrews. An assertive, auburn-haired winger with a slight build (in 1938, 5ft. 6ins; 10st. 7lbs). To Dundee from St Andrews FC, making his senior debut in 1934/35. Moved to Brechin City and then, in February 1937, Grimsby Town. Appeared in the Mariners' Div. 1 side on 23 occasions (2 goals) before crossing the Humber. Died 1983.

THOMAS F. SMITH
Left-half. Another Scot with a Dundee connection. He joined the Dens Park club from a junior side, Luncarty, making his senior debut in the 1932/33 season. From then until Dundee's relegation in 1938 Tom clocked up 163 Scottish League Div. 1 appearances, scoring 5 goals. The most experienced of the 1939 recruits.

CITY IN TWO WORLD WARS

1915-16 to 1918-19

In 1915, after a season of falling gates and bitter criticism that football should continue on pre-war lines in time of war, the professional game, in England, was abandoned for the duration of the conflict. Regional Leagues and unpaid players became the order of the day. Hull City, with a basis of their local players and a lengthy string of 'guests', took part in the Midland Section of the Football League.

The following is a list of those who made the most appearances in the course of those four seasons, with their most frequent position indicated, although the conditions of the day often resulted in players turning out in alternative positions.

Player	Usual position	Apps. (Max. 142)	Goals
Mercer, David	RW	142	48
Edelston, Joe	HB	130	1
Hendry, Nick	GK	115	—
Betts, Arthur	FB	106	—
Wigglesworth, Arthur	FB	101	—
Jacketts, George	HB	95	3
Wright, Tim	HB	77	14
Sheridan, J.	HB	72	2
Lee, Jack	LW	67	28
Hughes, Bobby (Northampton Tn.)	W	62	31
Pattison, Jack	HB	46	—
Smith, Joe (Bury & ex-City)	RW	34	4
McQuillan, Jack (Leeds City)	FB	31	2
Stevens, Sammy	CF	30	23
Ford, H. (Goole Town)	LW	30	2
'Wallis' (Otherwise Harry Walden of Bradford City)	CF	25	11
Pace, Arthur (Croydon Common)	IF	25	—
Potter, Cec (Norwich City)	IF	22	7
Slide, Bob	IF	20	7
Grimshaw, W. (Bradford City)	IR	18	6
Bradbury, J.	IF	17	4
Lyon, Jack	IL	15	7
Deacey, Charlie	CH	15	2
Chaplin, George (Bradford City)	FB	15	—
Osborn, F. (Preston N.E.)	IF	13	7
Bleakley, Tommy	HB	13	—
Nevin, Jack (Ayr United)	CH	13	—
Percival, H.	IL	11	3
Simmon, Harry	IF	11	2

1939-40 to 1945-46

The 1939-40 season had just started when war broke out. Immediately all football was stopped. Towards the end of October eight Regional Leagues came into operation. The Tigers were included in the North Eastern Region. Clubs once more made up their teams with guest players, although Hull City was well served by a nucleus of its own playing staff:

Player		Usual position	Apps. (Max. 142)	Goals
Watson, Arthur		LB	20	—
Curnow, Jack		GK	19	—
Gilmore, Pat		RH	19	—
Meens, Harold		CH	19	3
Smith, Tommy		LH	19	—
Anderson	(Goole T.)	IL	18	9
Woodhead, Cliff		RB	18	—
Robinson, Jack		RW	17	—
Prescott, Jack		CF	16	15
Davies, Dai		IR	15	3
Cunliffe, Arthur		LW	9	2
Richardson, Ernie	(Aldershot)	LW	9	1

For 1940-41 all the northern clubs were grouped together. City faced increasing difficulties in getting a team together, especially towards the end of the season. The club also had to contend with a considerable decline in attendances, and at the end of the season decided to close down for the duration of the war.

Player		Usual position	Apps. (Max. 23)	Goals
Woodhead, Cliff		LB	22	—
Meens, Harold		CH	20	—
Robinson, Jack		RH	19	—
Anderson	(Goole T.)	CF	18	11
Bly, Billy		GK	16	—
Ross, A. C.	(Chester)	RB	16	—
Barraclough, Billy	(Doncaster Rvs).	LW	15	2
Knott, Bert	(ex-Walsall)	IR	15	13
Cunliffe, Arthur		RW	14	5
Davies, Dai		IF	14	2
Bradley, G. J.	(Newcastle Utd.)	LH	11	—
Spivey, Dick	(Southport)	IL	9	2

In 1944 the Directors decided to resume playing, but having vacated the Anlaby Road ground, they were dependent on the goodwill of Hull F. C. and the Rugby League for the use of the Boulevard. The club's playing staff was by now scattered far and wide, so that the manager had a thankless task putting together a team consisting almost entirely of guests. At the turn of the year, when the 18 games to decide the champions of the Football League (North) were completed, City had called upon over fifty players. By the time the side had concluded its Second Championship fixtures the number approached ninety, and around half of them turned out just once. At the opposite end of the list were:

Player		Usual position	Apps. (Max. 23)	Goals
Harris	(West Ham)	LH	34	1
Bell, Ernie	(Mansfield Tn.)	RW	26	4
Curnow, Jack		GK	24	—
Beeson, G.	(Walsall)	RB	20	1
Glaister, George	(Blackburn Rvs.)	LW	18	6
Flinton	(Scarborough)	LW	16	3
Miller, David	(Middlesbrough)	IL	16	—
Beardshaw, Colin	(Bradford City)	CH	14	—
Symons, Jack		FB	12	—
Montgomery, Stan	(ex-Romford)	HB	10	4
Stokes, E.	(Sheffield Wed.)	LB	10	—
Howe, Les	(Tottenham H.)	IF	9	5

Glaister was joint leading scorer along with Bert Knott, although Bert notched his half-dozen in exactly one sixth of the number of games George played!

With the resumption of Rugby League on peace-time lines in 1945-46, Hull City was unable to use the Boulevard. Reconstruction of housing and industry meant that there were no materials available for building the stands at Boothferry Park until early in 1946, and the club's former ground was being used by the Hull Amateurs F.C., so that the Tiger was inactive for another season.

HULL CITY
F.A. CUP RECORD

1904-05 to 1983-84

(Goal scorers in brackets)

1904-05

Sat. 17th September   Preliminary Qual. Round
v Stockton   Away*   Drew   3-3   Attce: 4,000

Whitehouse; Leiper, Jones; Martin, Wolfe, Raisbeck; O. W. Mackrill (1), Rushton, Howe (1), Spence (1), Wilkinson.

Thurs 22nd September   Replay
v Stockton   Away   Lost   1-4   Attce: 4,000

Whitehouse; Leiper, Jones; Martin, Wolfe, Raisbeck; O. W. Mackrill, Rushton, Howe, Spence (1), Wilkinson.

* Hull City gave up ground advantage. Their ground, the Boulevard, was required by Hull F.C. for R.L. match.

1905-06

Sat. 7th October   First Qual. Round
v Grimethorpe Utd.   Home*   Won   8-1   Attce: 2,000

Spendiff; Langley, Jones; Browell, Robinson (1), Gordon; Simmon, Wilson, (2), Joe Smith (3), Howe (2), Raisbeck.

Sat. 28th October   Second Qual. Round
v Denaby United**   Away   Won   2-0   Attce: 3,000

G. W. Cook; Davies, Brooks; Martin, Carney, Frost; Lavery, Thornton, Rushton, Jack Smith (2), Manning.

Sat. 18th November   Third Qual. Round
v Leeds City   Home   Abandoned after 50 min. (fog)
                               Without score   Attce: 3,000

Spendiff; Langley, Jones; Browell, Robinson, Gordon; Manning, Wilson, Joe Smith, Jack Smith, Raisbeck.

Wed. 22nd November   Third Qual. Round
v Leeds City   Home   Drew   1-1   Attce: 3,000

Spendiff; Langley, Jones; Browell, Robinson, Gordon; Manning, Wilson, Rushton, Jack Smith, Raisbeck (1).

Wed. 29th November   Replay
v Leeds City   Away   Won   2-1   Attce: 8,000

Spendiff; Jones, Davies; Browell, Robinson, Raisbeck; Manning, Spence, Rushton (1), Gordon, Joe Smith (1).

Sat. 9th December   Fourth Qual. Round
v Oldham Athletic   Home   Won   2-1   Attce: 4,000

Spendiff; Davies, Jones; Browell, Robinson, Gordon; Manning, Jack Smith (1), Rushton, Howe (1), Raisbeck.

Sat. 13th January   First Round Proper
v Reading   Home   Lost   0-1   Attce: 9,000

Spendiff; Davies, Jones; Browell, Robinson, Raisbeck; Manning, Spence, Rushton, Gordon, Joe Smith.

* Grimethorpe gave up ground advantage.
** First team unable to postpone League fixture with Manchester United, so that the Reserves had to go to Denaby.

City exempt from Qualifying Competition after this season.

1906-07

Sat. 12th January   First Round
v Tottenham Hotspur   Away   Drew   0-0   Attce: 28,000

Spendiff; Hedley, McQuillan; Browell, Robinson, Gordon; Manning, Jack Smith, Rushton, Joe Smith, E. G. D. Wright.

Thurs. 17th January   Replay
v Tottenham Hotspur   Home   Drew*   0-0   Attce: 21,795

Spendiff; Hedley, McQuillan; Browell, Robinson, Gordon; Manning, Jack Smith, Rushton, Joe Smith, E. G. D. Wright.

Mon. 21st January   Second Replay
v Tottenham Hotspur   Away**   Lost   0-1   Attce: 20,000

Spendiff; Hedley, McQuillan; Browell, Robinson, Gordon; Manning, Jack Smith, Howe, Joe Smith, E. G. D. Wright.

* Abandoned after ten minutes extra time (Bad light)
** City agreed to play at Tottenham for £150 in addition to their half share of the gate.

1907-08

Sat. 11th January   First Round
v Woolwich Arsenal   Away   Drew   0-0   Attce: 15,000

Spendiff; Hedley, McQuillan; Browell, Robinson, Gordon; Joe Smith, Jack Smith, Temple, Martin, E. G. D. Wright.

Thurs. 16th January   Replay
v Woolwich Arsenal   Home   Won   4-1   Attce: 16,000

Spendiff; Hedley, McQuillan; Browell, Robinson, Martin; Joe Smith, Jack Smith (1), Shaw (2), Temple (1), E. G. D. Wright.

Sat. 1st February   Second Round
  v Aston Villa   Away   Lost   0-3   Attce: 35,000
  Spendiff; Hedley, McQuillan; Browell, Robinson, Martin; Joe Smith, Jack Smith, Shaw, Temple, E. G. D. Wright.

1908-09

Sat. 16th January   First Round
  v Chelsea   Home   Drew   1-1   Attce: 18,000
  Roughley; Stephenson, McQuillan; G. Browell, Robinson, Gordon; Joe Smith, Jack Smith, Temple (1), Gilberthorpe, E. G. D. Wright.

Wed. 20th January   Replay
  v Chelsea   Away   Lost   0-1   Attce: 30,000
  Roughley; Stephenson, McQuillan; G. Browell, A. Browell, Gordon; Joe Smith, Jack Smith, Temple, Gilberthorpe, E. G. D. Wright.

1909-10

Sat. 15th January   First Round
  v Chelsea   Away   Lost   1-2   Attce: 38,000
  Roughley; Nevins, McQuillan; G. Browell, A Browell, Gordon; Joe Smith, Temple (1), Jack Smith, W. Smith, E. G. D. Wright.

1910-11

Sat. 14th January   First Round
  v Bristol Rovers   Away   Drew   0-0   Attce: 9,666
  Roughley; Nevins, McQuillan; McIntosh, A. Browell, Gordon; Joe Smith, Temple, T. Browell, W. Smith, E. G. D. Wright.

Thurs. 19th January   Replay
  v Bristol Rovers   Home   Won   1-0   Attce: 13,000
  Roughley; Nevins, McQuillan (1); McIntosh, A. Browell, Gordon; Joe Smith, Temple, T. Browell, W. Smith, E. G. D. Wright.

Sat. 4th February   Second Round
  v Oldham Athletic   Home   Won   1-0   Attce: 17,000
  Roughley; Nevins, McQuillan; W. Wright, A. Browell, Gordon; Joe Smith, Temple (1), T. Browell, W. Smith, E. G. D. Wright.

Sat. 25th February   Third Round
  v Newcastle United   Away   Lost   2-3   Attce: 46,531
  Roughley; Nevins, McQuillan; W. Wright, A. Browell, Gordon; Joe Smith (2), Temple, T. Browell, W. Smith, E. G. D. Wright.

1911-12

Sat. 13th January   First Round
  v Oldham Athletic   Away   Drew   1-1   Attce: 12,000
  Roughley; Nevins, McQuillan; W. Wright, A. Browell, Gordon; Joe Smith, Chapman, Best (1), Temple, Neve.

Tues. 16th January   Replay
   v Oldham Athletic   Home   Lost   0-1   Attce: 13,112
   Roughley; Nevins, McQuillan; W. Wright, A. Browell, Gordon; Joe Smith, Chapman, Best, W. Smith, Neve.

1912-13

Sat. 11th January   First Round
   v Fulham   Away   Won   2-0   Attce: 10,000
   Hendry; Nevins, McQuillan; W. Wright, O'Connell, Gordon; McDonald, Fazackerley (1), Stevens (1), Goode, E. G. D. Wright.

Sat. 1st February   Second Round
   v Newcastle United   Home   Drew   0-0   Attce: 18,250
   Hendry; Nevins, McQuillan; W. Wright, O'Connell, Gordon; McDonald, Fazackerley, Stevens, Goode, E. G. D. Wright.

Wed. 5th February   Replay
   v Newcastle United   Away   Lost   0-3   Attce: 32,278
   Hendry; Nevins, McQuillan; W. Wright, O'Connell, Gordon; McDonald, Fazackerley, Stevens, Boyton, E. G. D. Wright.

1913-14

Sat. 10th January   First Round
   v Bury   Home   Drew   0-0   Attce: 12,000
   Hendry; Pattison, Morgan; Edelston, O'Connell, McIntosh; McDonald, J. Lyon, Stevens, Halligan, Lee.

Wed. 14th January   Replay
   v Bury   Away   Lost   1-2   Attce: 12,808
   Hendry; Pattison, Morgan; Edelston, O'Connell, McIntosh; McDonald, J. Lyon, Stevens, Halligan, Lee (1).

1914-15

Sat. 9th January   First Round
   v West Brom. Albion   Home   Won   1-0   Attce: 12,625
   Hendry; Morgan, Betts; Edelston, Deacey, Wright; Mercer, Cameron, Stevens (1), Halligan, Lee.

Sat. 30th January   Second Round
   v Northampton Town   Home   Won   2-1   Attce: 13,000
   Hendry; Pattison, Betts; Edelston, Deacey, Wright; Mercer, Cameron, Stevens (2), Halligan, Lee.

Sat. 20th February   Third Round
   v Southampton   Away   Drew   2-2*   Attce: 15,607
   Hendry; Betts, Morgan; Edelston, Deacey, Wright; Mercer, Cameron (1), Stevens, Halligan, Lee (1).

Sat. 27th February   Replay
v Southampton   Home   Won   4-0   Attce: 11,000
Hendry; Betts, Morgan; Edelston, Deacey, Wright; Mercer, Cameron (1), Stevens (2), Halligan, Lee (1).

Sat. 6th March   Fourth Round
v Bolton Wanderers   Away   Lost   2-4   Attce: 24,379
Hendry; Betts, Morgan; Edelston, Deacey (1), Wright; Mercer, Cameron, Stevens (1), Halligan, Lee.

* Extra time in first meeting by special arrangement this season.

1915-16 to 1918-19
No competition

1919-20

Wed. 14th January   First Round
v Sunderland   Away   Lost   2-6   Attce: 35,586
Hendry; Bell, Betts; Edelston, Deacey, Wright; Hughes, Mercer, Stevens (2), Morrall, Lee.

(Postponed from Sat. 10th due to snow at Roker Park pitch).

1920-21

Sat. 8th January   First Round
v Bath City   Home   Won   3-0   Attce: 11,600
Mercer; Cheetham, Bell; Collier, Gilhooley, Bleakley; Crawford (1), Brandon, McKinney, Sergeaunt (1), Wilson (1).

Sat. 29th January   Second Round
v Crystal Palace   Away   Won   2-0   Attce: 21,000
Mercer; Cheetham, Bell; Collier, Gilhooley, Bleakley; Crawford (1), Brandon, McKinney, Sergeaunt, Wilson (1).

Sat. 19th February   Third Round
v Burnley   Home   Won   3-0   Attce: 26,000
Mercer; Cheetham, Bell; Collier, Gilhooley, Bleakley; Crawford, Brandon (2), McKinney, Sergeaunt, Wilson (1).

Sat. 5th March   Fourth Round
v Preston North End   Home   Drew   0-0   Attce: 27,000
Mercer; Cheetham, Bell; Collier, Gilhooley, Bleakley; Crawford, Brandon, McKinney, Sergeaunt, Wilson.

Thur. 10th March   Replay
v Preston North End   Home   Lost   0-1   Attce: 32,853
Mercer; Cheetham, Bell; Collier, Gilhooley, Bleakley; Crawford, Brandon, McKinney, Sergeaunt, Wilson.

1921-22

Sat. 7th January   First Round
v Middlesbrough   Home   Won   5-0   Attce: 23,000
Mercer; Lodge, Bell; Collier, Gilhooley, Bleakley (1); Crawford (1), Coverdale (2), Mills (1), Flood, Hughes.

HULL CITY A.F.C. SEASON 1922/23

Back row: J. Collier, J. W. Lodge, W. H. Mercer, M. Bell, D. C. Bew, T. Bleakley.
Front: J. F. Crawford, D. McKinney, G. S. Martin, R. Coverdale, A. Thom.

Sat. 28th January   Second Round
v Nottingham Forest   Away   Lost   0-3   Attce: 28,000
Mercer; Lodge, Bell; Collier, Gilhooley, Bleakley; Crawford, Coverdale, Mills, Flood, Hughes.

1922-23
Sat. 13th January   First Round
v West Ham United   Home   Lost   2-3   Attce: 14,000
Mercer; Gibson, Bell; Middlemiss, Bew, Bleakley; Crawford (1), Mills (1), Wood, Coverdale, Thom.

1923-24
Sat. 12th January   First Round
v Bolton Wanderers   Home   Drew   2-2   Attce: 28,603
Mercer; Gibson, Bell; Collier, Bleakley, Johnson; Richardson, Martin (1), Mills (1), Lewis, Thom.

Wed. 16th January   Replay
v Bolton Wanderers   Away   Lost   0-4   Attce: 40,315
Mercer; Gibson, Bell; Collier, Bleakley, Johnson; Richardson, Martin, Mills, Lewis, Thom.

1924-25
Sat. 10th January   First Round
v Wolv. Wanderers   Home   Drew   1-1   Attce: 22,689
Maddison; Gibson, Bell; Collier, O'Brien, Bleakley; Richardson, Martin, Mills (1), Howarth, Thom.

Thur. 15th January   Replay
v Wolv. Wanderers   Away   Won   1-0   Attce: 24,447
Bell; Gibson, McGee; Collier, O'Brien, Bleakley; Richardson, Hamilton, Mills (1), Martin, Thom.

Sat. 31st January   Second Round
v Crystal Palace   Home   Won   3-2   Attce: 20,805
Bown; McGee, Bell; Collier, O'Brien, Bleakley (1); Richardson, Hamilton, Mills (2), Martin, Thom.

Sat. 21st February   Third Round
v Leicester City   Home   Drew   1-1   Attce: 27,000
Maddison; Gibson, McGee; Collier, O'Brien (1), Bleakley; Thomas, Hamilton, Mills, Martin, Thom.

Thurs. 26th February   Replay
v Leicester City   Away   Lost   1-3   Attce: 19,864
Maddison; Gibson, McGee; Collier, O'Brien, Bleakley; Thomas, Hamilton (1), Mills, Martin, Thom.

1925-26
Sat. 9th January   Third Round*
v Aston Villa   Home   Lost   0-3   Attce: 26,000
Maddison; McGee, Bell; Lee, O'Brien, Bleakley; Richardson, Martin, Whitworth, Mills, Thom.

* Cup rounds reorganised from this season.

HULLO! HULL, HOW ARE YOU? GOING ALONG, NICELY THANK YOU! :: By Jos. Walker

BELL   WYPER   GUYAN   TAYLOR   MADDISON   SWAN   SULLIVAN   MARTIN   HOWIESON   DIXON   LLOYD

The inter-war period saw the heyday of the soccer caricaturist. Every national and regional newspaper seemed to have its own locally-based artist (Hull had the famous Ern Shaw, for instance). Among the very best was Jos. Walker, whose work appeared from around 1919 for the next 30 years. This 1927 cartoon of City running on to the field is an excellent example of Walker's brilliance.

1926-27

Sat. 8th January   Third Round
v West Brom. Albion   Home   Won   2-1   Attce: 18,000

Maddison; McGee, Bell; Sullivan, Dixon, Bleakley; Martin, Scott (1), Cowan (1), Whitworth, Taylor.

Sat. 29th January   Fourth Round
v Everton   Home   Drew   1-1   Attce: 22,000

Maddison; McGee, Bell; Swan, Dixon, Sullivan; Horne, Scott, Whitworth, Martin (1), Taylor.

Wed. 2nd February   Replay
v Everton   Away   Drew   2-2 aet   Attce: 45,000

Maddison; McGee, Bell; Swan, Dixon, Sullivan; Martin, Scott (1), Guyan (1), McLaughlin, Taylor.

Mon. 7th February   Second Replay
v Everton   at Villa Park   Won   3-2   Attce: 16,800

Maddison; McGee, Bell; Swan, Dixon, Sullivan; Martin (1), Scott, Guyan (1), Whitworth (1), Taylor.

Sat. 19th February   Fifth Round
v Wolv. Wanderers   Away   Lost   0-1   Attce: 48,948

Maddison; McGee, Bell; Swan, Dixon, Sullivan; Martin, Scott, Guyan, Whitworth, Taylor.

1927-28

Sat. 14th January   Third Round
v Leicester City   Home   Lost   0-1   Attce: 23,141

Maddison; Gibson, Bell; Dixon, Watson, Bleakley; Martin, Alexander, Nelson, Howieson, Taylor.

1928-29

Sat. 12th January   Third Round
v Bradford (P.A.)   Home   Drew   1-1   Attce: 23,000

Maddison; Goldsmith, Bell; Dixon, Childs, Bleakley; Alexander, Starling, McDonald (1), Weaver, Taylor.

Wed. 16th January   Replay
v Bradford (P.A.)   Away   Lost   1-3   Attce: 21,072
Maddison; Goldsmith, Bell; Dixon, Childs, Bleakley; Alexander, Starling, McDonald (1), Weaver, Taylor.

1929-30

Sat. 11th January   Third Round
v Plymouth Argyle   Away   Won   4-3   Attce: 28,923
Gibson; Goldsmith, Bell; Walsh, Childs, Gowdy; Taylor, Alexander (3), Mills, Howieson, Duncan (1).

Sat. 25th January   Fourth Round
v Blackpool   Home   Won   3-1   Attce: 23,000
Gibson; Goldsmith, Bell; Walsh, Childs, Gowdy; Taylor, Alexander (1), Mills (1), Starling (1), Duncan.

Sat. 15th February   Fifth Round
v Manchester City   Away   Won   2-1   Attce: 61,574
Gibson; Goldsmith, Howieson; Walsh, Childs, Gowdy; Taylor (1), Alexander, Mills (1), Starling, Duncan.

Sat. 1st March   Sixth Round
v Newcastle Utd.   Away   Drew   1-1   Attce: 63,486
Gibson; Goldsmith, Bell; Walsh, Childs, Gowdy; Taylor, Starling, Alexander (1), Howieson, Duncan.

Thurs. 6th March   Replay
v Newcastle Utd.   Home   Won   1-0   Attce: 32,930
Gibson; Goldsmith, Bell; Walsh, Childs, Gowdy; Taylor, Starling, Alexander, Howieson (1), Duncan.

Sat. 22nd March   Semi-final
v Arsenal   at Elland Road   Drew   2-2   Attce: 47,549
Gibson; Goldsmith, Bell; Walsh, Childs, Gowdy; Alexander, Starling, Mills, Howieson (1), Duncan (1).

Wed. 26th March   Replay
v Arsenal   at Villa Park   Lost   0-1   Attce: 43,676
Gibson; Goldsmith, Bell; Bleakley, Childs, Gowdy; Cartwright, Starling, Mills, Howieson, Duncan.

1930-31

Sat. 10th January   Third Round
v Blackpool   Home   Lost   1-2   Attce: 17,000
Gibson; Goldsmith, Bell; Walsh, Childs, Gowdy; Alexander, Longden, Raleigh, Weldon, D. Duncan (1).

1931-32

Sat. 28th November   First Round
v Mansfield Town   Home   Won   4-1   Attce: 10,000
Maddison; Woodhead, Rodgers; Newton, Wrack, Mills; Munnings (1), A. Duncan, Speed (1), Wainscoat (2), D. Duncan.

Sat. 12th December   Second Round
v New Brighton   Away   Won   4-0   Attce: 4,835
Maddison; Woodhead, Rodgers; Newton, Hill, Mills; Munnings (1), A. Duncan, Speed (2), Wainscoat (1), D. Duncan.

Sat. 9th January   Third Round
v Stoke City   Away   Lost   0-3   Attce: 22,180
Gibson; Goldsmith, Rodgers; Newton, Hill, Mills; Munnings, Raleigh, Speed, Wainscoat, D. Duncan.

1932-33

Sat. 26th November   First Round
v Stalybridge Celtic   Away   Won   8-2   Attce: 6,641
Maddison; Goldsmith, Woodhead; Gardner, Hill (1), Denby; Forward (1), Duncan, McNaughton (1), Wainscoat (4), Sargeant (1).

Sat. 10th December   Second Round
v Carlisle United   Away   Drew   1-1   Attce: 10,365
Maddison; Goldsmith, Woodhead; Gardner, Hill, Mills; Forward, Duncan, McNaughton, Wainscoat, Sargeant (1).

Thurs. 15th December   Replay
v Carlisle United   Home   Won   2-1 aet   Attce: 12,000
Maddison; Goldsmith, Woodhead; Gardner, Hill, Mills, Forward (1), Duncan, McNaughton, Wainscoat (1), Sargeant.

Sat. 14th January   Third Round
v Sunderland   Home   Lost   0-2   Attce: 22,566
Maddison; Goldsmith, Woodhead; Gardner, Longden, Denby; Forward, Duncan, McNaughton, Mills, Sargeant.

1933-34

Sat. 13th January   Third Round
v Brentford   Home   Won   1-0   Attce: 18,000
Maddison; Goldsmith, Woodhead; Gardner, Hill, Melville; Hubbard (1), Duncan, McNaughton, Denby, MacKenzie.

Sat. 27th January   Fourth Round
v Manchester City   Home   Drew   2-2   Attce: 25,000
Maddison; Goldsmith, Woodhead; Gardner, Hill (1), Melville; Hubbard, Duncan, McNaughton, Longden, Sargeant. Other scorer: Dale, o.g.

Wed. 31st January   Replay
v Manchester City   Away   Lost   1-4   Attce: 49,042
Maddison; Goldsmith, Woodhead; Gardner, Hill, Denby; Hubbard, Duncan, McNaughton (1), Longden, Sargeant.

1934-35

Sat. 12th January   Third Round
v Newcastle Utd   Home   Lost   1-5   Attce: 23,000
Maddison; Quantick, Woodhead; Longden, Tabram, Helsby; Hutchison, Hubbard, Charlton (1), Wright, Thorley.

HULL CITY A.F.C. SEASON 1934/35

Back row: Joe Beck (trainer), C. Woodhead, J. H. Quantick, G. Maddison, W. D. Tabram, T. Helsby, J. H. Hill (manager).
Front row: E. Longden, D. Hutchison, A. Duncan, D. Wright, J. Acquroff, E. Thorley.

1935-36

Sat. 11th January Third Round
v West Brom. Albion   Away   Lost   0-2   Attce: 27,505
Maddison; Quantick, Woodhead; Foster, Tabram, Denby; Hubbard, Sharp, Jordan, Acquroff, Thorley.

1936-37

Sat. 28th November First Round
v York City   Away   Lost   2-5   Attce: 7,700
Maddison; Annables, Woodhead; Denby, Tabram, Treanor; Mayson (1), Hubbard (1), Best, Holmes, Wilkinson.

1937-38

Sat. 27th November First Round
v Scunthorpe United   Home   Won   4-0   Attce: 6,000
Goodall; Woodhead, Parker; Robinson, Blyth, Hardy; Hubbard, Fryer, MacNeill (2), Davies, Pears (2).

Sat. 11th December Second Round
v Exeter City   Away   Won   2-1   Attce: 10,297
Goodall; Woodhead, Parker; Robinson, Blyth, Hardy; Hubbard (1), Fryer (1), MacNeill, Davies, Pears.

Sat. 8th January Third Round
v Huddersfield Town   Away   Lost   1-3   Attce: 25,442
Goodall; Woodhead, Parker; Robinson, Blyth, Hardy; Hubbard, Fryer, MacNeill, Davies, Pears (1).

1938-39

Sat. 26th November First Round
v Rotherham United   Home   Won   4-1   Attce: 8,000
Darling; Woodhead, Dowen; Robinson, Blyth, Hardy; Huxford, Hubbard (2), MacNeill, Davies (1), Cunliffe (1).

Sat. 10th December Second Round
v Chester   Away   Drew   2-2   Attce: 9,905
Ellis; Woodhead, Dowen; Robinson, Blyth, Hardy; Hubbard, Richardson, MacNeill, Davies (2), Cunliffe.

Thurs. 15th December Replay
v Chester   Home   Lost   0-1   Attce: 9,000
Ellis; Woodhead, Dowen; Robinson, Blyth, Hardy; Hubbard, Richardson, MacNeill, Davies, Cunliffe.

1939-40 to 1944-45

No competition

1945-46

Hull City did not participate

1946-47

Sat. 30th November   First Round
   v New Brighton   Home   Drew   0-0   Attce: 21,895
   Bly; Watson, Meens; Greenhalgh, Brown, Mills; Chadwick, McGorrighan, Lester, Peach, Brownsword.

Wed. 4th December   Replay
   v New Brighton   Away   Won   2-1 aet Attce: 7,688
   Bly; Watson, Meens; Greenhalgh, Brown, Mills; Knott, Peach, Lester (1), McGorrighan, Chadwick (1).

Sat. 14th December   Second Round
   v Darlington   Away   Won   2-1   Attce: 8,077
   Bly; Watson, Meens; Greenhalgh, Brown, Mills; Davies, Peach (1), Lester (1), McGorrighan, Chadwick.

Sat. 11th January   Third Round
   v Blackburn Rovers   Away   Drew   1-1   Attce: 23,500
   Bly; Watson, Meens; Greenhalgh, Brown, Mills; Hassall, Peach, Cook (1), McGorrighan, Chadwick.

Thurs. 16th January   Replay
   v Blackburn Rovers   Home   Lost   0-3   Attce: 30,501
   Carter; Watson, Fowler; Greenhalgh, Brown, Mills; Davidson, Davies, Cook, McGorrighan, Hassall.

1947-48

Sat. 29th November   First Round
   v Southport   Home   Drew   1-1 aet Attce: 20,000
   Hannaby; Hassall, Taylor; Greenhalgh, Meens, Berry; Reagan, Harrison, Lester, Gallacher (1), Bloxham.

Sat. 6th December   Replay
   v Southport   Away   Won   3-2   Attce: 11,000
   Bly; Hassall, Taylor; Greenhalgh, Meens, Mellor; Reagan (1), Gallacher, Richardson (1), McGorrighan (1), Bloxham.

Sat. 13th December   Second Round
   v Cheltenham Town   Home   Won   4-2   Attce: 21,000
   Bly; Hassall, Johnson; Greenhalgh, Meens, Berry; Reagan (1), Gallacher, Richardson (3), McGorrighan, Bloxham.

Sat. 10th January   Third Round
v Middlesbrough   Home   Lost   1-3   Attce: 40,179
Hannaby; Hassall, Taylor; Greenhalgh, Meens, Mellor; Reagan, Moore, Murphy (1), Richardson, Harrison.

1948-49

Sat. 27th November   First Round
v Accrington Stanley   Home   Won   3-1   Attce: 21,926
Bly; Taylor, Berry; Greenhalgh, Meens, Mellor; Harrison, Jensen (1), Moore, Carter (2), Burbanks.

Sat. 11th December   Second Round
v Reading   Home   Drew   0-0 aet Attce: 29,692
Bly; Taylor, Berry; Greenhalgh, Meens, Mellor; Harrison, Buchan, Jensen, Carter, Burbanks.

Sat. 18th December   Replay
v Reading   Away   Won   2-1   Attce: 21,920
Bly; Taylor, Berry; Greenhalgh, Wright, Mellor; Harrison, Jensen, Moore (2), Buchan, Bloxham.

Sat. 8th January   Third Round
v Blackburn Rovers   Away   Won   2-1   Attce: 33,200
Bly; Taylor, Berry; Greenhalgh, Meens, Mellor; Harrison, Jensen, Moore (1), Buchan (1), Bloxham.

Sat. 29th January   Fourth Round
v Grimsby Town   Away   Won   3-2   Attce: 26,505
Bly; Taylor, Berry; Greenhalgh, Meens, Mellor; Harrison, Jensen, Moore (2), Buchan, Carter (1).

Sat. 12th February Fifth Round
v Stoke City   Away   Won   2-0   Attce: 46,738
Bly; Taylor, Berry; Greenhalgh (1), Meens, Mellor; Harrison, Jensen, Moore (1), Buchan, Carter.

Sat. 26th February Sixth Round
v Manchester United   Home   Lost   0-1   Attce: 55,019
Bly; Taylor, Berry; Greenhalgh, Meens, Mellor; Harrison, Jensen, Moore, Buchan, Carter.

1949-50

Sat. 7th January   Third Round
v Southport   Away   Drew   0-0   Attce: 15,500
Bly; Hassall, Taylor; Jensen, Bowler, Mellor; Harrison, Revie, Moore, Carter, Burbanks.

Thurs. 12th January Replay
v Southport   Home   Won   5-0   Attce: 28,018
Bly; Hassall, Taylor; Greenhalgh (1), Bowler, Mellor; Harrison (1), Revie (1), Moore (1), Carter, Burbanks (1).

127

Sat. 28th January   Fourth Round
v Stockport County   Away   Drew   0-0   Attce: 26,600
Bly; Hassall, Taylor; Greenhalgh, Bowler, Mellor; Harrison, Revie, Moore, Jensen, Carter.

Thurs. 2nd February   Replay
v Stockport County   Home   Lost   0-2   Attce: 24,556
Bly; Hassall, Taylor; Greenhalgh, Bowler, Mellor; Harrison, Jensen, Moore, Carter, Burbanks.

1950-51

Sat. 6th January   Third Round
v Everton   Home   Won   2-0   Attce: 36,468
Robinson; Hassall, Jensen; Revie, Berry, Harris; Harrison, Carter (1), Ackerman, Gerrie (1), Burbanks.

Sat. 27th January   Fourth Round
v Rotherham United   Home   Won   2-0   Attce: 50,040
Robinson; Hassall, Jensen; Revie, Berry, Harris; Harrison (1), Carter (1), Ackerman, Gerrie, Burbanks.

Sat. 10th February   Fifth Round
v Bristol Rovers   Away   Lost   0-3   Attce: 31,000
Robinson; Hassall, Varney; Revie, Meens, Harris; Harrison, Carter, Ackerman, Jensen, Burbanks.

1951-52

Sat. 12th January   Third Round
v Manchester United   Away   Won   2-0   Attce: 43,517
Robinson; Hassall, Jensen; Harris, Berry, Durham; Harrison (1), Carter, Gerrie (1), Todd, Burbanks.

Sat. 2nd February   Fourth Round
v Blackburn Rovers   Away   Lost   0-2   Attce: 45,000
Robinson; Hassall, Jensen; Harris, Berry, Durham; Linaker, Carter, Gerrie, Todd, Burbanks.

1952-53

Sat. 10th January   Third Round
v Charlton Athletic   Home   Won   3-1   Attce: 37,531
Robinson; Hassall, Phillips; Harris (1), Davidson, Durham; K. Harrison, Horton (1), Gerrie, Jensen (1), Cripsey.

Sat. 31st January   Fourth Round
v Gateshead   Home   Lost   1-2   Attce: 37,063
Robinson; Phillips, Jensen; Harris, F. Harrison, Durham; Murray, Horton, Gerrie (1), Todd, Cripsey.

1953-54

Sat. 9th January   Third Round
   v Brentford   Away   Drew   0-0   Attce: 16,000
   Bly; F. Harrison, Jensen; Harris, Berry, Durham; K. Harrison, Horton, Crosbie, Ackerman, Cripsey.

Thurs. 14th January   Replay
   v Brentford   Home   Drew   2-2 aet   Attce: 20,126
   Bly; F. Harrison, Jensen; Harris, Berry, Durham; K. Harrison, Horton (1), Crosbie (1), Ackerman, Cripsey.

Mon. 18th January   Second Replay
   v Brentford   at Doncaster   Won   5-2   Attce: 10,176
   Bly; F. Harrison, Jensen; Harris, Berry, Durham; K. Harrison, Horton (2), Crosbie (2), Ackerman (1), Cripsey.

Sat. 30th January   Fourth Round
   v Blackburn Rovers   Away   Drew   2-2   Attce: 33,000
   Forgan; F. Harrison, Jensen; Harris, Berry, Durham; K. Harrison (1), Horton, Crosbie (1), Ackerman, Bulless.

Thurs. 4th February   Replay
   v Blackburn Rovers   Home   Won   2-1   Attce: 23,446
   Bly; F. Harrison, Jensen; Harris, Berry, Durham; K. Harrison, Horton, Crosbie, Ackerman (1), Bulless (1).

Sat. 20th February   Fifth Round
   v Tottenham Hotspur Home   Drew   1-1   Attce: 46,791
   Bly; F. Harrison, Jensen (1); Harris, Berry, Durham; K. Harrison, Horton, Crosbie, Ackerman, Bulless.

Wed. 24th February   Replay
   v Tottenham Hotspur Away   Lost   0-2   Attce: 52,936
   Bly; F. Harrison, Jensen; Harris, Franklin, Durham; Phillips, Horton, Crosbie, Ackerman, Bulless.

1954-55

Sat. 8th January   Third Round
   v Birmingham City   Home   Lost   0-2   Attce: 25,920
   Bly; Dennison, Jensen; Horton, Berry, Durham; K. Harrison, Downie, Ackerman, Mannion, Dryburgh.

1955-56

Sat. 7th January   Third Round
   v Aston Villa   Away   Drew   1-1   Attce: 33,285
   Bly; Neal, Jensen; Davidson, Porteous, Bulless; Atkinson, Clarke (1), Mortensen, Bradbury, Cripsey.

Thurs. 12th January   Replay
   v Aston Villa   Home   Lost   1-2   Attce: 15,670
   Bly; Neal, Jensen; Davidson, Porteous, Bulless; Atkinson (1), Clarke, Mortensen, Bradbury, Cripsey.

1956-57

Sat. 17th November   First Round
   v Gateshead   Home   Won   4-0   Attce: 12,260
   Bly; Harrison, Durham; Collinson, Feasey, Bulless; Stephens, Clarke, Mortensen (2), Bradbury (1), Cripsey (1).

Sat. 8th December   Second Round
   v York City   Home   Won   2-1   Attce: 24,155
   Bly; Harrison, Durham; Collinson, Feasey, Davidson; Stephens, Clarke, Mortensen, Bulless (2), Cripsey.

Sat. 5th January   Third Round
   v Bristol Rovers   Home   Lost   3-4   Attce: 22,752
   Bly; Harrison, Durham; Collinson, Feasey, Davidson; Stephens (1), Clarke (2), Bradbury, Bulless, Cripsey.

1957-58

Sat. 16th November   First Round
   v Crewe Alexandra   Home   Won   2-1   Attce: 10,773
   Bly; Davidson, Durham; Collinson, Nielson, Bennion; Stephens, Clarke (1), Bradbury (1), Bulless, Cripsey.

Sat. 7th December   Second Round
   v Port Vale   Away   Drew   2-2   Attce: 14,358
   Bly; Feasey, Durham; Collinson, Nielson, Davidson (1); Stephens, Clarke, Bradbury (1), Bentley, Bulless.

Mon. 9th December   Replay
   v Port Vale   Home   Won   4-3 aet Attce: 17,403
   Bly; Feasey, Durham; Collinson, Nielson, Davidson; Stephens, Clarke, Bradbury (2), Bentley, Bulless (1). Other scorer: Cleary, O.G.

Sat. 4th January   Third Round
   v Barnsley   Home   Drew   1-1   Attce: 21,868
   Fisher; Harrison, Durham; Collinson, Feasey, Davidson; Stephens, Clarke, Bradbury (1), Bulless, Cripsey.

Wed. 8th January   Replay
   v Barnsley   Away   Won   2-0   Attce: 20,890
   Fisher; Harrison, Durham; Collinson, Feasey, Davidson; Stephens, Clarke (1), Bradbury, Bulless (1), Cripsey.

Wed. 29th January   Fourth Round
   v Sheffield Wednesday Away   Lost   3-4   Attce: 47,119
   Bly; Harrison, Durham; Collinson, Feasey, Davidson; Stephens (1), Clarke, Bradbury (1), Bulless (1), Cripsey.

   (Postponed from Sat. 25th due to condition of Hillsborough pitch).

1958-59

Sat. 15th November   First Round
v Stockport County   Home   Lost   0-1   Attce: 17,441
Bly; Harrison, Durham; Collinson, Feasey, Garvey; Clarke, Bradbury, Smith, Coates, Bowering.

1959-60

Sat. 9th January   Third Round
v Fulham   Away   Lost   0-5   Attce: 22,100
Bly; Davidson, Bulless; Feasey, Garvey, Collinson; Clarke, Sewell, Shiner, Gubbins, Bradbury.

1960-61

Sat. 5th November   First Round
v Sutton Town   Home   Won   3-0   Attce: 8,402
Fisher; Davidson, Garvey; Collinson, Feasey, Bulless; Clarke, Sewell (1), Chilton, Price (1), Gubbins (1).

Sat. 26th November   Second Round
v Darlington   Away   Drew   1-1   Attce: 8,553
Fisher; Davidson, Garvey; Collinson, Feasey, Bulless; Clarke, Price (1), Chilton, McMillan, Gubbins.

Mon. 28th November   Replay
v Darlington   Home   Drew   1-1 aet   Attce: 18,125
Fisher; Davidson, Garvey; Collinson, Feasey, Bulless; Clarke, Price, Chilton (1), McMillan, Gubbins.

Mon. 5th December   Second Replay
v Darlington   at Elland Road   Drew   1-1*   Attce: 9,721
Fisher; Davidson, Garvey; Collinson, Feasey, Bulless; Clarke, Price (1), Chilton, McMillan, Stocks.

Mon. 12th December   Third Replay
v Darlington   at Doncaster   Drew   0-0 aet   Attce: 5,313
Fisher; Davidson, Garvey; Collinson, Feasey, Bulless; Price, Sewell, Chilton, McMillan, Clarke.

Thurs. 15th December   Fourth Replay
v Darlington at Middlesbrough   Won   3-0   Attce: 19,366
Fisher; Davidson, Garvey; McMillan, Feasey, Bulless; Clarke (1), Price, Gubbins (1), Sewell, King (1).

Sat. 7th January   Third Round
v Bolton Wanderers   Home   Lost   0-1   Attce: 18,771
Fisher; Davidson, Garvey; McMillan, Feasey, Bulless; Clarke, Price, Chilton, Sewell, Gubbins.

* Extra time not played due to heavy condition of pitch.

1961-62

Sat. 4th November   First Round
   v Rhyl   Home   Won   5-0   Attce: 7,451
   Fisher; Davidson, Garvey; Collinson, Feasey, McMillan (1); Clarke, McSeveney (1), Chilton (2), Henderson (1), Crickmore.

Sat. 25th November   Second Round
   v Bradford City   Home   Lost   0-2   Attce: 10,124
   Fisher; Davidson, Bulless; Collinson, Feasey, McMillan; Clarke, McSeveney, Chilton, Henderson, Crickmore.

1962-63

Sat. 3rd November   First Round
   v Crook Town   Home   Won   5-4   Attce: 9,484
   Williams; Davidson, Garvey; Sharpe, Feasey, McMillan; Clarke, Price, Chilton (1), Henderson (2), McSeveney (2).

Sat. 24th November   Second Round
   v Workington   Home   Won   2-0   Attce: 8,686
   Williams; Davidson, Sharpe; Collinson, Garvey, McMillan; Clarke, Henderson, Chilton, Cummins, McSeveney (2).

Mon. 11th February*   Third Round
   v Leyton Orient   Away   Drew   1-1   Attce: 9,752
   Williams; Davidson, Sharpe; Collinson, Garvey, McMillan; Clarke, Henderson, Chilton (1), Cummins, McSeveney.

Tues. 19th February   Replay
   v Leyton Orient   Home   Lost   0-2 aet   Attce: 14,214
   Williams; Davidson, Sharpe; Collinson, Garvey, McMillan; Clarke, Henderson, Chilton, Cummins, McSeveney.

   * After numerous postponements.

1963-64

Sat. 16th November   First Round
   v Crewe Alexandra   Home   Drew   2-2   Attce: 10,013
   Swan; Davidson, Butler; Garvey, Feasey, Sharpe; Clarke, Wilkinson, Chilton (1), Henderson, Shaw (1).

Wed. 20th November   Replay
   v Crewe Alexandra   Away   Won   3-0   Attce: 7,955
   Swan; Davidson, Butler; Garvey, Feasey, Sharpe; McSeveney, Wilkinson (2), Chilton, Henderson (1), Shaw.

Sat. 7th December   Second Round
   v Wrexham   Away   Won   2-0   Attce: 8,186
   Swan; Davidson, Butler; Garvey, Feasey, Sharpe; Clarke, Wilkinson, Chilton (1), Henderson (1), Shaw.

Sat. 4th January Third Round
v Everton   Home   Drew   1-1   Attce: 36,478
Williams; Davidson, Butler; Collinson, Feasey, McMillan; Clarke, Wilkinson (1), Chilton, Henderson, McSeveney.

Tues. 7th January Replay
v Everton   Away   Lost   1-2   Attce: 56,613
Williams; Davidson, Butler; Collinson, Feasey, McMillan; Clarke, Wilkinson, Chilton, Henderson, McSeveney (1).

1964-65

Sat. 14th November First Round
v Kidderminster Harriers Away   Won   4-1   Attce: 6,619
Swan; Davidson, Butler; Collinson, Milner, Summers; Young, Wilkinson (2), Chilton, Heath (1), McSeveney (1).

Sat. 5th December Second Round
v Lincoln City   Home   Drew   1-1   Attce: 10,167
Swan; Davidson, Butler; Collinson, Milner, Summers (1); Wilkinson, Wagstaff, Chilton, Heath, McSeveney.

Wed. 9th December Replay
v Lincoln City   Away   Lost   1-3   Attce: 8,383
Swan; Davidson, Butler; Collinson, Milner, Summers; Clarke, Wagstaff, Chilton, Henderson, McSeveney (1).

1965-66

Sat. 13th November First Round
v Bradford (P.A.) Away   Won   3-2   Attce: 11,487
Swan; Davidson, D. Butler; Jarvis, Milner, Simpkin; Henderson, Wagstaff, Chilton (1), Houghton (1), I. Butler (1).

Wed. 8th December Second Round
v Gateshead   Away   Won   4-0   Attce: 5,935
Swan; Davidson, D. Butler; Jarvis, Milner, Simpkin; Henderson (1), Wagstaff (1), Chilton, Houghton (1), I. Butler (1).

Sat. 22nd January Third Round
v Southampton   Home   Won   1-0   Attce: 28,851
Swan; Davidson, D. Butler; Jarvis, Milner, Simpkin; Henderson, Wagstaff, Chilton, Houghton (1), I. Butler.

Sat. 12th February Fourth Round
v Nottingham Forest Home   Won   2-0   Attce: 38,055
Swan; Davidson, Brown; Jarvis, Milner, Houghton; Henderson, Wagstaff, Chilton, Heath (2), I. Butler.

Sat. 5th March Fifth Round
v Southport   Home   Won   2-0   Attce: 38,871
Swan; Davidson, D. Butler; Jarvis, Milner, Simpkin; Henderson, Wagstaff, Chilton (2), Houghton, I. Butler.

Sat. 26th March   Sixth Round
v Chelsea   Away   Drew   2-2   Attce: 46,924
Swan; Davidson, D. Butler; Jarvis, Milner, Simpkin; Henderson, Wagstaff (2), Chilton, Houghton, I. Butler.

Thurs. 31st March   Replay
v Chelsea   Home   Lost   1-3   Attce: 45,328
Swan; Davidson, D. Butler; Jarvis, Milner, Simpkin (1); Henderson, Wagstaff, Chilton, Houghton, I. Butler.

1966-67

Sat. 28th January   Third Round
v Portsmouth   Home   Drew   1-1   Attce: 29,381
McKechnie; Davidson, D. Butler; Jarvis, Milner, Simpkin; Henderson, Wagstaff, Chilton, Houghton (1), I. Butler. Sub: Wilkinson.

Wed. 1st February   Replay
v Portsmouth   Away   Drew   2-2 aet Attce: 33,107
McKechnie; Davidson, D. Butler; Jarvis, Milner, Simpkin; Henderson, Wagstaff, Chilton (1), Houghton (1), I. Butler. Sub: Wilkinson.

Mon. 6th February   Second Replay
v Portsmouth at Coventry   Lost   1-3   Attce: 18,448
Swan; Davidson, D. Butler; Jarvis, Corner, Simpkin; Henderson, Wagstaff, Chilton (1), Houghton, I. Butler. Sub: Wilkinson.

1967-68

Sat. 27th January   Third Round
v Middlesbrough   Away   Drew   1-1   Attce: 28,509
McKechnie; Banks, D. Butler; Greenwood, Wilson, Simpkin; Houghton, Wagstaff, Chilton (1), Wilkinson, I. Butler. Sub: Henderson.

Wed. 31st January   Replay
v Middlesbrough   Home   Drew   2-2 aet Attce: 33,916
McKechnie; Banks, D. Butler; Greenwood, Wilson, Simpkin; Houghton, Wagstaff (2), Chilton, Wilkinson, I. Butler. Sub: Henderson.

Wed. 7th February   Second Replay
v Middlesbrough   at York   Lost   0-1   Attce: 16,524
McKechnie; Banks, D. Butler; Greenwood, Wilson, Simpkin; Houghton, Wagstaff, Chilton, Wilkinson, I. Butler. Sub: Henderson.

1968-69

Sat. 4th January   Third Round
v Wolv. Wanderers   Home   Lost   1-3   Attce: 27,526
McKechnie, Greenwood, Beardsley, Pettit, Wilson, Simpkin, Jarvis, Wagstaff, Chilton (1), Houghton, I. Butler. Sub: Wilkinson.

1969-70

Sat. 3rd January   Third Round
v Manchester City   Home   Lost   0-1   Attce: 30,271
McKechnie, Banks, Beardsley, Greenwood, Wilson, Simpkin, Jarvis, Houghton, Chilton, Wagstaff, I. Butler. Sub: Lord.

1970-71

Sat. 2nd January   Third Round
v Charlton Athletic   Home   Won   3-0   Attce: 19,926
McKechnie, Banks, de Vries, Greenwood, Neill, Simpkin, Lord, Houghton (1), Chilton, Wagstaff (1), Butler (1). Sub: Pettit.

Sat. 23rd January   Fourth Round
v Blackpool   Home   Won   2-0   Attce: 34,752
McKechnie, Banks, de Vries, Wilkinson, Neill, Simpkin, Greenwood, Lord, Chilton (1), Wagstaff (1), Butler. Sub: Houghton.

Sat. 13th February   Fifth Round
v Brentford   Home   Won   2-1   Attce: 29,709
McKechnie, Banks, de Vries, Wilkinson, Neill, Simpkin, Lord, Houghton (1), Chilton (1), Wagstaff, Butler. Sub: Greenwood.

Sat. 6th March   Sixth Round
v Stoke City   Home   Lost   2-3   Attce: 41,452
McKechnie, Banks, de Vries, Wilkinson, Neill, Simpkin, Lord, Houghton, Chilton, Wagstaff (2), Butler. Sub: Pearson.

1971-72

Sat. 15th January   Third Round
v Norwich City   Away   Won   3-0   Attce: 22,044
McKechnie, Banks, de Vries, Wilkinson, Neill, Knighton, McGill (1), Lord, Pearson, Wagstaff (1), Butler (1). Sub: Houghton.

Sat. 5th February   Fourth Round
v Coventry City   Away   Won   1-0   Attce: 24,621
McKechnie, Banks, de Vries, Wilkinson, Neill, Baxter, McGill, Lord, Pearson, Wagstaff (1), Butler. Sub: Houghton.

Sat. 26th February   Fifth Round
v Stoke City   Away   Lost   1-4   Attce: 34,558
McKechnie, Banks, de Vries, Wilkinson, Neill, Baxter, McGill, Lord, Kaye, Wagstaff (1), Butler. Sub: O'Riley.

1972-73

Sat. 13th January   Third Round
v Stockport County   Away   Drew   0-0   Attce: 8,294
McKechnie, Banks, Beardsley, Kaye, Neill, Knighton, McGill, Houghton, Pearson, Wagstaff, Greenwood. Sub: Holme.

Tues. 23rd January   Replay
v Stockport County   Home   Won   2-0   Attce: 13,593

McKechnie, Banks, Beardsley, Kaye, Neill, Knighton, McGill, Houghton (1), Pearson, Wagstaff (1), Greenwood. Sub: Holme.

Sat. 3rd February   Fourth Round
v West Ham United   Home   Won   1-0   Attce: 32,290

McKechnie, Banks, Beardsley, Kaye, Neill, Knighton, McGill, Houghton (1), Pearson, Holme, Greenwood. Sub: Butler.

Sat. 24th February   Fifth Round
v Coventry City   Away   Lost   0-3   Attce: 31,663

Wealands, Banks, Beardsley, Kaye, Neill, Knighton, McGill, Houghton, Pearson, Holme, Greenwood. Sub: Blampey.

1973-74

Sat. 5th January   Third Round
v Bristol City   Away   Drew   1-1   Attce: 8,969

Wealands, Banks, McGill, Galvin (1), Deere, Burnett, Holme, Lord, Pearson, Wagstaff, Greenwood. Sub: de Vries.

Tues. 8th January   Replay
v Bristol City   Home   Lost   0-1   Attce: 5,340

Wealands, Banks, McGill, Galvin, Deere, Burnett, Holme, Lord, Hemmerman, Wagstaff, Greenwood. Sub: de Vries.

1974-75

Sat. 4th January   Third Round
v Fulham   Away   Drew   1-1   Attce: 8,897

Wealands, Banks, Daniel, Galvin, Croft, Burnett, Grimes, Lord, Wood, Wagstaff (1), Greenwood. Sub: Deere.

Tues. 7th January   Replay
v Fulham   Home   Drew   2-2 aet Attce: 11,850

Wealands, Banks, Daniel, Galvin, Croft (1), Burnett, Grimes, Lord, Fletcher (1), Hemmerman, Greenwood. Sub: Deere.

Mon. 13th January   Second Replay
v Fulham   at Leicester   Lost   0-1   Attce: 4,929

Wealands, Banks, Daniel, Galvin, Deere, Burnett, McGill, Lord, Wood, Grimes, Greenwood. Sub: Fletcher.

1975-76

Sat. 3rd January   Third Round
v Plymouth Argyle   Home   Drew   1-1   Attce: 6,515

Wealands, Banks, McGill, Hawley, Croft, Roberts, Grimes (1), Lyall, Wood, Galvin, Greenwood. Sub: Haigh.

Tues. 6th January   Replay
   v Plymouth Argyle   Away   Won   4-1   Attce: 20,208
   Wealands, Daniel, Banks, Hawley (1), Croft, Roberts, Grimes, Lyall, Wood (2), Galvin, Greenwood. Sub: McGill. Other scorer: Sutton, own goal.

Mon. 2nd February*   Fourth Round
   v Sunderland   Away   Lost   0-1   Attce: 32,320
   Wealands, Daniel, de Vries, Hawley, Croft, Roberts, Galvin, Lyall, Wood, Fletcher, Stewart. Sub: Deere.

   * Postponed from Sat. 24th & Tues. 27th January due to snow.

1976-77

Sat. 8th January   Third Round
   v Port Vale   Home   Drew   1-1   Attce: 9,694
   Wealands, Daniel, de Vries, Bremner, Croft, Haigh, Nisbet (1), Lyall, Sunley, Hawley, Stewart. Sub: McIntosh.

Mon. 10th January   Replay
   v Port Vale   Away   Lost   1-3 aet   Attce: 10,668
   Wealands, Daniel, de Vries, Bremner, Dobson, Croft, Nisbet, Lyall, Sunley, Hemmerman (1), Haigh. Sub: McIntosh.

1977-78

Sat. 7th January   Third Round
   v Leicester City   Home   Lost   0-1   Attce: 12,374
   Blackburn, Nisbet, Daniel, Bremner, Dobson, Haigh, Hawker, Lord, Hawley, Sunley, Stewart. Sub: Bannister.

1978-79

Sat. 25th November   First Round
   v Stafford Rangers   Home   Won   2-1   Attce: 5,411
   Blackburn, Nisbet, de Vries, Horswill, Hood, Haigh, Warboys, Lord, Edwards (1), Bannister, Farley. Sub: Hawker. Other scorer: Sargeant, own goal.

Sat. 16th December   Second Round
   v Carlisle United   Away   Lost   0-3   Attce: 5,335
   Blackburn, Nisbet, de Vries, Croft, Horswill, Haigh, Galvin, Hood, Edwards, Bannister, Farley. Sub: Stewart.

1979-80

Sat. 24th November   First Round
   v Carlisle United   Away   Drew   3-3   Attce: 4,970
   Blackburn, Hood, Haigh (1), Skipper, Dobson, Nisbet, G. Roberts (1), Moss, Edwards, Tait (1), Hawker. Sub: Farley.

Wed. 28th November   Replay
v Carlisle United   Home   Lost   0-2   Attce: 6,657

Blackburn, Hood, Haigh, Hawker, Dobson, Nisbet, G. Roberts, Moss, Edwards, Bannister, Farley. Sub: McDonald.

1980-81

Sat. 22nd November   First Round
v Halifax Town   Home   Won   2-1   Attce: 4,024

Norman, Nisbet, Horswill, G. Roberts, J. Roberts, D. Roberts, Marwood, Norrie, Edwards (2), McClaren, Deacy. Sub: Flounders.

Sat. 13th December   Second Round
v Blyth Spartans   Home   Drew   1-1   Attce: 6,050

Norman, Nisbet, McNeil, Croft, G. Roberts, Richards, Marwood, McClaren, Edwards (1), Norrie, Deacy. Sub: Moss.

Tues. 16th December   Replay
v Blyth Spartans   Away   Drew   2-2 aet   Attce: 5,870

Norman, Nisbet, McNeil, Croft, G. Roberts, Richards, Marwood, McClaren, Edwards (1), Norrie (1), Deacy. Sub: Swann.

Mon. 22nd December   Second Replay
v Blyth Spartans at Elland Road   Won   2-1 aet   Attce: 5,914

Norman, Booth, McNeil, Croft (1), G. Roberts, J. Roberts, Marwood, McClaren, Edwards, Norrie (1), Deacy. Sub: Moss.

Sat. 3rd January   Third Round
v Doncaster Rovers   Home   Won   1-0   Attce: 10,709

Norman, Hoolickin, Ferguson, Croft, Richards, G. Roberts, Marwood, McClaren, Edwards, Norrie, Deacy (1). Sub: Booth.

Sat. 24th January   Fourth Round
v Tottenham Hotspur   Away   Lost   0-2   Attce: 37,432

Norman, Hoolickin, McNeil, Richards, Booth, J. Roberts, Marwood, McClaren, Edwards, Norrie, Deacy. Sub: Croft.

1981-82

Sat. 21st November   First Round
v Rochdale   Away   Drew   2-2   Attce: 2,722

Norman, McNeil, Booth, D. Roberts, Deacy, G. Roberts, Marwood, McClaren (1), Whitehurst (1), Mutrie, Swann. Sub: Richards.

Tues. 24th November   Replay
v Rochdale   Home   Drew   2-2 aet   Attce: 4,063

Norman, McNeil, Booth, D. Roberts, Deacy, G. Roberts, Marwood, McClaren, Whitehurst (1), Mutrie, Swann (1). Sub: Norrie.

Mon. 30th November   Second Replay
v Rochdale   at Elland Road   Won   1-0   Attce: 3,268

Norman, McNeil, Booth, D. Roberts, Deacy, G. Roberts, Marwood, McClaren (1), Whitehurst, Mutrie, Swann. Sub: Norrie.

Mon. 4th January*   Second Round
v Hartlepool United   Home   Won   2-0   Attce: 4,975
Norman, McNeil, Booth, D. Roberts, Deacy, G. Roberts, Marwood (1), McClaren, Norrie, Mutrie (1), Swann. Sub: Ferguson.

Mon. 18th January*   Third Round
v Chelsea   Away   Drew   0-0   Attce: 14,899
Davies, McNeil, Booth, D. Roberts, Deacy, G. Roberts, Marwood, Ferguson, Whitehurst, Mutrie, Swann. Sub: Flounders.

Thurs. 21st January   Replay
v Chelsea   Home   Lost   0-2   Attce: 13,238
Davies, McNeil, Booth, D. Roberts, Deacy, G. Roberts, Marwood, Ferguson, Whitehurst, Mutrie, Swann. Sub: Flounders.

* After several postponements.

1982-83

Sat. 20th November   First Round
v Sheffield United   Home   Drew   1-1   Attce: 9,152
Norman, McNeil, Booth, D. Roberts, Skipper, Swann, Marwood, McClaren, Whitehurst, Mutrie, G. Roberts. Sub: Flounders. Scorer: Kenworthy, own goal.

Tues. 23rd November   Replay
v Sheffield United   Away   Lost   0-2   Attce: 12,232
Norman, McNeil, Askew, D. Roberts, Skipper, Booth, Marwood, McClaren, Whitehurst, Mutrie, G. Roberts. Sub: Swann.

1983-84

Sat. 19th November   First Round
v Penrith   Away   Won   2-0   Attce: 1,828
Norman, McNeil, Hollifield, D. Roberts, Skipper, Booth, Marwood, Askew, Whitehurst (1), Flounders, G. Roberts (1). Sub: Massey.

Sat. 10th December   Second Round
v Rotherham United   Away   Lost   1-2   Attce: 6,885
Norman, McNeil, Booth, Askew, Skipper, Hollifield, Marwood, McClaren, Whitehurst, Flounders (1), G. Roberts. Sub: Swann.

TOMMY BROWELL
Among the most famous Tigers of all time.

HULL CITY LEAGUE CUP RECORD

1960-61 to 1983-84

Note: Where no First Round result is shown, the Tigers received a bye.

1960-61

Mon. 10th October   First Round
  v Bolton Wanderers   Home   Drew   0-0   Attce: 11,980
  Fisher; Davidson, Garvey; Collinson, Feasey, Bulless; Clarke, Price, Chilton, King, Gubbins.

Wed. 19th October   Replay
  v Bolton Wanderers   Away   Lost   1-5   Attce: 10,781
  Fisher; Davidson, Garvey; Collinson, Feasey, Bulless; Clarke, Sewell, Chilton, Price, Gubbins (1).

1961-62

Mon. 11th September   First Round
  v Bradford (P. A.)   Home   Won   4-2   Attce: 10,401
  Fisher; Davidson, Garvey; Collinson, Feasey, McMillan; Clarke, McSeveney, Chilton (2), Bulless, Crickmore (1). Other scorer: Atkinson, own goal.
  Gubbins (1).

Tues. 3rd October   Second Round
  v Bury   Away   Won   4-3   Attce: 8,204
  Fisher; Davidson, Garvey; Collinson (1), Feasey, McMillan; Clarke (1), McSeveney, Chilton (2), Bulless, Crickmore.

Wed. 15th November   Third Round
  v Sunderland   Away   Lost   1-2   Attce: 15,969
  Fisher; Davidson, Bulless; Collinson, Feasey, McMillan; Clarke, McSeveney (1), Chilton, Henderson, Crickmore.

1962-63

Mon. 24th September   Second Round
v Middlesbrough   Home   Drew   2-2   Attce: 10,640
Williams; Davidson, Bulless; Collinson (1), Garvey, McMillan; Clarke, Price, Chilton (1), Henderson, McSeveney.

Mon. 8th October   Replay
v Middlesbrough   Away   Drew   1-1 aet   Attce: 15,612
Williams; Davidson, Bulless; Collinson, Garvey, McMillan; Clarke (1), Price, Chilton, Henderson, McSeveney.

Wed. 10th October   Second Replay
v Middlesbrough   Home   Won   3-0 aet   Attce: 11,960
Williams; Davidson, Sharpe; Collinson, Garvey, McMillan; Clarke, Price (1), Chilton (1), Henderson, McSeveney (1).

Wed. 17th October   Third Round
v Fulham   Home   Lost   1-2   Attce: 20,308
Williams; Davidson, Sharpe; Collinson, Garvey, McMillan; Clarke, Price, Chilton (1), Henderson, McSeveney.

1963-64

Wed. 25th September   Second Round
v Exeter City   Home   Won   1-0   Attce: 9,313
Swan; Davidson, Butler; Sharpe, Milner, McMillan; Clarke, Henderson (1), Chilton, Cummins, McSeveney.

Wed. 16th October   Third Round
v Manchester City   Home   Lost   0-3   Attce: 13,880
Swan; Davidson, Butler; Sharpe, Feasey, McMillan; Clarke, Wilkinson, Chilton, Henderson, McSeveney.

1964-65

Tues. 22nd September   Second Round
v Southend United   Home   Drew   0-0   Attce: 4,012
Swan; Davidson, Butler; Sharpe, Feasey, McMillan; Clarke, Wilkinson, Corner, Henderson, McSeveney.

Mon. 28th September   Replay
v Southend United   Away   Lost   1-3   Attce: 5,089
Swan; Davidson, Butler; Garvey, Feasey, Summers; Wilkinson (1), Chilton, Corner, Henderson, Sharpe.

1965-66

Wed. 22nd September   Second Round
v Derby County   Home   Drew   2-2   Attce: 15,601
Williams; Davidson, D. Butler; Simpkin, Milner, Summers; Henderson, Wagstaff, Chilton, Houghton (2), I. Butler.

Wed. 29th September   Replay
  v Derby County   Away   Lost   3-4   Attce: 9,645
  Williams; Davidson, D. Butler; Simpkin (1), Milner, Summers; Henderson, Wagstaff (1), Chilton (1), Houghton, I. Butler.

1966-67

Wed. 20th August   First Round
  v Lincoln City   Away   Lost   0-1   Attce: 6,238
  Swan; Davidson, D. Butler; Jarvis, Milner, Simpkin; Henderson, Wagstaff, Chilton, Houghton, I. Butler. Sub: Heath.
  Note: D. Butler took over in goal after Swan came off injured.

1967-68

Tues. 12th September   Second Round
  v Queen's Park Rangers Away   Lost   1-2   Attce: 16,609
  McKechnie; Lees, Wilkinson; Jarvis, Banks, Simpkin; Greenwood, Wagstaff (1), Chilton, Houghton, Young. Sub: Lord.

1968-69

Wed. 14th August   First Round
  v Halifax Town   Away   Won   3-0   Attce: 4,493
  McKechnie, Greenwood, Beardsley, Jarvis, Simpkin, Pettit, Wilkinson (1), Wagstaff (1), Chilton (1), Houghton, I. Butler. Sub: Lord.

Wed. 4th September   Second Round
  v Brentford   Away   Lost   0-3   Attce: 11,485
  McKechnie, Banks, Beardsley, Pettit, Wilson, Greenwood, Jarvis, Wagstaff, Chilton, Simpkin, I. Butler. Sub: Houghton.

1969-70

Wed. 3rd September   Second Round
  v Norwich City   Home   Won   1-0   Attce: 10,824
  McKechnie, Banks, D. Butler, Pettit, Barker, Simpkin, Blampey, Wagstaff (1), Chilton, Houghton, I. Butler. Sub: Lord.

Wed. 24th September   Third Round
  v Derby County   Away   Lost   1-3   Attce: 31,603
  McKechnie, Banks, D. Butler, Pettit, Barker, Simpkin, Wilkinson, Wagstaff, Chilton (1), Houghton, I. Butler. Sub: Jarvis.

1970-71

Wed. 9th September   Second Round
  v West Ham United   Away   Lost   0-1   Attce: 19,264
  McKechnie, Beardsley, de Vries, Wilkinson, Neill, Simpkin, Lord, Houghton, Chilton, Wagstaff, Jarvis. Sub: P. Greenwood.

1971-72

Tues. 7th September   Second Round
v Liverpool   Away   Lost   0-3   Attce: 31,612
McKechnie, Banks, de Vries, Wilkinson, P. Greenwood, Knighton, Lord, Houghton, Pearson, Wagstaff, O'Riley. Sub: Simpkin.

1972-73

Tues. 5th September   Second Round
v Fulham   Home   Won   1-0   Attce: 6,352
Wealands, Banks, de Vries, Wilkinson, Kaye, Knighton (1), Lord, McGill, O'Riley, Greenwood, Butler. Sub: Houghton.

Tues. 3rd October   Third Round
v Norwich City   Home   Lost   1-2   Attce: 11,524
Wealands, Banks, de Vries, Wilkinson, Neill, Knighton, McGill, Houghton, Pearson, Wagstaff, Butler. Sub: Holme (1).

1973-74

Mon. 8th October   Second Round
v Leicester City   Away   Drew   3-3   Attce: 9,777
Wealands, Banks, McGill, Kaye, Deere, Blampey, Hawley, Galvin (1), Pearson, Wagstaff (1), Greenwood. Sub: Hemmerman. Other scorer: Whitworth, own goal.

Wed. 31st October   Replay
v Leicester City   Home   Won   3-2   Attce: 16,003
Wealands, Banks, de Vries (1), Blampey, Deere, Galvin, Hawley, Lord, Pearson (1), Wagstaff, Greenwood (1). Sub: McGill.

Tues. 6th November   Third Round
v Stockport County   Home   Won   4-1   Attce: 13,753
Wealands, Banks (1), de Vries, McGill, Deere, Galvin, Hawley, Lord, Pearson, Wagstaff (1), Holme (2). Sub: O'Riley.

Tues. 27th November   Fourth Round
v Liverpool   Home   Drew   0-0   Attce: 19,748
Wealands, Banks, McGill, Kaye, Deere, Galvin, Hawley, Lord, Pearson, Wagstaff, Greenwood. Sub: O'Riley.

Tues. 4th December   Replay
v Liverpool   Away   Lost   1-3   Attce: 17,120
Wealands, McGill, deVries, Kaye, Deere, Galvin, Hawley, Lord, Pearson, Wagstaff, Greenwood. Sub: O'Riley. Scorer: Lindsay, own goal.

1974-75

Wed. 11th September   Second Round
v Burnley   Home   Lost   1-2   Attce: 7,544
Wealands, Blampey, de Vries, Burnett, Deere, McGill, Grimes, Hawley, Fletcher (1), Wagstaff, Greenwood. Sub: Lord.

1975-76

Tues. 9th September   Second Round
   v Preston North End   Home   Won   4-2   Attce: 5,095
   Wealands, Banks, de Vries, Galvin, Croft, Roberts, Grimes, Lord (1), Wood (1), Fletcher, Greenwood (2). Sub: McGill.

Tues. 7th October   Third Round
   v Sheffield United   Home   Won   2-0   Attce: 9,536
   Wealands, Banks, de Vries, Stewart, Croft, Roberts, Hawley (1), McGill, Wood, Wagstaff, Greenwood (1). Sub: Daniel.

Tues. 11th November   Fourth Round
   v Doncaster Rovers   Away   Lost   1-2   Attce: 20,476
   Wealands, Banks, de Vries, Galvin, Croft, Haigh, Grimes, Hawley, Wood (1), Wagstaff, Greenwood. Sub: McGill.

1976-77

Tues. 31st August   Second Round
   v Orient   Away   Lost   0-1   Attce: 3,578
   Wealands, Daniel, de Vries, Haigh, Hawley, Croft, Gibson, Lyall, Sunley, Hemmerman, Stewart. Sub: Galvin.

1977-78

Wed. 31st August   Second Round
   v Southport   Away   Drew   2-2   Attce: 3,864
   Wealands, Nisbet, de Vries, Bremner, Croft, Roberts, Haigh (1), Stewart, Hawley, Bannister (1), Galvin. Sub: Sunley.

Wed. 14th September   Replay
   v Southport   Home   Won   1-0   Attce: 4,846
   Wealands, Nisbet, de Vries, Bremner, Croft, Roberts, Haigh, Galvin, Sunley, Bannister (1), Stewart. Sub: Grimes.

Tues. 25th October   Third Round
   v Oldham Athletic   Home   Won   2-0   Attce: 6,923
   Wealands, Nisbet, Daniel, Bremner (1), Dobson, Haigh, Galvin, Grimes, Sunley, Bannister (1), Stewart. Sub: Hawker.

Tues. 29th November   Fourth Round
   v Arsenal   Away   Lost   1-5   Attce: 25,922
   Wealands, Nisbet, de Vries, Bremner, Dobson, Roberts, Grimes, Haigh, Sunley, Bannister, Galvin. Sub: Hawley (1).

1978-79

Sat. 12th August   First Round, First Leg
   v Peterborough United   Home   Lost   0-1   Attce: 4,165
   Wealands, Nisbet, de Vries, Croft, Dobson, Haigh, Hood, Horswill, Edwards, Bannister, Farley. Sub: Hawker.

Tues. 15th August   First Round, Second Leg
v Peterborough United   Away   Won   2-1   Attce: 4,387
Wealands, Nisbet, de Vries, Croft, Dobson, Haigh (1), Hood, Horswill, Edwards, Bannister (1), Farley. Sub: Hawker.

Tues. 22nd August   Replay
v Peterborough United   Home   Lost   0-1   Attce: 4,990
Wealands, Nisbet, de Vries, Croft, Dobson, Haigh, Hood, Horswill, Edwards, Bannister, Farley. Sub: Lord.

1979-80

Sat. 11th August   First Round, First Leg
v Sheffield Wednesday   Away   Drew   1-1   Attce: 9,152
Blackburn, Nisbet, McDonald, Hawker, Dobson, Haigh, Roberts, Horswill, Edwards (1), Bannister, Phillips. Sub: Hood.

Tues. 14th August   First Round, Second Leg
v Sheffield Wednesday   Home   Lost   1-2   Attce: 7,059
Blackburn, Nisbet, McDonald, Hawker, Dobson, Haigh, Roberts (1), Horswill, Edwards, Bannister, Phillips. Sub: Hood.

1980-81

Sat. 9th August   First Round, First Leg
v Lincoln City   Away   Lost   0-5   Attce: 3,538
Norman, Nisbet, Haigh, Booth, J. Roberts, Richards, Marwood, G. Roberts, Edwards, Norrie, Moss. Sub: McClaren.

Tues. 12th August   First Round, Second Leg
v Lincoln City   Home   Lost   0-2   Attce: 2,933
Norman, Nisbet, Horswill, Booth, J. Roberts, Haigh, Norrie, G. Roberts, Edwards, Moss, McDonald. Sub: McClaren.

1981-82

Wed. 2nd September   First Round, First Leg
v Lincoln City   Away   Lost   0-3   Attce: 3,498
Norman, McNeil, Booth, Richards, Eccleston, Horswill, G. Roberts, Edwards, Deacy, Mutrie, Ferguson. Sub: Whitehurst.

Tues. 15th September   First Round, Second Leg
v Lincoln City   Home   Drew   1-1   Attce: 2,702
Norman, Hoolickin, Booth, Richards, Eccleston, Horswill, McClaren, Edwards, Whitehurst, Mutrie, Ferguson (1). Sub: Marwood.

1982-83

Tues. 31st August   First Round, First Leg
v Sheffield United   Away   Lost   1-3   Attce: 7,036
Norman, Swann, McNeil, D. Roberts, Skipper, Booth, Marwood, McClaren, Whitehurst (1), Mutrie, G. Roberts. Sub: Flounders.

Tues. 14th September   First Round, Second Leg
v Sheffield United   Home   Won   1-0   Attce: 7,119

Davies, McNeil, Askew, D. Roberts, Skipper, Booth, Flounders (1), McClaren, Whitehurst, Mutrie, G. Roberts. Sub: Swann.

1983-84

Tues. 30th August   First Round, First Leg
v Lincoln City   Home   Drew   0-0   Attce: 7,036

Norman, McNeil, Hollifield, D. Roberts, Skipper, Cockin, Marwood, Swann, Whitehurst, Massey, G. Roberts. Sub: Mutrie.

Wed. 14th September   First Round, Second Leg
v Lincoln City   Away   Lost   1-3 aet   Attce: 4,630

Norman, McNeil, Hollifield, D. Roberts, Skipper (1), Askew, Marwood, Swann, Whitehurst, Mutrie, G. Roberts. Sub: Massey.

ABOUT THE AUTHOR

Douglas Lamming was born in the Isle of Man in 1914, both parents belonging to old Lincolnshire families. He spent almost all his early life in that county and was educated at Queen Elizabeth's Grammar School, Horncastle. He became a valuer by profession, a Fellow of the Rating and Valuation Association, working throughout his career for local and central government departments. An inveterate football follower from childhood, he commenced keeping records after demobilisation from the RAF in 1946. This brought about an association with the late Morley Farror, culminating in their *A Century of English International Football, 1872–1972,* which is now widely regarded as a seminal work on British soccer. For some years now he has contributed reminiscence features and poetry to *Lincolnshire Life* as well as football articles. His poetry has appeared also in *The Dalesman.* In 1980 after many years he resumed drawing soccer caricatures, this time for publication, an aspect of his work which has appeared nationally besides being featured in club programmes, various AFS productions and elsewhere.

OTHER YORKSHIRE LOCAL INTEREST PUBLICATIONS FROM THE HUTTON PRESS

FED UP TO TOP ATTIC, by Bette Vickers. 312 pages with original cover drawing. Price: £4.50. ISBN 0 907033 16 4.

MARTHA: A Yorkshire Trilogy, Part 1, by Ruth Braithwaite. 132 pages with two photographs and two line-drawings. Price: £3.75. ISBN 0 907033 14 8.

BEN: A Yorkshire Trilogy, Part 2, by Ruth Braithwaite. 116 pages with original cover drawing. Price: £3.75. ISBN 0 907033 19 9.

COUNTRYMAN'S DIARY – LETTERS FROM A HULL SCHOOL. 36 pages with 27 letters and drawings by children. Price: £2.00. ISBN 0 907033 15 6.

PIE FOR BREAKFAST. Reminiscences of a Farmhand, by Harry Reffold. 116 pages with four photographs. Price: £3.25. ISBN 0 907033 17 2.

HORSES ON THE FARM. Recollections of Horse-Farming in Yorkshire, by Herbert L. Day. 84 pages with fourteen photographs. Price: £2.95. ISBN 0 907033 08 3.

MY LIFE WITH HORSES, by Herbert L. Day. 96 pages with eight photographs and original cover drawing. Price: £2.95. ISBN 0 907033 12 1.

TALES FROM THE WOLDS, by Herbert Johnson. 96 pages with six photographs. Price: £2.95. ISBN 0 907033 11 3.

CHURCHES OF THE WOLDS, by Christine R. Barker. Photographs by Rex W. Last. 36 large format pages with ten photographs. Price: £2.25. ISBN 0 907033 10 5.

THE YORKSHIRE WOLD RANGERS, by Angela Antrim, with line-drawings by the author. 120 pages. Price: £3.95. ISBN 0 907033 06 7.

SKETCHES OF DRIFFIELD, by Gary Sargeant with text by Christine Clubley. 40 large format pages. Price: £3.50. ISBN 0 907033 03 2.

ANY OLD IRON, the Story of the Yorkshire Farm Machinery Preservation Society, by E. Blanchard. 24 pages with seven photographs. Price: £1.95. ISBN 0 907033 18 0.

Price: £2.95   ISBN 0 907033 20 2